Mr. Marshall

The Rural Economy of Norfolk

Comprising the Management of Landed Estates and the Present Practice of

Husbandry in that County

Mr. Marshall

The Rural Economy of Norfolk
*Comprising the Management of Landed Estates and the Present Practice of
Husbandry in that County*

ISBN/EAN: 9783741144080

Manufactured in Europe, USA, Canada, Australia, Japa

Cover: Foto ©Thomas Meinert / pixelio.de

Manufactured and distributed by brebook publishing software
(www.brebook.com)

Mr. Marshall

The Rural Economy of Norfolk

THE
RURAL ECONOMY
OF
NORFOLK:

COMPRISING THE

Management of Landed Eſtates,

AND THE

PRESENT PRACTICE of HUSBANDRY
IN THAT COUNTY.

By Mr. MARSHALL,

(Author of MINUTES OF AGRICULTURE, &c.)
RESIDENT upwards of Two Years in NORFOLK.

THE SECOND EDITION.

IN TWO VOLUMES.
VOL. I.

LONDON:

Printed for G. NICOL, Bookſeller to his Majeſty, Pall-mall ;
G. G. and J. ROBINSON, Paternoſter-row ;
and J. DEBRETT, Piccadilly.

M,DCC,XCV.

ADDRESS

TO THE

PUBLIC.

THE utility of full and faithful Re-
gifters of the prefent practice of
Hufbandry, in well cultivated Diftricts,
occurred to me about ten years ago;—
when, in a journey of four or five hundred
miles through the central parts of the
Ifland, I experienced the inutility of a
tranfient view; but, at the fame time,
clearly faw the advantages which would
accrue from a TWELVEMONTH'S RESI-
DENCE in the immediate Diftrict of the
practice to be regiftered. At that time,
however, I was too bufily employed in
regiftering my own practice * to think of

* See MINUTES OF AGRICULTURE in SURREY.

extending

extending my Regifter, in any way, to the practice of others.—But being fortunately releafed from my connexion in Surrey, and having prepared for publication my EXPERIMENTS *and* OBSERVATIONS *concerning* AGRICULTURE *and the* WEATHER, I found leifure to reflect more maturely on the means of perfecting the fyftem, which I had, with much deliberation, fketched out, and which I had in part filled up, from my own practice.

In February 1780, I fubmitted to the Society of Arts in London, as the firft Society, profeffedly Agricultural, in the kingdom, the following Plan.

P L A N

FOR PROMOTING

AGRICULTURE.

THE knowledge of Agriculture either results from experience, simply; or is acquired through the united efforts of experience and theory.

Theory may facilitate, by analyzing the subject, and giving a comprehensive view of the science in general;---elucidate, by commenting on the experience already acquired;---accelerate, by proposing fit subjects for future investigations;---but cannot convey any certain information without the aid and concurrence of experience.

The experience of Agriculture is acquired through adequate observation, either on self-practice, or on the practice of others.

The practice of an individual, however, is generally limited to some particular

a 3   cular

cular branch of management, on some
certain soil and situation; and a general
knowledge of Agriculture must not be
expected from the practice of any one
man.

A man, nevertheless, who has spent
a long life in the practice of some certain
department, must necessarily have acquired a considerable share of knowledge of that particular department:
and it is probable, that were the knowledge of the individuals who excel in
the several departments of husbandry,
---were the knowledge of the ablest
farmers in the best-cultivated parts of
the island collected——English Agriculture would be found, at this day, to
be far advanced towards perfection.

But the individuals who excel in agriculture are unknown to each other;
and, if associated, could not probably
communicate their knowledge, with
any degree of precision: for their art
being the result of habit, it is too familiar to be minutely described. Their

farms

farms are the only records in which it
is regiftered, and even there it is as
fleeting as the hour in which it is performed. Nothing but actual obfervation, and immediately regiftering, in
writing, the feveral operations, as they
pafs throughout the year, can render
the practice of individuals of extenfive
fervice to the Public.

In fhort, the art of agriculture muft
ever remain imperfect while it is fuffered to languifh in the memory, and die
with the practitioner : RECORD, only,
can perpetuate the art ; and SYSTEM,
alone, render the fcience comprehenfive *.

Mr. Marfhall has already fubmitted
to the Public a regifter of his own
practice during five years ; compre-
hending a plan for acquiring agricultural knowledge, fyftematically, from

* What Dr. Johnfon fays of Language is applicable
to Agriculture——" Diction merely vocal is always
" in its childhood. As no man leaves his eloquence
" behind him, the new generations have all to learn."
—Journey to the Weftern Iflands of Scotland.

a 4   felf.

self-practice * ; which plan is equally
applicable to the practice of others ;
provided the obfervations be performed
without remiffion, and by one who is
accuftomed to agricultural obfervation.
He has alfo endeavoured to trace out
the foundation of a fyftem, fo far as his
own practice has extended.

His PRESENT PLAN is, to extend his
obfervations to the practice of others ;
more efpecially as it appertains to the
breeding, rearing, and fatting of cattle
---to the dairy management,---to the
management of fheep,---to the draining and watering of meadows,---and to
the grafs-land, or ley-management in
general.   After he is become proficient in thefe departments, his intentions
are to extend his SURVEY OF PROVIN-
CIAL AGRICULTURE to the arable or
plow-management.

His intended mode of obfervation is
this : Having pitched upon the branch
of management to be ftudied, and the

* See Experiments and Obfervations, as above.

diftrict

diftrict which excels in the practice of
that particular branch, he propofes to
fix his . place of refidence, during
TWELVE MONTHS, in a farm-houfe ;--
if poffible, in the houfe of the beft-
informed farmer in the diftrict pitched
upon ; and there, with daily attention,
minutely obferve and regifter the living
practice which furrounds him: not the
practice of theoretical, but of profef-
fional farmers ; or rather the provincial
practice of the diftrict, county, or country obferved ; neverthelefs attending to
improvements and excellencies, by
whomfoever practifed.

Nor is his plan confined merely to
obfervation : he means to acquire by
felf-practice a competent knowledge of
the MANUAL OPERATIONS incident to
the department of hufbandry which is
the immediate object of his ftudy ; as
alfo to collect fuch IMPLEMENTS and
UTENSILS as may appear peculiarly
adapted to the purpofes for which they
are feverally intended ; not fketches nor
models,

models, but the inftruments themfelves
which he has feen in common ufe;
and of whofe ufes he has acquired, by
manual practice, an adequate knowledge.

In order to furnifh himfelf with every
advantage which may forward his general defign, his further intentions are to
employ his leifure in taking a complete REVIEW OF WRITTEN AGRI-
CULTURE, from Fitz-Herbert, in 1534,
to the prefent time (excepting the
works of fuch authors as may be living
at the time of clofing the review);
and, after his judgment has been ma-
tured by a furvey of provincial practice to comprefs into as narrow a com-
pafs as may be, the ufeful information
relative to Britifh Agriculture, which
has been already recorded; whether it
appears in incidents and experiments
fufficiently authenticated, or in hints
which may furnifh fubjects for future
experiment.

Briefly,—his plan is, reciprocally to
receive and to offer information;—to

COR-

communicate provincial practice to the Public at large;——to collect and comprefs the ufeful information which is at prefent widely fcattered in almoft numberlefs volumes ;—and to reduce thefe joint accumulations of agricultural knowledge to fyftematic fcience : confequently, to offer to the prefent and fucceeding generations a comprehenfive SYSTEM OF ENGLISH AGRICULTURE, as it now ftands ;——and to raife it on a bafis fo ample and fcientific, as that future acquifitions may be added to it from time to time.

ON

ON THE EIGHTH of the fucceed-. ing month the Society were pleafed to pafs the following Refolutions :

" Resolved,
" That the collecting a general " knowledge of the Agriculture of " the kingdom, as propofed by Mr. " Marfhall, may be highly ufeful.

" Resolved,
" That as it is not the practice of the " Society to adopt the execution of " plans of this kind, the Society cannot " engage in the undertaking.

" Resolved,
" That Mr. Marfhall have liberty to " confult the Books of Agriculture in " the poffeffion of the Society, and to " infpect the feveral Machines and " Models in their repofitories."

THESE

THESE RESOLUTIONS, though
they afforded no real affiftance, ferved tö
eftablifh the ufefulnefs of the plan.   The
ineans of carrying it into execution remained now the only object of confideration.
An application to PARLIAMENT was
thought of, and ftrongly recommended,
but at a time when public economy had
become a neceffary and prevailing principle, and when the immediate prefervation
of the State called for every hour of parlia-
mentary deliberation, it would have been
highly improper to have attempted to
draw off the attention of Parliament to
any other object, however ufeful.

But being thut embarked, it was thought
advifeable to proceed fo far, at leaft, as to
make the Plan *known* to thofe whom it
particularly concerns ;—and it was accordingly communicated to feveral of the
principal Nobility, and to fome few Gentlemen of landed Property. Its reception,
however, was not fuch as I confidered it to
be entitled to ; and in this fpecimen there
were fufficient grounds to convince me of
what might be expected from INDIVI-
DUALS.

I there-

I therefore folded my Plan ;—with, however, a degree of *reluctance* ;--because I was confident that, were it carried into execution, it would be productive of much public good ;---but without any share of *regret* ;---because I had fully discharged my duty to my COUNTRY, to my *profession*, and to *myself*.

In Auguft 1780, I went down into Norfolk, as agent to Sir HARBORD HARBORD'S eftate ;---one of the firft in that county.

The management of *Eftates*, though a fifter-art to Agriculture, or the management of *Farms*, was in a manner new to me ; and, though intimately connected with my Plan, had never ftruck me, as being, what it really is, an infeparable department of RURAL ECONOMY. Eftate-Agency, it is true, has always been treated of by writers as a diftinct fubject ; but it has generally been found proper to explain, in the fame book, the leading branches of Agriculture ; for, beyond difpute, the management of an Eftate cannot be conducted

ducted with propriety by any man unacquainted with the management of a Farm.

Norfolk is not more celebrated for its system of husbandry, than for a superior knowledge in the management of landed Estates, which is there reduced to a regular business.

I was singularly fortunate in my situation. I had not only an opportunity of seeing the effects of improper management committed by those who had gone before me; but of profiting by my own experience (thereby much extended) in endeavouring to do away the evil effects.

With respect to husbandry, too, I had every advantage: I had an opportunity of employing my leisure in actual practice, on a large scale: the Agency, of course, afforded me an extent of country to range over, and make my observations upon, at will: and, I am happy in being able to add, a number of sensible men,---some of them at the head of their profession,---were always ready to give me,
without

without reserve, every information I
asked for.

Thus,--in a manner totally unforeseen
----I became poffeffed of an opportunity,
not only of extending my plan to an important purpofe I had not thought of, but
of executing the part I had propofed, in a
manner which the whole Landed Intereft
could not, without an Agency, have enabled me to have done.

I therefore embraced every opportunity
of regiftering the ufeful ideas which occurred, whether in hufbandry, or in
eftate-agency; but (I think proper to
mention in this place) without any view,
at that time, of carrying the whole of my
plan into execution. At length, however,
finding, that I could no longer conduct
the eftate, in a manner, which, to my
own mind, appeared to be right ;---I loft
no time in finifhing a Regifter of the
Rural Economy of the county; and, in
November 1782, I left Norfolk.

Having thought it neceffary to fay this
much, in explanation of the following
work;

THE
RURAL ECONOMY
OF
NORFOLK.

I.

THE DISTRICT.

THE County, confidered as a fubject of
RURAL ECONOMY, is aptly divifible
into EAST, WEST, and SOUTH NORFOLK.

THE SOUTHERN Hundreds partake of the
Suffolk practice; and, though well cultivated,
do not exhibit, in its purity, the NORFOLK
SYSTEM OF HUSBANDRY.

THE WESTERN divifion is either marfhy,
low land, applied chiefly to the dairy, after
the manner of Cambridgefhire; or open fheep-
walks and extenfive heaths, whofe flock are

VOL. I.   B   fheep

sheep and rabbits; or newly inclosed country
(chiefly of the last description), in which no
general plan of management has yet taken
place.

IN EAST NORFOLK, alone, we are to look
for that regular and long-established system of
practice which has raised, deservedly, the name
of Norfolk husbandmen; and which, in a
principal part of *this* District, remains unadul-
terated to the present time*.

THE CLIMATURE of East Norfolk is cooler
than that of other Districts, in this Island,
situated on the same degree of latitude; namely, fifty three degrees. The seasons, here, are
from a week to ten days later than they are in
the neighbourhood of the metropolis.

* The largest fortunes have been made by farmers in
West Norfolk: not, however, by any superior system of
management practised in that division of the county; but
through extensive tracts of sheep-walks, and other *fresh
ground*, held by individuals, having been *inclosed, marled,
broken up*, and subjected to the *management of East Norfolk*;
where farms being comparatively small, and having been
inclosed, marled, and plowed, time immemorial, there
was not *room* to make a MALLET,—a DURGATE,—or a
MARTIN. Viewing the state of husbandry in West
Norfolk collectively, it is much beneath that of the
District here described.

THE

THE SURFACE of this District, though the
foil be dry, is an almost uniform flat; except
a border toward the feacoast, which is broken,
and, in many places; bold and picturefque ;
and, excepting the more fouthern Hundreds,
in which marfhes, fens, and lakes, provincially
" BROADS," fome of them of confiderable
extent, abound.

THE RIVERS of Eaft Norfolk are fmall and
few in number ; but its RIVULETS are numerous ;—interfecting its flatted furface in a
fingular and happy manner.

INLAND NAVIGATIONS. Notwithftanding,
however, the fmallnefs of the rivers, the natural flatnefs of the country renders them
capable of being made navigable : the Yare
furnifhes a RIVER NAVIGATION between Yarmouth and Norwich ; as the Thyrn, called
the North River, does from Yarmouth, through
the Broads, to Dilham near North Walfham ;
and out of this proceeds a CANAL NAVIGA-
TION to Aylefham.

THE ROADS, notwithftanding King Charles
was pleafed to fay the county of Norfolk
was only fit to be cut out into roads for the reft
of his kingdom, are unpardonably bad ;—

narrow,

narrow, shaded, and *never mended:* they are numerous, however, especially the bridle roads; so that a traveller, on horseback, has generally the choice of two or three ways, of nearly equal length, to the same place. Not a foot of turnpike road in the District; excepting the road between Norwich and Yarmouth.

THE INCLOSURES are, in general, small, and the hedges high and full of trees. This has a singular effect in travelling through the country: the eye seems ever on the verge of a forest, which is, as it were by enchantment, continually changing into inclosures and hedgerows. There is not, generally speaking, a piece of woodland or a coppice in the whole District; and even plantations are thinly and partially scattered. A common or a heath (which not unfrequently occurs even in this part of Norfolk) is the only variety the face of the country affords. Some remnants of common fields still remain; but, in general, they are not larger than well sized inclosures. Upon the whole, East Norfolk at large may be said to be A VERY OLD-INCLOSED COUNTRY.

THE

THE TOWNS of East Norfolk are few : *Norwich, Yarmouth*, and *North Walsham*, are its principal MARKETS. But the smaller PORTS of *Blakeney, Cromer*, and *Munsley*, are beneficial in assisting to draw off the produce of the District; especially that of the northern Hundreds.

For a particular description of the Fleg Hundred, see MIN. 106.

Of the eastern coast, see MIN 112.

Of Blowfield Hundred and the Yarmouth Marshes, see MIN. 118.

B 3   ESTATES.

2.

E S T A T E S.

FORMERLY, in this Diſtrict, were many ſmall Owners—Yeomen—provincially called " Stateſmen," who cultivated their own eſtates. —There were. inſtances of entire pariſhes being occupied by this reſpectable claſs of men. But, among other evil effects of that inordinate paſſion for farming which prevailed ſome years ago, the decline of the independency of this country is a ſtriking one.

The yeomanry, heretofore independant and reſpected, ſeeing men, whom they had lately held as their inferiors, raiſed, by an exceſſive profit which had recently been made by farming, to a degree of affluence ſuperior to their own, and living in a ſtyle of extravagance their anceſtors had been ſtrangers to, became diſſatisfied with the homelineſs of their ſituation in life, and either launched out
into

into extravagances ill fuited to their income,
or *voluntarily* fold their comparatively fmall
patrimonies, in order that they might, agreeably with the fafhion or frenzy. of the day,
become great farmers.

By this means many of thofe comfortable
places which were thickly fcattered over Eaft
Norfolk, have fallen into the hands of men of
fortune ; and are now become united with
their large eftates.

There are, neverthelefs, fome few fmall
owners ftill remaining ; but very few of the
poffeffions, even of thofe, are FREEHOLD ; the
COPYHOLD tenure being prevalent throughout
the Diftrict ; which contains fome very extenfive, and, even to this day, lucrative,
MANORS.

3.

FARMS.

THE FARMS of Eaſt Norfolk are principally *incloſed*; there being, as has been already obſerved, few common fields at preſent
in this Diſtrict; and theſe few are in general
very ſmall; ten, twenty, or thirty acres; cut
into patches and ſhreds of two or three acres,
down to half an acre, or, perhaps, a rood
each *.

But another ſpecies of intermixture, much
more diſagreeable to the occupier, is here ſingularly prevalent. It is very common for an
incloſure, lying, perhaps, in the centre of an
otherwiſe entire farm, to be cut in two by a
ſlip of glebe or other land lying in it; and ſtill
more common for ſmall incloſures to be ſimi-
larly ſituated.

* The central parts of the Diſtrict are more particularly ſpoken of: towards the north coaſt, ſome pretty
extenſive common fields ſtill remain open; and ſome few
in the ſouthern Hundreds.

Theſe

Thefe inconveniences have, no doubt, arifen from common fields having been inclofed by piecemeal, without the general confent of the proprietors. They are, however, inconveniencies which are every year decreafing: many beneficial exchanges of intermixed lands have lately taken place, and many more equally advantageous remain yet to be made (fee Min. 4. on this fubject).

But notwithftanding thefe intermixtures and irregularities are ftill too prevalent, and notwithftanding fcattered and " one-fided" farms are fingularly abundant, there are many compact ring-fence farms to be met with in the Diftrict.

The sizes of farms, at prefent, are of the middle caft; few under fifty pounds, and fewer above three hundred pounds a year. Formerly they were much fmaller; but the numerous little places of the yeomanry having fallen into the hands of men of fortune, and being now incorporated with their extended eftates, are laid out into farms of fuch fizes, as beft fuit the intereft, or the conveniency, of the prefent proprietors.

THE

THE CHARACTERISTIC OF FARMS, in this District, is, invariably, ARABLE UPLAND;— with, generally, a small proportion of moory grassland, called MEADOW. Many, however, of the smaller farms, and some of those of considerable size, have no grassland whatever belonging to them. In this case MARSHES, or GRAZING GROUNDS, at, perhaps, twenty or thirty miles distance, are frequently hired by the occupiers of these farms.

But, viewing the District at large, the grassland bears so small a proportion to the arable, that its distinguishing characteristic is that of an ARABLE COUNTRY.

SOILS.

4.

S O I L S.

A SINGULAR uniformity of foil prevails throughout this country: there is not, perhaps, an acre in it, which does not come under the idea of a SANDY LOAM.

Its quality, however, varies widely, both as to texture and productiveness. The northern part of the District abounds with barren heaths and unfertile inclosures; while the southern Hundreds are principally covered with a richer, deeper, highly productive foil.

The foil, in general, however, may be termed shallow: perhaps six, perhaps five, inches may be taken as the medium depth.

Immediately under the cultivated foil, a hard crust—provincially "the PAN"—occurs universally; and, under this, substrata of various qualities: an unfathomable ocean of *sand* may be considered as the prevailing substratum. In some places a hungry *gravel*, but more frequently an absorbent *brickearth*, is the immediate
mediate

mediate SUBSOIL. *Marl* fometimes rifes to near the furface, but feldom fo high as the *pan*.

This feems to be univerfally confidered as a diftinct fomething, poifonous in its nature, and partaking neither of the foil nor the fubfoil. It is not my intention to ridicule this received opinion; it may be well founded; but, to me, the pan appears to be a production not of nature, but of art; or, to fpeak more accurately, a confequence of the Norfolk culture carried on, time immemorial, with the Norfolk plow;—whofe broad flat fhare being held invariably in a horizontal pofition, and (unlefs in fallowing) invariably at the fame depth, the furface of the fubfoil becomes formed, by the action of the fhare, the preffure and fliding of the heel of the plow, and the trampling of the horfe, into a firm even floor, upon which the foil is turned, and re-turned, in the fame manner it would be, if fpread on a floor of ftone, or other material.

But be this as it may, and whether the pan be a natural or a factitious production,—it is a fact well eftablifhed, that breaking it up by plowing below the accuftomed depth, is very injurious to fucceeding crops.

Two

Two reafons may be offered in explanation
of this effect; the pan, year after year, and,
perhaps, century after century, has been a
receptacle of the feeds of weeds; which, by
being trodden or otherwife preffed into it,
have remained there, locked up from the fun
and air, and thereby deprived of the power
of vegetation. But no fooner are thefe feeds
releafed from their confinement by being
brought to the furface with the plow, than
they vegetate in myriads, to the annoyance
of the crop.

The other reafon is this :—the firm clofe
contexture of the pan renders it in a degree
watertight; it is, at leaft, a check to the
rain-water, which finks through the foil; pro-
longing its ftay in the fphere of vegetation.
But the pan being broken, the filter is no
more; and the rain, which is not immediately retained by the foil, efcapes irretrievably into an infatiable bed of fand,—or fome
other abforbent fubfoil.

For, if we except a few quickfands, which
occur on the margins of meadows, and the
peat bogs which occupy their areas, there is not,
in the Diftrict, an acre of retentive subsoil.

The

The Norfolk foil, however, is not without its partial evils:—" fcalds" are as pernicious in Norfolk, as quickfands and fpringy patches are in cold-foiled countries; and, what is worfe, they are, perhaps, incurable; while a partial retentivenefs may be eafily removed.

Thefe SCALDS are probably occafioned by a partial abforbency; namely, by a *more* abforbent fubfoil being interfperfed in patches among one which is *lefs* abforbent; and, generally, perhaps, by " heads" or prominent parts of the univerfal fubftructure fand, rifing up through a ftratum of brickearth; in the manner that " heads of marl" fhoot up towards the furface: as will be defcribed in the next fection.

For inftances of the abforbency of the Norfolk fubfoil, fee MIN. 59.

For obfervations on the ditchmould of Norfolk, fee MIN. 77.

For obfervations on the foils of the Fleg Hundreds, fee MIN. 106.

For general obfervations on the friability of the Norfolk foils, fee MIN. 106.

For

For obfervations on the foil of the eaftern coaft, fee MIN. 112.

For obfervations on the foil of Blowfield Hundred, fee MIN. 118.

For inftance of fcalds being injured by wet weather, fee MIN. 121.

5·

M A N U R E S.

UNDER this head I purpofe to enumerate the different *fpecies* of manure; and defcribe, fo far as the obfervations I have been able to make will enable me, their refpective *natures.*

The principal fpecies made ufe of in this Diftrict are :—

Marl,	Dung,
Clay,	Compoft,
Mould,	Teathe of cattle,
Lime,	Sheepfold,
Afhes,	Soot, Rapecake,
	Maltduft, &c.

The

I. The grand foffil manure of Norfolk is
MARL; through whofe fertilizing quality,
judicioufly applied, lands, which feem by
nature to have been intended as a fcanty
maintenance for fheep and rabbits, are rendered capable of fattening bullocks of the
largeft fize, and of finifhing them in the
higheft manner.

There are, in this Diftrict, two fpecies of
marl, very diftinct in their general appearances;
though their quality of fertilizing be fimilar.

The central and northern parts of the
Diftrict abound, univerfally, with a whitifh-
coloured CHALK MARL; while the Fleg Hundreds, and the eaftern coaft, are equally fortunate in a grey-coloured CLAY MARL.

The firft has, in all probability, been in
ufe as a manure many centuries : there are
oaks of confiderable fize now going to decay
in pits which have obvioufly been heretofore
in ufe, and which, perhaps, ftill remain in
ufe, as marlpits.

The ufe of clay marl, as a manure, feems
to be a much later difcovery ; even yet, there
are farmers who are blind to its good effect;
becaufe it is not *marl*, but " clay ;" by which
name it is univerfally known.

The

The name, however, would be a thing of
no import, were it not indiscriminately applied to unctuous earths in general, whether
they contain, or not, any portion of calcareous matter. Nothing is " marl" which is
not white ; for, notwithstanding the county
has been so long and so largely indebted to its
fertilizing quality, her husbandmen, even in
this enlightened age, remain totally ignorant
of its distinguishing properties : through
which want of information much labour and
expence is frequently thrown away.

One man seeing the good effect of the Fleg
clay, for instance, concludes that all clays are
fertile ; and, finding a bed of strong brick
earth upon his farm, falls to work, at a great
expence, to " claying :"—while another ob-
serving this man's miscarriage, concludes that
all clays are unprofitable ; and, in consequence, is at an expence, equally ill applied,
of fetching " marl" from a great distance ;
while he has, perhaps, in his own farm, if
judiciously sought after, an earth of a quality
equally fertilizing with that he is throwing
away his time and his money in fetching.

This is a ſtrong evidence of the utility of chemical knowledge, in the inveſtigation of foſſil manures.

Before I left the county, I collected a variety of ſpecimens of marls, clays, and ſoils of different parts of it. Theſe, with a ſtill greater variety which I have collected in other parts of the kingdom, I hope to find leiſure, at ſome future time, to analyze ; and, from the reſults, endeavour to draw ſome general inferences.

At preſent I ſhall confine myſelf to

1. The chalk marl of Thorp-market, in the Hundred of North Erpingham ;

2. The clay marl of Hemſby, in the Hundred of Eaſt Fleg ;

3. The ſoft chalk of Thorp-next-Norwich ; commonly called Norwich marl ; and to

4. The hard chalk of Swaffham.

1. CHALK MARL of THORP-MARKET.

The natural ſituation of the white marls of this Diſtrict is ſingular : they do not lie in ſtrata, as foſſils in general do ;—nor in a continuation of rock, like chalk and limeſtone ;

but

but in diftinct maffes, of different figures and magnitydes, rifing with irregular heads toward the furface, and finking to, perhaps, ten, perhaps twenty feet deep, and fometimes to a depth unfathomed. If the abyfs of fand, in which they lie buried, could be rendered tranfparent, thefe *clouds* of marl would, I apprehend, be feen fcattered under the furface of this country, in refemblance of the clouds of vapour, which we frequently, in fummer, fee fufpended in the atmofphere.

The general appearance of thefe marls differs not only in different beds or " jams;" but the fame jam generally affords marl of different appearances and qualities: the upper part is ufually fouler and more friable, while the lower parts of the jam are of a purer, firmer, more chalk-like nature ; and are ufually interfperfed with " chalkftones;"——namely, lumps of *chalk*, firm enough to be ufed in writing ; and with *flints*, fimilar to thofe ufually found in chalkpits of other diftricts.

The fpecimen before me was taken from the middle of a tenfoot jam. The general appearance is that of a dirty, rough, friable

chalk ;

chalk ; its *colour* being fomewhat darker, and
its *contexture* fomewhat fofter, and more
brittle, than the common writing chalks of
Surrey and Kent.

In the open air, it *breaks* readily, and in-
corporates freely with the foil.

In water, it *falls* in a manner inftanta-
neoufly * ; but *diffolves not*, in any proportion, in this element †.

In the fire, it lofes more than one third of
its weight ‡, and burns to *lime* §.

* A piece of this *marl* plunged into water fell with
a fmart crackling noife in a few feconds: but a fmall
piece of *chalk* contained in it, received no change from
the water. Hence we have a fimple *differential teft* of
thefe two foffils.

† One hundred grains——pulverized, dried, weighed,
placed in a filter, flooded repeatedly with cold and
warm water, dried, weighed—received not the fmalleft
perceptible diminution of weight.

‡ A piece, weighing fifty grains, retained in a ftrong
fire three hours, loft eighteen grains and a half;
weighing, when cool, thirtyone grains and a half.

§ The pit from whence the fpecimen made ufe of
in this analyfis was taken, being worked as a lime-quarry,
I had repeated opportunities of obferving the effect of
the lime, both as a manure and as a building-material.
Its ftrength and operation, in both cafes, are, as far as
common obfervation can judge, fimilar to thofe of the
chalk limes of Surrey and Kent.

In

In the acid of sea salt, the principal part of it is *dissolved,* and taken up by the acid; leaving a small proportion, of gross earthy matter, undissolved. Of one hundred grains of this marl,—pulverized, dried, weighed, mixed with water, and saturated with this acid,—eighty-five grains pass through the filter; leaving a residue of fifteen grains: two thirds of which is palpable, consisting chiefly of sand and flint; one third a fine impalpable claylike matter; mixing freely with water;—some part of it subsiding with reluctance.

A solution of salt of tartar, added to the filtered liquor, precipitates the *whole* of the dissolved matter; in a *snow-white powder:* which being retained two hours and a half in a strong fire, loses five twelfths of its weight *, and is concreted into a porous, friable, *ash-coloured* mass of quicklime; which being re-suspended in acid, and again precipitated, regains the weight lost in the fire, and regains its *snowy whiteness.*

---

* Thirty grains of the powder perfectly dried, lost somewhat more than twelve grains and a half; the lime, when taken out of the crucible, weighing somewhat less than seventeen grains and a half.

There-

Therefore, it is highly probable, that the soluble matter of this marl is a pure, or nearly a pure, *calcareous earth* *.

We may therefore venture to fet down, as the component parts of one hundred grains of this marl, which may be taken as a fair fpecimen of the white marls of this Diftrict,

85 grains of chalk,
10 grains of fand,
5 grains of clay.
___
100 grains.

2. The CLAY MARL of HEMSBY.

In its natural ftate, it is fituated in extenfive beds or jams of confiderable depth (fee MIN. 106). Its *colour*, when dry, fomewhat lighter than that of fullersearth, flightly tinged with fpecks of a yellowifh brown colour : its *contexture* that of a gritty. fullersearth, interfperfed with granules of white chalk.

* The lime has a perceptible, but very faint *yellowifh* tint. By the addition of a tincture of galls the ultimate filtered liquor becomes turbid : a *white* mucilage fubfides ; leaving a tranfparent *green* liquor. A tincture of galls added to the lime water, before the addition of the acid, has a fomewhat fimilar effect. But, previous to the calcination, tincture of galls produces no change whatever upon this marl, either in a dilated or a diffolved ftate.

In

In the open air, it *breaks* into fmall fquares; and mixes freely with the foil.

In water, it *falls* readily; but *diffolves not*.

In the fire, it burns to *brick* *.

In the acid of fea falt, part of it is diffolved; but the major part is indiffoluble. Of one hundred grains, fortythree grains, only, pafs through the filter; leaving a refiduum of fiftyfeven grains; fifty grains of which is an impalpable claylike matter; the remaining feven grains palpable; chiefly fand; but mixed with fome beautifully coloured granules and fragments.

A folution of falt of tartar precipitates the whole of the diffoluble matter; which falls of a *pure white*; but dries to a *fomewhat yellowifh* powder; which in burning lofes exactly five twelfths of its weight; and concretes into a mafs of *fulphurcoloured lime:* which being

* A piece weighing fifty-two grains was kept in a ftrong fire more than two hours. Its *colour* was changed to a *faint red*, or fiefhcolour; its *contexture* to that of a hard-burnt brick, unchangeable in water; its weight forty grains. Being pulverized and faturated with the acid, the filtered liquor afforded, by an addition of the alkali, a *greyecloured* mucilage, which fell reluctantly, and dried to a *pale cinnamoncoloured* fubftance.

In the open air *.——

In water, it neither *falls* †, nor *diſſolves*.

In the fire, it burns to *lime*, loſing one third of its weight in the fire.

In the acid of ſea ſalt, almoſt the whole of it is diſſolved. Of one hundred grains, ninety-eight paſs through the filter; leaving only two grains of reſidue. Principally a dark brown ruſt-like matter; fine enough to lodge itſelf *in* the pores of the paper, leaving only a few particles of ſand *upon* the filter.

A ſolution of the ſalt of tartar precipitates the diſſolved matter in a *white mucilage*, which dries to a *yellowiſh white powder*; which, being retained three hours in a ſtrong fire, loſes a portion of its weight, and is converted into a friable maſs of *yellowiſh white* quicklime: which being re-diſſolved and re-precipitated,

---

* Having omitted to make an *intentional obſervation* on this circumſtance, I cannot ſpeak to it poſitively; but, from the ſmall quantity uſually ſet on, and the ſhort time it laſts, as well as from *general obſervation*, I believe, that it mixes readily with the ſoil.

† A piece, the ſize of a hazel nut, lay ſeveral hours in water without undergoing the leaſt change.

regains

regains its weight, and falls in a *snow-white mucilage*, which dries to a *nearly white powder*.

Therefore, one hundred grains of this chalk contains,

Ninetyeight grains of a matter diſſoluble in the acid of ſea ſalt, and is probably a pure, or nearly a pure, *chalk* ; and,

Two grains of indiſſoluble matter, whoſe properties I have not, yet, ſufficiently aſcertained.

This chalk contains the greateſt proportion of diſſoluble matter,—or, in other words, is the pureſt calcareous earth, I have yet analyzed. The chalk of Betchworth Hill (a continuation of Box Hill, near Dorking in Surrey), celebrated as a manure (for which purpoſe it is fetched, twelve or fourteen miles, by the farmers of Suſſex), affords a reſiduum of more than one tenth of its weight : whereas the chalk of Thorp-next-Norwich affords only one fiftieth.

4. The Hard Chalk of Swaffham.

In its natural ſtate, it is ſituated in an extended rock, riſing to near the ſurface, and worked ten or twelve feet deep, as a lime-quarry.

quarry. Its *colour* nearly white : its *contexture* that of a *hard* Kentish chalk ; but mellows, I find, by keeping in a dry situation. When taken from the quarry (in 1782), it was too hard to mark freely; now (1786), it is sufficiently soft for the purpose of writing.

· *In water*, it remains perfectly concrete.

In the acid of sea salt, it, in a manner wholly, dissolves; the solution being almost limpid : but, in filtering, a soil of a dark brown colour, and a few (perhaps twenty) particles of sand are left in the filter.

A solution of salt of tartar precipitates the dissolved particles, in a *snow-white powder*.

Therefore, this chalk is, *in its natural state*, NEARLY A PURE CALCAREOUS EARTH.

II. MOULD.—Besides what come under the idea of marls and clays, a variety of other earths are industriously sought after by the Norfolk husbandmen; for the purpose of bottoming their farmyards and dunghills; with a view to catch the drainage of the dung. The dung and the mould are afterwards turned up and mixed together; by which means the mould becomes saturated with vegetable juices communicated to it by the dung : and it is a common

mon obſervation, that the mould thus prepared " lies longer in the ground"—is a more permanent manure, than the dung itſelf.

This is not improbable ; for crude unmixed dung, buried in lumps, and diſſolved in the ſoil by heavy rains, is liable, no doubt, to be carried away, in part, below the vegetative ſtratum ; eſpecially of a light ſoil : therefore, to arreſt and fix it, before it be carried upon the land, ſeems to be, in the management of ſuch a ſoil at leaſt, highly judicious.

This piece of good management is talked about in moſt countries, and practiſed perhaps by ſome few individuals ; but in Norfolk, a light land country, it is the univerſal practice*.

The principal ſource of this mould—provincially " manner"—is the ſhovellings of ditches; which, in this country, are found to contain in themſelves a ſingularly fertilizing property. This rich mould is not compoſed of the ſediment of the waſhings of the adjoining incloſures ; many of the ditches, perhaps,

* I mean, to bottom dungheaps with a ſtratum of mould. It is not equally univerſal to turn over and mix the dung and mould together ; but this is frequently done by good huſbandmen. It is not, however, in every caſe, eligible. A dungheap, formed _in the ſpring_, for turneps, would, in a _dry_ ſeaſon, be injured by ſuch treatment.

never

never having, from the time of making to the time of scouring, admitted a current of water; but confists altogether of dead weeds, leaves of the hedge, and the mouldering of the bank and the fides of the ditch.

The effect of the air of Norfolk upon the Norfolk foil expofed in this manner is extraordinary: the moft barren rufty fubftratum expofed for a few years in the face of a ditchbank, is changed into a rich black mould, of a fertilizing quality. This change, in a greater or lefs degree, takes place in every country; but I have not obferved it, any where, fo obvious as it is in this Diftrict. *Perhaps*, the fea air, acting upon a loofe porous foil, may affift in producing this change. Be this as it may, it is an interefting fact; by which, perhaps, Norfolk hufbandmen, at leaft, might profit (fee MIN. 77. on this fubject).

Another fource of " manner" is *ufelefs turf*. The backs of ditchbanks—the borders of fences in general—the fides of lanes, and the nooks of yards, &c. &c. which, in other places, are fuffered to remain, from generation to generation, the nurfery of weeds, are, by the Norfolk farmers, turned up into ridges, to rot the roots, &c. of the grafs and weeds, and to receive

ceive the melioration of the air; which done, it
is carted, in due feafon, to the paryard, or
dungheap.

Another fpecimen of manure much coveted
here is "mergin"—that is, the rubbifh of old
buildings.—Scaftone walls afford a great quantity of this valuable article; which, from its
immediate effect, and its duration, taken jointly, is confidered, by fome, as being fuperior to
marl, mould, or even dung itfelf; efpecially
upon fcalds, and hot burning foils. It is fometimes mixed with dung; but more commonly
fet on alone.

III. LIME is in good repute, though not in
general ufe, as a manure; hufbandmen in Norfolk being, like hufbandmen in other places, of
different opinions refpecting the value of lime.
This difference in opinion will ever remain,
while general conclufions are drawn from particular incidents. The effect of lime upon
different foils is as various as the foils themfelves; and nothing but experiment can determine whether it will, or will not, be beneficial
to a given foil.

It is ufed by many judicious farmers, even
after marl, with fuccefs. Upon hot burning
foils

foils it is generally found of the greatest efficacy; and is perhaps the most effectual cure of "scalds" which has yet been discovered: from these and other circumstances, lime is here considered as a *cold* manure.

IV. ASHES.—These are not in estimation as a manure in this country: even those of the hearth are in a degree neglected.

The meadows and fens abound with peatbogs, which in some places would be considered as inestimable sources of manure. The peat of the meadows would no doubt afford an ample supply of ashes; but those of the fens, being wholly composed of the roots, &c. of aquatics, burn down to an inconsiderable quantity of ashes, of a white colour, and of a volatile nature, like those of paper. Even the small quantity they afford is not considered, by men who stand high in their profession, as a valuable manure.

Sodburning is not, I believe, practised in any degree: I never, at least, met with an instance of it; nor, indeed, with any instance in which ashes were intentionally produced solely as a manure; except one, in which anthills were burnt for this purpose (fee MIN. 6).

V. DUNG.

V. Dung.—The *quality* of dung is here attended to with greater precifion than in moft other Diftricts.

"Town muck" ftands firft. Norwich affords a fupply to the country round it; while Yarmouth produces, for its neighbourhood, a muck of a fingular quality.

Yarmouth is in a manner furrounded by marfhes and the fea; ftraw, of courfe, becomes there a dear article. This, and the vicinity of the feafhore, has eftablifhed a practice, which I believe has been in ufe time immemorial, of *littering* ftables with fea fand inftead of ftraw. As the bed becomes foiled or wet, frefh fand is fcattered on, until the whole is in a degree faturated with dung and urine: the ftall is then cleared and a frefh bed of fand laid in. By this means muck of a quality fingularly excellent is produced: it is fetched by the farmers of the Fleg Hundreds to a very great diftance.

The "muck" of the "paryard," too, is efteemed of various qualities.—That of the ftable, made from horfes fed on hay and corn, is reckoned the beft; that from *fatting* cattle the next; while that of *lean* cattle, and of *cows* in particular, is confidered as of a very inferior quality;

quality; even though turneps make a part of
their food. The dung of fuch cattle, kept on
ftraw, alone, is efteemed of little or no value.
And, what may appear extraordinary to many,
the muck from the ftraw which is trodden,
only, is by fome thought to be better than that
from the ftraw which is eaten by lean ftock.

VI. Compost.—This may be faid to be the
common manure of the Diftrict; for there is
very little dung fet on without being firft mixed,
in the yard, or in the field, with mould, marl,
or other " manner." See Mould.

Sometimes a confiderable proportion of
" manner" is added to the dung: I have known
a compoft of one part marl, one part mould,
and the third part dung, ufed in common, by a
very induftrious judicious farmer, with fuccefs.

It feems to be a fact, well eftablifhed, that
although marl, alone, will not anfwer on land
which has been recently marled; yet, mixed
with dung, it produces a beneficial effect.

VII. Teathe.—This is a provincial term,
conveying a compound idea, for which we have
no Englifh word. When we make ufe of the

term *fold*, as applied to the fertilizing effect of
fheep pent upon land, we do not mean to convey an idea merely of the fæces they leave behind them, in this cafe, but alfo of the urine, the
trampling, and perhaps of the perfpiration, and
the warmth, communicated to the foil by the
practice of folding.   *Teathe* in like manner is
applied to the fertilizing effect of cattle, upon
the land upon which they are foddered with
turneps or other food; whether that fertilizing effect be produced by their dung—their
urine—their treading—or by their breath—
their perfpiration—and the warmth of their
bodies.

This term is applied likewife to fheep and
other ftock: nor is it confined to ftock fhut up
within narrow limits, but is extended to pafturing ftock; implying, collectively, the returns
which they make to the lands they depafture.

The teathe of cattle is, like their dung,
eftimated according to the quality of the food,
and the quality of the cattle which confume it.
The teathe of fat heavy bullocks, at head-keep,
is efteemed very beneficial to the lands of Norfolk; while that of cows and lean ftock is, the
" jamming" apart, confidered of little value.

VIII.

VIII. SHEEPFOLD.—There are few sheep kept in this District; and the fold is not in use; except by a very few principal farmers; and by some gentlemen who keep large tracts in hand. The value of sheepfold is well understood; but the main object of the East Norfolk husbandry is bullocks; and the farmers, by their practice, seem well aware that sheep among cattle are unprofitable stock.

IX. SOOT is in good repute; and, near the towns, is in use. RAPECAKE is also in good esteem, in some parts of the District; as are MALTCOOMBS, in places where they can be had at a reasonable price.

For the *application*, and the *method of applying* these various manures, see the article MANURE PROCESS.

For the method of *raising farm-yard manure*, see FARM-YARD MANAGEMENT.

For an instance of *burning ant-bills* for manure, see MIN. 6.

For an instance of utility of the *shovelling of a sheepfold* to grassland, see MIN. 10.

For an instance of the use of *sheepfold* to barley, see MIN. 11.

D 2   For

For experiments on *different manures* for wheat, fee MIN. 18.

For a calculation on the value of *fheepfold*, fee MIN. 18.

For experiments and obfervations on the action of *lime*, fee MIN. 29.

For reflections on *bullock teathe*, upon the fair-ftead of St. Faith's, fee MIN. 31.

For a defcription of the *Fleg clay*, fee MIN. 106.

For obfervations on the effect of *calcareous earths* on ftiff land, fee MIN. 106.

For a defcription of the *marl and clay of the coaft*, fee MIN. 112.

FARMERS.

6.

F A R M E R S.

I DO NOT mean to hold out the farmers of Norfolk as a separate order of men: farmers, in every country, have, in their dress, their manner, their conversation, and their acquirements, a striking resemblance: neverthelefs, in every country, I find fome diftinguifhing characteriftic.

The farmers of Norfolk are ftrongly marked by a liberality of thinking, and, in confequence, by an opennefs in their manner and converfation. This may be accounted for: many of them have been, and fome of them ftill are, rich: this has led them to mix, in a greater or lefs degree, with what is called the World; of which their leafes render them independant. A tenant-at-will, be his riches what they may, is a fubaltern in fociety; in which he dares not to mix, left his landlord, or his landlord's affociates, fhould be pleafed to take offence.

D 3 Thus

Thus the clergy, and thofe men of fmall income who·fall under the denomination of country 'fquires, are in moft places looked up to by farmers; while in Norfolk they are con-fidered, by the principal farmers at leaft, as belonging to the fame order of fociety*.

The

* As an inftance of the *complacency* and *good breeding* (I do not mean *complaifance* or *politenefs*) of the fuperior clafs of Norfolk farmers, I will relate the circum lances of de-portment which occurred to myfelf, at a farm-houfe, at which I flept accidentally.

Our hoft having given ftrict orders, and fome perfonal attention, refpecting our horfes, the company were led into a fpacious kitchen, characterized by cleanlinefs and a chearful fire. A decent upper-fervant prefented herfelf. Supper was ordered, and a bottle of wine, in a neat fa-fhionable decanter, fet upon the table. A fmart, but not extravagant, fupper foon made its appearance. The houfekeeper waited in an adjoining room, and a maid-fervant at the table, with a degree of propriety and de-corum frequently unfeen in the houfes of thofe who call themfelves gentlemen. A trifling incident proved the good fenfe, if not the good breeding, of our hoft and his family. Forgetting that I was at the table of a *Norfolk farmer*, I afked for an article of the fide-board which was not at hand. The fervant went out of the room as if to fetch it; but inftead of returning, the houfekeeper came in to make an apology for not happening to have it in the houfe: fhe withdrew: the maid-fervant returned; while

the

The lower claſs of Norfolk farmers, however, are the ſame plain men, which farmers in
general are, in every other country; living in a
great meaſure with their ſervants. Another
claſs live in the kitchen with their ſervants, but
eat at a ſeparate table; while the upper claſſes
have their "keeping rooms" and other commodious apartments.

In general they riſe early, breakfaſt early,
and dine univerſally at twelve o'clock, at leaſt
the ſervants. This is well adapted to the Norfolk practice of going what are called two journies a day, with the plowteams: the men reach
home by dinner-time; and having refreſhed

the converſation went on without any notice being taken,
or any obſervation whatever being made on the aukward-
neſs of the circumſtance.

In the morning when I returned from a walk, I found,
in a decently, but not extravagantly, furniſhed parlour,
two tables ſet out; one with tea equipage, the other with
napkins, bread and butter, ham, radiſhes, &c. The
houſekeeper ſat at the former, placed on one ſide of the
room, and made tea; which was brought to us at our
table on the other: and this without the leaſt ſhew of
parade or formality. In ſhort, the whole treatment had
ſo much the air of that free-and-eaſy reception which I
had formerly experienced on the eſtate of a Weſt-India
Planter, that it was with ſome difficulty I could believe
myſelf in the houſe of an Engliſh farmer.

D 4   themſelves

themfelves and their horfes, are ready to ftart
again at one to two o'clock for the afternoon
journey. ,

For caufes of their prefent decline with
refpect to riches, fee MIN. 58,

7.

W O R K M E N.

WORKMEN, here, as in other places, are
divifible into YEARLY SERVANTS and DAY-
LABOURERS.

At the public hiring of YEARLY SERVANTS,
an excellent cuftom fubfifts in this Diftrict:
The High-Conftable of the Hundred in which
a ftatute is held, holds, at the fame time and
place, what is called a "petty feffions;" at
which the hiring and its attendant circumftances are, or may be, regiftered; which regifter becomes, in cafes of difpute, either between mafter and fervant, or between parifh
and parifh, a ufeful record.

In

In refpect to DAYLABOURERS, two remarkable circumftances are united; namely, hard work and low wages! A Norfolk farm labourer will do as much work for one fhilling, as fome two men, in many other places, will do for eighteenpence each. There is an honefty, I had almoft faid an honour, about them, when working by the day, which I have not been able to difcover in the daylabourers of any other country.

For an evidence corroborating thefe obfervations, fee MIN. 98.

For reafons accounting for their activity, fee MIN. 100.

For an inftance of ftill greater exertion, fee MIN. 106.

HORSES.

8.

H O R S E S.

HORSES are the only beasts of labour made use of in the Norfolk husbandry : there is not, perhaps, one OX worked in the county.

The farm-horses of Norfolk were, formerly, a small brown-muzzled breed ; light-boned ; but stood hard work, and hard keep, in a remarkable manner; and two of them were found quite equal to the Norfolk plow in the Norfolk soil.

Of late, stallions, of the heavier black breeds of Lincolnshire, Leicestershire, &c. have been fashionable; and at present (perhaps unfortunately for the country) the true Norfolk breed is almost entirely worn out.

I have heard sensible old men regret this ; and complain heavily against the present breed: they eat up too much of their corn, and are not so active as their favorite " old sort."

The present breed, however, are by no means heavy : on the contrary, being yet as a

mongrel

mongrel kind between the two breeds, they
are, compared with the elephants of Lincolnshire, a light, punch, active, little horse.

The singular breed of Suffolk is, at present,
the fashionable *cross*; and, to my mind, a very
judicious one: for, although this strange *variety* of the equestrian species—or, to speak
from appearances, this half-horse half-hog race
of animals—are not so handsome, in harness, as
the present beautiful breed of Leicestershire;
they appear to me, from a knowledge of both
kinds, to be better adapted to the Norfolk
husbandry. Their principal fault is a flatness
of rib: if this could be improved, they would,
in my opinion, be the first breed of draught-
horses in the kingdom.

It is, however, the lighter, more active
part of them, which is best adapted to the Norfolk husbandry. Had the original Norfolk
breed been crossed with these, instead of the
slugs of the Fens, the produce could not have
failed of being excellent.

Five horses are here called " a teamer," and
are usually placed under the care of one
" teamerman ;" who, in more leisure-times,
plows with two of them in the morning, and
with

with other two in the afternoon ; but, in general, a labourer, or a boy, works one pair of them while the teamerman works the other pair, two journies a day ; having always, in this cafe, one horfe at reft.

But in feedtime, more particularly in " barley feel," the fifth horfe goes to harrow ; every horfe upon the farm going to work at fix or feven in the morning, and ftays till twelve : goes out again at one or two, and remains at work till fix or feven.

In a waggon upon the road, five horfes are univerfally in ufe.

Whether upon the road or on the farm, the common practice is for the horfes to trot with empty carriages.

Formerly, this admirable cuftom was carried too far : inftead of trotting for difpatch, races were run, at full fpeed, upon the road.   The lead was the goal contended for : a forehorfe which would, at a word or a fignal, break out at full fpeed, was, by the young men who took delight in the diverfion of " roading," confidered as invaluable. Many waggons, and fome necks, having been broken by this dangerous amufement, it is, at prefent, a good deal laid afide ; though not yet entirely left off. I have

myfelf

myfelf feen a race of this kind : a following
team broke out, upon a common, and, un-
mindful of the ruts, hollow-ways, and rough-
neffes, contended for the lead ; while the leading team as eagerly ftrove to keep it ; both of
them going at as full a gallop as horfes in har-
nefs could go, for a confiderable diftance ; the
drivers ftanding upright in their refpective waggons. The clofe of the race was the moft dangerous part of it ; for fo foon as the forehorfe
of the team which broke out, found that he
had gained the lead, he rufhed eagerly into the
road ; which, in that place, happening to be
hollow, it appeared to me miraculous that
no mifchief was done. Savage, however, as
this cuftom may feem, the prefent fpirit of
activity may be, in fome meafure, indebted to
it ; and whenever it is wholly laid afide, I
hope it will be from motives of prudence,
rather than from a want of fpirit and inclination
to continue it.

THE KEEP OF HORSES in Norfolk, notwithftanding the work they go through, is lefs expenfive than that of other places, where large
unwieldy horfes feem to be kept for ftate, rather
than for labour. This, though prevalent in
many well cultivated diftricts, is an evident
absurdity.

absurdity. There may be cases, in which heavy loads are to be drawn short distances, and where the number of horses is limited, as in London ; in which cases, heavy powerful horses may be eligible ; but, from the observations I have been able to make, a compact horse is much fitter for the varied employments upon a farm ; and, with respect to keep, a main consideration in the choice of a farm horse, the advantage is greatly in favor of small horses. The present breed in Norfolk, still retaining a considerable portion of the original blood, is kept at half the expence at which many farm horses, in different parts of the kingdom, are supported.

In the leisure months of winter, barley straw is, in general, their only rack meat; and thro' winter and spring, they are suppered up with it ; except, perhaps, in the hurry of barley feedtime ; against which a reserve of clover hay is made ; provided the teamerman does not make away with it before that time. A Norfolk farmer has a similar difficulty in preventing his men from stealing hay, as those of other countries have to keep them from pilfering more than their allowance of corn.

I met with one instance, in which a judicious regulation was made, with respect to horse hay.

At

At Michaelmas, the master sets apart what he considers as a sufficient quantity to last to the close of barley seedtime. This allowance he consigns wholly to the care of his men ; who never fail to husband it in such a manner as to have the necessary reserve at barley seel; whereas before he fell upon this regulation, his horses were either worked down to skeletons, or he was obliged to buy hay for them at that season.

With respect to corn, a bushel each horse, a week, is, in the busiest season, considered as an ample allowance ; in more leisure times a much less quantity suffices.

Oats are the usual horsecorn ; but barley, when cheap or unsaleable, is sometimes given to horses.   In this case, it is generally " *malted*;" that is, steeped, and afterwards spread abroad, for a few days, until it begin to vegetate ; and, in this crisis, is given to the horses: It is thought to be less heating in this state, than it is when given to the horses in its natural state.

Chaff is universally mixed with horsecorn : the great quantities of corn grown in this country afford, in general, a sufficiency of *natural* chaff ; so that *cut chaff* is not much in use :

the

the chaff, or rather the awns, of barley, which,
in fome places, are thrown as ufelefs to the
dunghill, are here in good efteem as horfe
provender.   Oat chaff is defervedly confidered as being of a much inferior quality.

The fummer keep of horfes, is, almoft wholly,
clover :—fome few tares are grown, but the
quantity is inconfiderable.

Soiling horfes, in the ftable, is not here a
practice ; except for baiting in the daytime ;
the horfes being univerfally kept out at night ;
and, generally, in clover lays.

A fingular expedient, to prevent their breaking pafture, is here practifed :—Horfes inclined
to this vice are chained, two-and-two, by the
fore feet ; one end of a chain, about a yard
long, being faftened with a fhackle to the near
foot of one horfe, and the other end to the off
foot of the other.   This, however, though an
excellent way of preventing their rambling, is
a dangerous practice : accidents frequently happen. I knew an inftance of two horfes, coupled
in this manner, falling into a marl pit twenty
feet deep ; and though one of them miracu-
loufly efcaped, in a great meafure unhurt, the
other was mangled in a manner equally fingular,
                                              and,

and died on the spot. Accidents apart, the practice is a good one : horses accustomed to be coupled in this manner, become, in a striking manner, tractable and civil to each other; so that their feeding and sleeping is not so much interrupted, as in theory might be conceived.

Another practice, singular I believe to Norfolk, is that of "roping" horses, not only in common fields, but in inclosures : thus, instead of turning the horses loose into a piece of clover, the practice is to tedder them upon it; beginning on one side, and clearing the herbage as they go. This is a middle way between soiling and pasturing : it saves the expence of mowing, and carrying to the stable; but does not eat up the herbage so clean as soiling does: on the other hand, it is more saving of herbage than pasturing is; but there is not only trouble and expence; but a degree of risk, in roping.

Vol. I.   E   IMPLE-

9.

I M P L E M E N T S.

I. THE WAGGONS of Norfolk are of the middle fize and middle height: higher than thofe of Glouceſterſhire ; but lower than thofe of the midland counties. They are very numerous : upon a middleſized farm, three or four are ufually kept ; carts being feldom ufed here (notwithſtanding the levelnefs of the country) in getting in harveſt. However, to render carts ufeful in harveſt—more efpecially if waggons are wanted — a fingular expedient is here put in practice. With a common dung cart and a pair of old waggon ſhaſts and fore wheels, a carriage is formed ; which, partaking both of a cart and a waggon, is called a

II. 'MAPHRODITE. The points of the ſhaſts reſt on the bolſter of the fore wheels, to which they are faſtened. A copſe, or foreladder, fimilar to that which is fometimes fixed upon a cart ſhafts, but longer, is alfo ſupported by the

the bolster, projecting over the horse in front, in the manner of the foreladder of a waggon; the length and the breadth of the top of the " 'maphrodite" being the same, or nearly the same, as those of a waggon. In a hilly country, where carts are in a manner useless in harvest, these CART-WAGGONS would be found extremely convenient.

III. THE CARTS of Norfolk have a singularity pertaining to them. The shafts, instead of being fixed hinge-wise to the axle, or to the bottom of the cart, are a continuation of the side-pieces of the bottom itself: of course, the Norfolk carts do not *tilt* in the manner in which carts in general do.

In setting on manure, a long bellyband is made use of; so that the shafts rise with the fore part of the cart; the shaft horse being the only stay to its tilting up entirely. Nor is this an uncommon circumstance; the shaft horse, in this case, remaining upon his hind legs until he be drawn down again by the fore horses. This, to common observation, is an aukward and a *barbarous* custom: I have not, however, been able to hear of a shaft

E 2   horse

horse receiving any great injury from this
practice *.

Marling, it is highly probable, brought it
into use: the wear-and-tear of carts in this
rugged operation is endless; the simplest,
strongest, and least expensive cart has, of
course, been, for ages; the study of Norfolk
husbandmen; and it is probable that a more
simple, a stronger, or a less expensive cart cannot be devised than that described above;
which is in common use in this District.

Carts of the common construction, of which
there are some few used here, for particular
purposes, are called TUMBRELS.

IV. THE NORFOLK PLOW is still more singular in its construction than the Norfolk cart;
and, what is equally singular, it is, in a manner
wholly, confined to the county of Norfolk.
The first I saw was at Thetford, and I do not
recollect to have seen one plow of any other
construction while I remained in the country,
nor one of that construction since I left it.

It is true, this implement has been distri-

* A broad soft bellyband, of leather or hemp, ought
however to be used on this occasion. The sharp iron
chains which are frequently made use of, are painful to
the ox at least.

buted,

buted, at different times, in almost every Diftrict in the kingdom; but it has not, I believe,
been *adopted* in any one of them;—except
perhaps in Nottingham Forest.

There is no doubt of the excellency of the
Norfolk plow in cultivating the Norfolk soil;
or any soil which is similar to it; namely, a
shallow, sandy loam, free from obstructions.
But the width, and general shape, of the share
render it utterly incapable of being worked in
a strong soil, in which stones or other obstructions abound: and the usual manner of setting
the hind part of the " plat" or mouldboard,
equally prevents it from turning, properly, a
deep square furrow.

The peculiarities of its construction are principally these :—the wheels are taller, and their
tackle more complex, than those of other small
plows; the form of the wheels themselves
being, however, beautifully simple. The share
is unusually broad, flat, and blunt at the point.
The *mouldboard* is not of wood, but of iron,
sometimes wrought sometimes cast *; being a

* *Cast-iron shares* have lately been invented, and a pa-
tent procured for them, by a person of Norwich. For
the Norfolk plow, in the Norfolk soil, they appear, from

separate ſtrong *plate*, twiſted into a form reſembling the mouldboard of the modern
little plow of Yorkſhire and other Diſtricts ;
which, it is probable, has been copied from the
Norfolk "plat." Another thing remarkable
in the Norfolk plow, though not ſingular to it,
is its having only one handle.

There are readers, perhaps, who will expect that a drawing and dimenſions of the Norfolk plow, and, perhaps, of the other implements peculiar to the country, ought to have
been given in this work ; in order that copies
of them might have been made in other
Diſtricts. The idea, in theory, is plauſible ;
and I have myſelf, as writers in general on the
ſubject of huſbandry have, ſpent much time in
the purſuit of it. Experience, however, has
convinced me that, with reſpect to myſelf at
leaſt, it has been time ill-ſpent: I have found
even patterns inſufficient guides to workmen :
ſo much depends on minutiæ in the conſtruc-

the ſpecimens I have ſeen of them, to be a valuable invention. If they can be made *firm* enough to ſtand in a
ſtony ſoil, and hard enough to retain a ſufficient edge in a
gravel, they muſt prove, to agriculture in general, a moſt
valuable acquiſition. *Jan.* 1787.

tion

tion of the more complex implements of agriculture. Nay, the very implement which gives rise to these observations, constructed in Norfolk in the most complete manner, and furnished with every necessary appendage, has lain useless upon a soil it suited, until a Norfolk plowman was sent to hold it! How unreasonable, then, to expect utility from a drawing of it!

These circumstances are not singular to the Norfolk plow; I have known them attend other implements transferred from one part of the island to another: and I will beg leave to observe, here, in general terms, that whoever wishes to introduce an implement which is in use in some distant District, would do well to have it not only constructed, but set to work, in the country where it is in use; and I will venture to add, that success cannot be insured unless a person accustomed to the working of it accompanies it, and sets it to work in the District into which it is intended to be introduced.

This is, no doubt, an expensive way of proceeding; but it is a certain one: while every other expedient is throwing away, or at least

risking,

rifking, a certain expence, without any other certainty whatever.

Suppofe the Norfolk plow, for inftance, to be tranfported one hundred miles,—and the charges of a man, a horfe, and a light cart, to be from fixpence to a fhilling a mile,—the expence,—to a large occupier, in a country where a fandy foil, free from obftructions, and with an abforbent fubfoil, is worked by three horfes at length with a driver,—would not be an object*.   Plowing with two horfes without a driver, inftead of three with a driver, is, perhaps, the greateft faving which can . be introduced upon a farm: and, for the foil abovementioned, it would be difficult to con- ftruct a better plow than that which is now, and has been time immemorial, in common ufe in Norfolk.

If I were to hazard an improvement of the Norfolk plow, it would be the addition of another handle; and to change the practice of driving with a whip (to my mind a very auk-

* In thefe days of fpirited improvements in hufbandry, when fifty to a hundred guineas are given for one year's ride of a ram, five pounds for the introduction of a ufe- ful implement cannot be deemed extravagant.

ward

ward bufinefs) to that of driving with whipreins, in the Yorkfhire manner; a practice,
the excellency of which I have myfelf experienced in different Diftricts.

The Norfolk rein is one continued "line"
paffing from the bridle of one horfe, through a
ftaple fixed on the underfide of the handle of
the plow, to the bit of the other horfe; the
plowman holding his plow with the left hand,
and carrying a fhort whip in his right. In
difficult work the right hand, whip-and-all, is
applied to the handle of the plow; the plowman walking, in this cafe, in a pofture and
with a gait, which, to a ftranger, appears
extremely aukward; and nothing, but the
want of another handle, could render it fuffer-
able to the plowman himfelf.

The Norfolk line has, in fetting out a frefh
furrow, a feeming advantage over whipreins.
In this difficult work, at which the Norfolk
plowmen are fingularly expert, the loofe part
of the line is gathered up in the right hand, fo
that the plowman has, with the fmalleft motion of his hand, one way or other, a perfect
command of both horfes; but if, in this operation, he tie the two ends of the whipreins
together,

together, letting the left-hand one ride beneath
a pin, or in a hook, placed under the handle
for that purpofe, the advantage of the Norfolk
line is thereby fully obtained.

The Norfolk *barrow* is adapted to the foil—
light and fhort-tined.—Each harrow has its
horfe :—that is, each horfe draws a feparate
harrow ;—three or four harrows being fometimes drawn abreaft, without being, as in other
places, intimately connected together.

V. The roller of this country is very fimple and *very light*. This, confidering the nature of the foil, is extraordinary.

The farm-rollers, in general, have no fhafts
—perhaps only two loofe pieces of wood, about
two feet and a half long, with a hole near one
end, to receive the gudgeon of the roller, and
a hook or eye at the other, to hook the trace
to : fometimes two rails are fixed in between
the two end-pieces, framewife, with two hooks
or ftaples in the front rail to hook the horfe to,

In evidence of the lightnefs of the Norfolk
roller, I do not recollect to have feen more
than one horfe ufed in a common farm roller ;
and this one horfe, befides drawing the implement,

ment, has ufually carried the driver; it being
the fingular cuftom of this country to " ride at
roll :" an employment, however, which generally falls to the fhare of a young boy, or an old
man.

Notwithftanding the high degree of cultivation in which the lands of Norfolk are undoubtedly kept, no country perhaps has lefs
variety of implements.

There is not perhaps a *drill*, a *borfeboe*, or
fcarcely a *borferake*, in Eaft Norfolk. I faw
one *fpikey roller* for the purpofe of indenting
the furface of a clover lay once plowed for
wheat (fee the article WHEAT): but this, I
believe, was never in common ufe.

There is, however, one implement, received into the Norfolk hufbandry, which is probably a Norfolk invention, and peculiar to the
county: I have not met with it, at leaft, out of
this country:—I mean the

VI. SNOW-SLEDGE.—This beautifully fimple implement is ufed for uncovering turneps
buried under a deep fnow. It is fimply three
deal or other boards, from one to two inches
thick, ten or twelve inches deep, and feven to
nine feet long, fet upon their edges in the form

of

of an equilateral triangle, and ftrongly united,
with nails or ftraps of iron, at the angles; at
one of which is faftened, by means of a double
ftrap, a hook or an eye, to hang the horfes to.
This being drawn over a piece of turneps covered with fnow, forces up the fnow into a
ridge on each fide, while between the ridges a
ftripe of turneps is left bare; without having
received any material injury from the operation.

VII. TIMBER-CARRIAGES. Although timber-carriages may not, in ftri&tnefs, be faid to
belong to hufbandry, a defcription of them
does not fall inaptly under the prefent head.
They are in Norfolk, as in moft other places,
of two kinds: the four-wheeled carriage—provincially, ("a drug;"—and the pair of wheels—
provincially, "a gill."—The laft is moft in ufe;
and of this only I mean to fpeak:—not fo
much of its conftru&tion, as of the manner of
ufing it.

The conftru&tion of the Norfolk gill is fimilar to that of the timber-wheels of moft other
countries: namely, a pair of tall wheels, with
a crooked axletree, furmounted by a block;
to which axle is fixed a pair of fhafts, or fometimes a fingle pole, only.

But

But the method of using them, here, is different from that which I have observed in other places; where the only use they are put to is to raise the butt end of a large timber to be drawn a short distance; the top end being suffered to drag behind upon the ground, to the injury of the turf, or the road, it is drawn upon.

In Norfolk, a large stick of timber, or perhaps three or four smaller ones, are entirely slung to the axle; so that, in drawing, no part of them whatever touches the ground; the top end being generally drawn foremost, and the end toward the horses always the heaviest.

The method of taking up a piece of timber is this: the horses being taken off, the wheels are run, by hand, astride the timber to be slung, until the axle is judged to be a few inches behind the balance-point: or, which is better, a chain is first put round the timber, and the wheels run up to it. It is difficult to ascertain the exact place of fixing the chain, by the eye; nevertheless, a person accustomed to sling timber in this manner, will come very near the truth. The chain hooked, and the axle brought into its proper situation, the shafts, or pole, is thrown back in the usual manner; the chain

carried

carried over the block; brought round the pole; its end made faft; and the fhafts or pole drawn down again by the horfes; by which means the timber is lifted from the ground, and fufpended to the axle.

If the required point of balance be not hit upon the firft trial, the fhafts are fuffered to rife again, the chain is unhooked, and fhifted to its proper fituation: the fhafts being again pulled down, are bound, by an iron trace or fmall chain, clofe down to the timber; while another fmall chain or trace is faftened round the foremoft end to hook the horfes to; *the team drawing by the timber, not by the pole or fhafts.*

The utility of having a fuperbalance of weight forward is twofold:—if the piece were flung in exact equilibrium, it would, upon the road, be in perpetual vibration; thereby rendering the pull unfteady, and extremely inconvenient to the horfes; whereas by throwing the balance forward, the traces are conftantly kept down in their proper place, and the pull becomes uniform: if, however, too much weight were to be thrown forward, the draught of the horfes would not raife the point from the ground; the friction would, of courfe, increafe the draught, and the road be at the fame time hurt.

hurt. It therefore follows, that the proper weight to be thrown forward is enough to prevent a vibration, but not so much as to prevent the point from being raised from the road by the draught of the horses upon level ground.

The other advantage by a superbalance forward, is gained in going down a hill; in which case, the draught not being wanted, the point, of course, falls to the ground, and serves as a pall to regulate the motion of the carriage; if the superbalance alone be not sufficient to check the too great rapidity of the motion, the driver adds his own weight. Likewise, if, in ascending a hill, the balance be lost; he, in like manner, seats himself upon the fore part of the load, thereby keeping it down to its proper level.

This method of conveying timber may, it is possible, be in use in other Districts; but I have not seen it practised any where except in Norfolk. I know it to be an excellent, but not a common practice: I have, therefore, been induced to give this description of it.

T A X E S.

10.

T A X E S.

UNDER this head I shall class
Landtax,
Tithe,
Poor's Rates.

I. THE LANDTAX, in this District, runs
at about eighteen pence to two shillings upon
the present rents.

II. TITHE. The District is mostly tithe-
able; but tithe is here seldom taken in kind.
The rents paid, in three principal parishes in
this neighbourhood, are:

North Walsham, about two shillings and
nine pence, rectorial; and one shilling, vicarial; an acre, all round.

South-Reps, about three shillings each acre
of arable land, for rectorial and vicarial.
This parish is allowed to be reasonably rented.
The rector resides in the parish.

North-Reps, for great and small, three
shillings an acre all round; though much bad
land in the parish.

N. B.

N. B. In *Rowton*, a small parish of poor land, about two shillings for corn and fallow, two-and-sixpence for clover and turneps, and one penny halfpenny for each cow and calf, as a modus for meadow.

III. POOR'S RATE. In the year 1782, and for some years preceding, the poor's rate of

North Walsham was about five shillings and sixpence upon the pound, rackrent.

South Reps, three shillings and sixpence upon the rackrent.

North-Reps, four shillings upon the same.

Rowton, three shillings upon the same.

Erpingham, (a considerable parish) three-and-sixpence upon the same.

It must be observed, however, that the period under notice being in the war, the wives and families of militiamen were a principal cause of raising the poor's rates to the above high pitch.

II.

GENERAL MANAGEMENT

OF

ESTATES.

THE MANAGEMENT of landed eſtates, in this Diſtrict, is conducted on a plan, which is not generally known, and is ſeldom if ever executed, in other parts of the kingdom ; where receiving, twice a year, by a plain rentroll, is frequently the ſum of management.

Formerly, it was the invariable practice of the Diſtrict for landlords not only to build, but to repair; alſo to furniſh gates ready-made ; plant and cut hedges ; and even repair the ditches of their tenants ; reſerving to themſelves the hedgewood ; and, in effect, a degree of poſſeſſion of the buildings and fences ; the tenant having, of courſe, only a partial poſſeſſion of the farm he rented. And the ſame ſyſtem of management, with ſome few alterations, prevails to the preſent time.

This

This renders the immediate superintendency of a large estate in Norfolk a busy and unbroken scene of employment. The summer months are not more actively employed in attending to REPAIRS, than the winter months are in the management of FENCES.

But these and other articles I shall consider separately; comprizing under the present head such general matter, only, as necessarily occurs upon every leased estate.

I. TENANCY.   *Tenants-at-will* are thinly scattered. LEASES, either for a *term*, or from *year-to-year*, are universal. *Leases for life* are rarely heard of in this District.

II. TERM.   The term, formerly, was twenty-one years ; but the advance of produce which took place some years ago, producing, as it ever will do, an advance of rent, the tenant who had then just entered on a lease of twenty-one years, became, for a series of years, under-rented : the consequence is, gentlemen, in general, refuse to grant leases of longer term than fourteen years, and many . curtailed them to seven years ; a term, in my opinion, much too short.

F 2   Articles

Articles from year-to-year are very prevalent, especially among smaller tenants; and, in many respects, they are preferable to a short term; which is a tie to both parties, without being, in general, advantageous to either.

Marling is the principal improvement of a Norfolk farm; but who would marl on a seven years leafe? Where much marling is to be done, fourteen years is too short a term;—and though landlords may once have felt the inconveniencies of twenty-one years leafes, it is probable that tenants, who have of late years taken leafes of that length, will, before their expiration, experience, in their turn, feelings of a similar nature.

III. RENT. The medial rent of the District may be laid at twelve shillings an acre : toward the North coast the soil is lighter, and less productive, than it is in more central parts of the District ; but on the Eastern coast and in the southern Hundreds it is much more fertile, letting from eighteen to twenty shillings an acre.

In general, the District is very highly rented: there are lands in the kingdom,—I will venture to say within twenty miles of the metropolis,— which let at eight shillings an acre, yet are, in their nature, equally fertile as those of Norfolk, which

which let currently for ten to twelve shillings.
Nothing can account for this but the superiority of the Norfolk husbandry; and the
quick dispatch which prevails in every department of the Norfolk system of management.

IV. COVENANTS. Covenants of leases are, in
Norfolk, as in other Districts, various as leases
themselves: the particular circumstances of an
estate, and the special matter of agreement
between landlord and tenant, will ever produce
this variety, in a greater or less degree : nevertheless, every country has its natural covenants, and its prevailing fashions, as to re-
strictions and indulgences.

These fashions, however, alter ; and an improvement has recently taken place, upon some
of the first estates in Norfolk, with respect to
the REPAIRS of buildings and fences; the tenant
now covenanting to pay half the workmen's
wages.   This has two valuable effects :—the
tenant thereby pays a stricter attention to the
workmen employed; and becomes more careful of those things which, heretofore, he had no
interest in preserving.

V. No department of the management of an
estate gives more uneasiness to both landlord

F 3   and

and tenant than do REMOVALS, or exchanges of
tenants; and every covenant which facilitates
this unpleafant bufinefs is valuable. The fhift-
ing of tenants is no where conducted with
greater eafe than in Norfolk; where, it is
probable, leafes have been long in ufe; and
where removals from farm to farm are become
familiar.

VI. THE TIME OF RECEIVING RENTS, in Norfolk, is, pretty generally, Chriftmas and Midfummer; landlords giving their tenants three
months credit. Chriftmas, however, is of all
others the worft time of the year for this purpofe: many ferious evils arife from it (fee
MIN. 47, on this fubject). The firft of March
and the firft of June appear to be the moft
eligible rentdays in Norfolk.

VII. The following HEADS OF A LEASE will
place the general management of a Norfolk eftate in a clear and comprehenfive point of view.
They are not, either in form or fubftance,
copied, precifely, from the leafe in ufe upon
any particular eftate; but exhibit, I believe, a
pretty faithful outline of the modern Norfolk
leafe.

LANDLORD

LANDLORD AGREES, 1. to let, certain specified premises, for a term, and at a rent, previously agreed upon.

2. ALSO to put the buildings, gates, and fences in tenantable repair.

3. ALSO to furnish rough materials, and pay half the workmen's wages in keeping them in repair, during the term of the demise; wilful or negligent damage excepted.

4. ALSO to furnish the premises with such ladders as may be wanted in doing repairs, or in preserving the buildings, in case of high wind, fire in chimneys, &c. (an excellent clause).

5. ALSO to furnish rough materials for keeping the gates, gateposts, styles, &c. &c. in repair; or to furnish the materials ready cut out; tenant paying the usual price of labour for cutting out.

6. ALSO to pay half the expence of such shores and ditches as he, or his agent, shall direct to be made or renewed.

LANDLORD RESERVES, 1. all minerals, fossils, marls, clays; with liberty to work mines, quarries and pits, and to burn lime and bricks upon the premises; likewise to carry away ſuch minerals, &c. &c.; excepting ſuch marl, or clay, as may be wanted for the improvement of the farm.

2. Also, all timber trees, and other trees and woods, underwood *and hedgewood*; with liberty to fell, convert, char, and carry off ſuch timber or other woods; excepting ſuch thorns and buſhes as ſhall be ſet out by landlord, for making and repairing fences; provided the thorns, &c. ſo ſet out be cut in the winter months; excepting, however, out of this proviſo, ſuch few as may be wanted in the courſe of the ſummer months, for ſtopping accidental gaps.

3. Also, full liberty of planting timbertrees in hedges, or on hedgebanks; with a power to take to himſelf, after twelve months notice given, ſome certain number of acres of land for the purpoſe of raiſing timber trees, other trees, or underwood; allowing the tenant ſuch yearly rent, &c. for the land ſo taken, as two arbitrators ſhall fix.

4. Also, a power of altering roads, AND of incloſing commons, or waſte lands, without the controul of the tenant; to which intent, all commonright is uſually reſerved,

in form, though feldom *in effect,* to the landlord,

5. ALSO, the cuftomary liberty to view
buildings, do repairs, and, confequently, to
bring and lay materials.

6. LASTLY, the right of fporting and de-
ftroying vermin.

TENANT AGREES, 1. to pay the ftipulated
rent half-yearly ; and within thirty days after
it be due ; under forfeiture of the leafe ; and,
further, to pay the laft halfyear's rent two
months, or a longer time, before the expiration of the term.

2. ALSO, to do all carriage for repairs (within a fpecified diftance) ; AND to find all iron-
work and nails ; AND to furnifh wheat-ftraw
for thatching ; AND to pay half the workmen's
wages, and find them with fmall beer.

3. ALSO, to do all ditching, &c. fet out
by landlord (provided the quantity fet out do
not exceed one tenth of the whole) ; AND to
pay half the workmen's wages, and find them
in fmall beer ; AND to defend with hurdles,
or otherwife, all fuch young hedges as fhall be
expofed, in fpring and fummer, to the browz-
ings of pafturing ftock.

4. ALSO,

4. ALSO, to make, or pay for making, fuch gates, &c. as fhall be wanted upon the farm during the term of the demife; and to hew, or to pay for hewing, all neceffary gate-pofts; and to put down and hang, in a workman-like manner, fuch gates and gate-pofts, at his own fole expence; as well as keep all the old gates on the premifes in tenantable repair.

5. ALSO, not to affign over, nor, in any other way, part with poffeffion of his farm; but to make it his conftant refidence during the term of the leafe. Nor to take any other farm; nor to purchafe any lands adjoining, or intermixed with it; without the licence and confent of landlord; under forfeiture of the leafe.

6. ALSO, not to break up any meadow, pafture, or furze ground, under the penalty of ten pounds an acre a year. NOR to cut " flags," that is, turves, under fifty fhillings a hundred.

7. ALSO, not to lop or top any timber-tree, under the penalty of twenty pounds: NOR other tree, under ten pounds: NOR cut under-wood or hedgewood (except as before excepted)

under

under ten pounds a load. But, on the contrary, to preserve them from damage as much as may be; and, if damaged by others, to give every information in his power, under the penalty of twenty pounds.

8. Also, not to take more than two crops of corn without a whole year's fallow,—a crop of turneps twice hoed,—or a two years lay,— intervening, under the penalty of ——.

9. Also, to consume on the premises all hay, straw, and other stover; and not to carry off, or suffer to be carried off, any part, under pretence of being tithe compounded for, or under any other pretence whatever, under the penalty of ten pounds, for every load carried off.

10. Nor to carry off, nor suffer to be carried off, any dung, muck, &c. under five pounds a load.

11. Nor to impair the foundations of the buildings round the dungyard, by scooping out the bottom of the yard too near the buildings; but to keep up a pathway three feet wide between the dungpit and the foundations (an excellent clause).

12. Also,

12. Also, not to stock any part of the premises with rabbits; but to endeavour, as much as may be, to destroy them.

13. Also, *during the last two years of the lease*, not to take in any agistment stock.

14. Also, *in the last year*, not to suffer swine to go loose without being yoked and rung.

15. Also, *in the last year*, to permit land-lord, or incoming tenant, to sow grass seeds over the summer corn; AND to harrow them in, gratis; AND, not to feed off the young grasses after harvest.

16. Also, *in the last year*, not to sow less than —— acres of fallow, of, at least, three plowings and suitable harrowings, with two pints an acre of good, marketable, white-loaf turnep-seed; AND, in due time, to give the plants two hoings (*or, if the crop miss, to give the fallow two extra plowings*) in a husbandlike manner; AND, at the expiration of the term, to leave such turneps growing on the premises; free from wilful or neglectful injury; under the penalty of —— pounds an acre.

17. Also,

17. Also, to permit landlord or incoming tenant to begin, on or after the first day of July, *in the laft year*, to break up the two years lay (hereafter agreed to be left) for wheat fallow, or any other purpofe; AND to harrow, ftir, and work the said fallows; and to carry and fpread dung or other manure thereon, without moleftation.

18. Also, *in the laft year*, to permit landlord, or incoming tenant, to lay up hay, or other fodder, on the premifes, and to protect it thereon.

19. Also, to lay up and leave upon the premifes, *at the expiration of the leafe*, all the hay of the laft year (or of any preceding year, if unconfumed at the expiration of the term) except —— loads, which tenant is allowed to carry off.

20. Also, to lay up, in the ufual barns and rick yards, the laft year's crops of corn; together with the tithe, if compounded for; AND to thrafh them out, *in proper feafon*; and in fuch manner that the ftraw, chaff, and colder fhall be injured as little as may be.

21. Also, *at the expiration of the term*, to leave no lefs than —— acres of olland, of

two

two years laying (including that which may
have been broken up by landlord or incoming
tenant) and which shall have been laid down
in a husbandlike manner, after turneps or a
summer fallow, and with not less than twelve
pounds of clover, and half a peck of ray
grass, seeds an acre—under the penalty of——
pound an acre. Also not less than —— acres
of olland, of one year's laying, to be laid down
as above specified, under the penalty of——
pound an acre.

22. Also, *at the expiration of the term*, to
leave all the yard manure, produced in the
last year of the lease, piled up in a husbandlike manner, on the premises; excepting such
part of it as may have been used for the turnep crop; and excepting such other part as
may have been used by landlord, or incoming
tenant, for wheat.

23. Also, *at the expiration of the term*, to
leave the buildings, ladders, gates, fences, wa-
ter-courses, &c. &c. in good and tenantable
repair; landlord in this, as in every other case,
performing his part as above agreed to *.

* Also, upon such parts of an estate as lie near the
residence of the owner, it is customary for the tenant to
agree

TENANT TO BE ALLOWED, 1. the full value
of all the hay left upon the premifes, of the laft
year's growth, or of the growth of any preceding year; provided the quantity of old hay
do not exceed —— loads.

2. ALSO, the full value of the turneps left
on the premifes; or the accuftomed price for
the plowings, harrowings, and manuring; at
his own option.

3. ALSO, the feedage of the lays broken up,
by the landlord or the incoming tenant, from
the time of their being broken up until the
expiration of the term the enfuing Michaelmas; ALSO, for all damage arifing in carrying
on manure or otherwife.

4. ALSO, the feedage of the young clovers,
from harveft to Michaelmas.

5. ALSO, the ufe of the barns and rick-
yards for fummer corn until Mayday; and
for winter corn until the firft of July next enfuing.

agree to furnifh annually, a certain number of loads of
ftraw, according to the fize of his farm; ALSO to do the
carriage of a certain number of loads of ccals; ALSO to
keep dogs, warn off fportfmen, and fuffer them to be
profecuted in his name: remnants, thefe, of the antient
bafe tenures of foccage and villanage.

6. ALSO

6. Also, (by way of a confideration for the ftover) the cuftomary price for thrafhing and dreffing the corn; the landlord, or incoming tenant, ALSO carrying the fame to market, gratis: provided the diftance required to be carried does not exceed —— miles, and the quantity required to be carried, at one journey, be not lefs than —— coombs.

All the above ALLOWANCES to be referred to two arbitrators; one to be chofen by each party, in Michaelmas week; and the amount awarded to be immediately paid down, by the landlord, or the incoming tenant.

For the method of conducting *exchanges of intermixed lands*, in Norfolk, fee MIN. 4.

For the *time of receiving rents*, fee MIN. 47.

For the operation of a *rife of rent*, fee MIN. 58.

For an inftance of IMPROVEMENT by *rabbit-warren*, fee MIN. 79.

For inftance of IMPROVEMENT by *building-leafes*, fee MIN. 106.

For an IMPROVEMENT by *inclofure*, fee MIN. 137.

Note. Befides the above particulars, refpecting the general management of eftates, I find myfelf poffeffed of a variety of others, on the more immediate connection between landlord and tenant; but they cannot, with ftrict propriety, be publifhed in the prefent volumes.

12.

12.

BUILDINGS and REPAIRS.

THE FARMERIES of Norfolk are, in general, large and convenient. Many of them
have been the residencies of that yeomanry,
which, as has been already observed, is now
nearly extinct.

I. THE DWELLING HOUSE, in general, is commodious: kitchen and " backhouse ;" parlour; and, on the larger farms, a " keeping
room," in which the master and his family sit
apart from the servants.

II. THE BARNS of Norfolk are superior to those
of every other county; numerous and spacious. No farm has less than three thrashing
floors; some farms five or six, and these of
unusual dimensions. Twentyfour feet by eighteen is considered as a wellsized floor; twenty
by fifteen, a small one. Indeed, a floor of less
dimensions is ill adapted to the Norfolk method of cleaning corn; which is universally
effected by casting it with shovels from one end

of the floor to the other. To obtain this ne-
ceſſary length of floor, a porch on one or both
ſides of the barn, is almoſt univerſal. A leanto
porch, with double doors to let out an empty
waggon, and with a range of leanto ſheds or
hovels on either ſide, continuing the roof of
the barn, without a break to the eaves of the
porch and ſheds, is at preſent, deſervedly, in
good eſtimation.

III. BARN FLOORS are of plank, " lumps" (a
kind of bricks), or clay: the laſt are moſt prevalent; and although they be conſidered as inferior to the firſt, they are in better eſteem in
Norfolk than in moſt other places; for a Norfolk farmer is aware that what he loſes by the
handle of his corn, thraſhed on a clay floor, he
regains by *meaſure*; for the ſame duſt which
gives the roughneſs of handle in the ſample,
prevents the corn, thus ſoiled by the clay's
bearing up, from ſettling ſo cloſe in the buſhel,
as that which has been thraſhed on a clean
wooden floor.

IV. THE STABLES are no way peculiar; except in their having, in general, " a hayhouſe"
adjoining to them, inſtead of a haychamber
over

over them; a cuftom which is at once wafteful both of hay and houferoom: at prefent, however, it is the practice to raife ftables high enough to admit of hay chambers over them; with floors, not of boards, but of clay; which is cheaper, and, in other refpects, much preferable to board floors.

V. Cow houses are unknown in a Norfolk farmery: a fmall " fuckling place" and a " calves' houfe" are the only buildings appropriated to cattle: except

VI. Bullock sheds, which are fometimes (but not generally) erected; more efpecially in the fouthern Hundreds of this Diftrict. See Min. 118.

VII. The hogsty of Norfolk is fingular, though not particularly excellent: inftead of creeping into a pigfty, in the manner ufually done, a Norfolk farmer walks into his " pighoufe," at a door fimilar to thofe of his other outbuildings; the building is of courfe higher and more expenfive, but certainly more commodious, than in the ufual form.

VIII. Granaries are few: I faw none upon feparate pillars; and but very few over.

G 2　　　　IX. Wag-

IX. WAGGON SHEDS. Thefe in general are commodious. I met with a CART SHED on an admirable plan. The width equal to the cart and fhafts; open in front; with a bank of earth on the back part, about eighteen inches high, and of fuch a width as juft to take the wheels before the tail of the cart reach the back of the fhed: the cart is backed in, the horfe taken out, and the cart fuffered to tilt: the bank receives the tail, while the fhafts rife under the eaves of the front—dry,—and out of the way of cattle: the horfe is put in with equal facility: the backband, which remains faft at both ends, is entered into the groove of the faddle, and the fhafts pulled down.

X. RICK YARDS in general are fmall, owing to the capacioufnefs of the barns. It is pretty common, and very convenient, to have a rick frame at one or both ends of the barn, with a pitching hole, in at which the corn is houfed, without the affiftance of team labour. Sometimes thefe ftacking places at the ends of barns are inclofed, without having a frame for the ftack; which being houfed immediately after the firft clearing of the barn, the inclofure afterwards

terwards makes an admirable foldyard for calves or yearling cattle.

XI. FOLDYARDS—provincially,"paryards," in general, are warm and fnug: the outer fence is moftly " battoned ;" namely, made with pofts, and three or four wide ftrong rails, or " battons ;" an inch to one inch and a half thick, and eight or nine inches wide ; the lower ones being placed clofe enough for an effectual fence againft fwine. Thefe in autumn are fometimes lined with tall thorn faggots, efpecially on the bleaker fides. The area is *parted* into feparate yards with common pofts and rails, to which fimilar faggots (provincially, " kidds") are faftened : this, at a fmall expence, keeps the different fpecies of ftock feparate, and renders their apartments comfortable.

XII. DRINKING PITS, notwithftanding the abforbency of the Norfolk foil, are common to moft farm yards. It feems probable that they have, formerly, been made by art, and with much judgment ; as in general they retain the water very perfectly. At prefent, however, the art, if known, is out of ufe: indeed the RIVU-

LETS which abound in so singular a manner in Norfolk, preclude, in some measure, the use of artificial watering places, except in or near farm yards : besides, WELLS, in general, are so shallow, and their water so excellent, that both of them might, without extreme incon- venience, be dispensed with.

THE BUILDING MATERIALS of Norfolk are, 1. BRICKS, which are here manufactured with great skill. The materials are good : the subsoil, in many places, is naturally a very fine brick earth, without any admixture being required.

Besides the common *red* brick, of which the buildings of a farm are generally constructed, Norfolk is celebrated for an admirable *white*, or rather STONE-COLOURED BRICK, which, except on a near view, has all the effect of a well-co- loured stone. Of this brick the first houses in the county are built : for so expert are the moulders of this excellent material, that cor- nices and even columns, with their pedestals and capitals, are formed of it.

This superiority in brickmaking is, how- ever, one of those efforts of necessity, which are frequently productive of excellency in in- vention : there is not, generally speaking, a
stone

stone in the county; excepting a few flints, thinly scattered among the soil; and excepting the *sea stone*, which, near the coast, is used instead of bricks.

2. SEA STONES, however, are, in unskilful hands, a dangerous material to build with; for, being globular, their own weight, if the wall be high and run up hastily, is sufficient to crush it to the ground : and, when carried up deliberately, if the lime be bad, or the mortar injudiciously made, sea-stone walls are liable to part; having nothing but the mortar to bind them together. Their durability is their best recommendation; for, though the wall decay, the stones still are there; and it is highly probable that many of the stones which were used in the first buildings of that material are still in use. When they are found among ruins, upon or near the site to be built upon, they may, if skilfully set (and especially if the quoins and jams be carried up with bricks), be a very eligible building material.

Weatherboarding is made little use of in Norfolk;—in ordinary buildings, *clay daubing* sometimes is used as a substitute.

3. With respect to the materials of the HOUSE-CARPENTER, *oak* is generally used for door and

G 4 window

window frames: alfo for wallplates and fills
of every kind, and for beams, when it can be
had.   But in a country where the growth of
oak is confined, in a great meafure, to the
hedge-rows, it cannot be expected that a full
fupply can be fpared for building. *Afh* and *elm*
are ufed as fubftitutes; and, in a maritime
country, *foreign timber* is had at a reafonable
price.

4. COVERINGS are principally of *pantile* or of
reed;—many *ftraw* roofs remain; but, at prefent, few new ones are put on.

REED is, at prefent, the favorite roof; and
is of all others (good flate excepted) the moft
eligible for farm buildings.   A reed roof properly laid, will lie fifty years without touching;
and thirty or forty more, with only adjufting
("driving") it, and levelling the hollows with
a little frefh reed.   At an hundred years old,
it may be relaid; and will then, if laid upon
the upper parts of the roof, laft through a
confiderable part of another century.

It is principally cut from the margins of the
" broads;" and is carried, perhaps, forty or
fifty miles into the central and northern parts
of the county.

A cover-

A covering of reed is, in the firft inftance,
coftly: but when its durability, and the high
degree of prefervation in which it keeps the
roof are taken into the account, it is of all
others the cheapeft covering; befides its being,
whether in the extreme of heat or cold, the
moft comfortable.

The price of reed, in the place of its growth,
is from three pounds to three guineas a hundred; containing fix fcore fathom; each fathom
(compofed of five or fix fheaves) meafuring
fix feet in circumference. A hundred of reed
will cover five fquares of roof: the laying is
a halfpenny a yard, or four fhillings and twopence a fquare; and the tar-rope and rods for
faftening it on, coft eighteen pence a fquare:
fo that a covering of new reed cofts about
eighteen fhillings a fquare, containing one
hundred fquare feet; befides carriage, and
what is called " roofing;" namely, a cap of
wheat ftraw placed upon the ridge, in a fomewhat fimilar manner, and for the fame purpofe,
as ridge tiles are put on.

This capping, which is done in a moft effectual, but in a tedious and expenfive, manner,
cofts in materials and workmanfhip about
fixteen

fixteen pence each foot In length ; which, upon a roof of fixteen feet and a half fpar, is an additional expence of four fhillings each fquare of reeding.

The carriage is in proportion to the diftance. Taking twenty miles as a medium diftance ; and one fhilling a mile as a medium price ; the expence is twenty fhillings a " load" of fixty fathom, or forty fhillings a hundred ; which laying five fquares is a further addition of eight fhillings a fquare : therefore the whole expence of a covering of reed fetched twenty miles may be laid at thirty fhillings a fquare *:

I am the more minute on this head, as I fee this valuable material entirely neglected, as a covering for buildings, In moft parts of the kingdom.

5. The FLOORING MATERIALS of this Diftrict are, for upper floors, *deal, afh, elm,* and *peplar* boards: fometimes *clay* is ufed for cottages, and for common garrets; but, for the ground floor, *fquare bricks,*————paving tiles———— provincially, " pavements"—are, in farm houfes, the almoft univerfal flooring: even the beft rooms, of the

* For the method of laying reed and fetting on the roofing, fee Min. 32.

first

firſt farm houſe, are generally laid with this material; which is manufactured in an excellent
manner, of various colours, and of various dimenſions, from nine inches to eighteen inches
ſquare. Two pavements of the laſt dimenſion
make, for a common room, an excellent
HEARTH.

6. LIME is made from marl, entirely; this
Diſtrict affording neither limeſtone nor chalk:
Weſt Norfolk, however, abounds with a ſpecies
of hard foſſil—provincially, "caulk"—a kind
of hard chalk—from which lime of a tolerably
good quality is burnt. See MANURE, p. 26.

Lime is univerſally *burnt* with *coals*, and
generally in *drawing kilns*: it coſts from ſeven
to eight ſhillings a chaldron (more or leſs according to the diſtance of the carriage of the
coals), and is ſold for nine ſhillings to ten
ſhillings a chaldron *.

Bricks are burnt principally in *kilns*; few
in *clamps*: the bottom of the kiln is always
ſet with bricks; while the upper parts are
occaſionally filled with tiles, pavements, and
other ware.

For

* 1782.Oct. 26. Four chaldron and a half of coals (thirty-
ſix buſhels) burned thirty-four chaldron thirty buſhels of
lime

For the *price of building materials*, &c. fee
LIST OF RATES.

For the method, and expence, of making
baychamber floors with clay, fee MIN. 15.

For obfervations on the coping of *gables,*
fee MIN. 25.

For the method of *laying reed*, and fetting
on ridge caps, fee MIN. 32.

For the method of *laying pantiles* on reed,
&c. fee MIN. 33.

For obfervations on *check beams* acrofs barn-
floors, fee MIN. 35.

lime (thirty-two bufhels). In general, however, thirty-
two chaldron is the produce of that quantity : this is
fomewhat more than *feven* chaldron of lime to a chaldron
of *fea*-coals.

One chaldron of coals and carriage four miles	1	17	6
Labour, at twenty-pence a chaldron of lime,	0	11	8
Horfe and cart for moving marl, - -	0	1	0
	£ 2	10	2

Seven chaldron, at feven fhillings and twopence a chaldron,   -   -   -   £ 2 10 2

I have known a quantity fold, for manure, at eight
fhillings a chaldron.

The chalk of Swaffham yields about *five* chaldron of
lime (thirty-two bufhels) to one chaldron of *fea*-coals
(of thirty-fix bufhels).

For

For obfervations on the utility of *laying tiles on mortar*, fee MIN. 48.

For obfervations on *buttreffes*, fee MIN. 60.

For obfervations on the *general management* of repairs, fee MIN. 64.

Por the effects of a *high wind*, fee MIN. 91.

For general obfervations on the *refidence of workmen*, fee MIN. 92.

For defcription of a *farm yard* in Fleg, fee MIN. 106.

For obfervations on *farmyard walls*, fee MIN. 115.

For obfervations on *feaftone walls*, fee M. 116.

For the defcription of a *bullock fhed* in Blowfield Hundred, fee MIN. 118.

For the method of building a hog ciftern, fee MIN. 131.

13.

GATES and DEAD FENCES.

IT has already been mentioned as a practice of Norfolk, for landlords to furnish their
tenants with GATES ready-made.

This, when an estate is intended to be made
the most of, and where the tenants, being under lease, have no right to expect other indulgences than the lease gives them, is a good
practice ; for when rough timber is allowed,
even though it be set out, a designing tenant
will generally get the advantage, let the estate
be ever so well looked after.

It is reasonable, however, and is, now, on
some estates customary, in this case, to charge
the tenant for sawing and making up ; also for
hewing posts ; and for sawing out such parts
of gates as are wanted for repairs ; which, as
well as putting down posts and hanging new
gates, is generally done at the expence of the
tenant, who sometimes, but not always, finds
gate irons.

It

It is a practice, not uncommon here, to drive hooks on both sides the hanging-post ; in order that the gate may be shifted to this or that side, as the pasturing stock are shifted : and sometimes I have seen two gates hung upon the same post; one on either side : a most effectual guard, when both sides are in pasture.

The prevailing DEAD FENCE is *battoning* (see FOLDYARD); the tenant being charged for hewing posts and sawing battons, in the same proportion he is for gates or gatestuff; namely, the full expence of workmanship.

Even STILES are frequently provided, and charged for, in the same way, by landlords.

For an instance of *ivy* being serviceable to a *seastone fence wall*, see MIN. 9.

For general observations on *farmyard fence walls*, see MIN. 115.

For the method of setting a *furze-faggot fence*, see MIN. 135.

14.

L I V E   H E D G E S.

THE WOODLANDS of Eaſt Norfolk being few, UNDERWOOD, either in *woods* or in *coppices*, is in a manner unknown.   The HEDGEROWS, alone, may be ſaid to furniſh the Diſtrict with *timber*, *topwood*, and *underwood.*

Old hedges, in general, abound with oak, aſh, and maple ſtubs, off which the wood is cut every time the hedge is felled; alſo with pollards, whoſe heads are another ſource of firewood; which, in a country where coals can be had only by ſea, is of courſe ſought after : yet it is a fact, as notorious as it is intereſting, that Eaſt Norfolk does not experience, to any degree of inconveniency, a want either of timber or firewood; although its entire ſupply may be ſaid, with little latitude, to be from hedgerows.

It is probably from this circumſtance, that hedgewood is ſuffered to ſtand to ſo great an

age

age and growth as it does in Norfolk. Twelve
or fourteen years is confidered as a moderate
growth ; twenty, and even thirty years it is
fometimes permitted to remain without cutting.
The "ftubwood," it is true, by this means acquires a degree of utility and bulkinefs; but
the "thorns" are in the mean time overhung
and deftroyed.

It appears by the HEADS OF A LEASE * that
the topwood, the ftubwood, and the loppings
of timber, if any, belong to the landlord. They
are, however, in general, of more value to the
occupier of the land than to any other perfon ;
befides the tenant having a degree of claim to
the refufal of them ; and it is cuftomary to fell
them to him at a moderate valuation.

I. THE METHOD OF VALUING HEDGEWOOD is
as follows : the tenant having been confulted ,
and the particular hedge or hedges to be felled, in
any given feafon, having been determined upon ,
each *top* is (or ought to be) valued and minuted
feparately ; carrying the *ftubwood* in the eye
until fome certain quantity is gone by.   But a
readier method is, I am told, fometimes practifed ; namely, that of walking by the fide of
the hedge without particularizing the indivi-

* Page 72.

duals; or, which is ftill fhorter, but ftill lefs
accurate—that of ftanding at one end, and,
by merely glancing the eye along it, putting
down a random valuation.

II. But valuing the tops and ftubwood, though
done in the moft accurate manner, is by no
means all that is neceffary to be done in fetting
out what is called "ditching:" every TIMBER
TREE, and every POLLARD, ftanding in the hedge
to be felled, fhould be cautioufly attended to.

The timbers which are going to decay, or
which, to appearance, will receive injury before
the next fall of the hedge, fhould be *marked
to come down:* if gate-pofts be wanted upon
the farm, fuch pollards as are fit for that purpofe fhould be fet out; alfo all fuch pollards
as are already dead, or will not to appearance
bear a top equal to their prefent value, before
the next fall of the hedge, ought to be valued
to the tenant as firewood.

III. Other very material things to be attended
to, are the YOUNG OAKLINGS rifing among the
hedgewood; as well as the "STANDS," and the
GROWING TIMBERS; which ought to be *pruned,*
and *fet up,* in fuch a manner, as to give freedom
to the hedge and the herbage growing under
them;

them; and at the fame time to encreafe their own value, by giving them length and cleannefs of ftem.

This part of the bufinefs, however, ought not to be left to the ditchers; but fhould be performed by fkilful woodmen, fent round for the purpofe (fee MIN. 5. on this fubject).

It may be needlefs to add, that to go through this various bufinefs properly, paffing once along the hedge is not fufficient: the timbers, pollards, and timberlings, fhould firft be infpected, and, if requifite, marked; by which means the quantity of firewood will be more fully afcertained, and its valuation, by this double view, be rendered more accurate*.

* Left the reader fhould think that I am here deviating from the plan of this part of the work, by entering into the didactic where defcription only was neceffary, more efpecially as fimilar directions are fcattered in the Minutes; I beg leave to obferve, that the fubject appears to me to be of fo much importance, and to have been fo flightly, if at all, touched upon by writers, that it ought to be placed in every point of view which will throw frefh light upon it. And although I may, in another work, have treated very fully upon this fubject, I neverthelefs think it proper to detail, in this, the incidents and reflections which have arifen, immediately, out of my practice and obfervation in Norfolk.

IV. THE

IV. The treatment of old hedges.
The hedgewood being felled to the ſtub, and
the pollards headed, the ditch is ſcoured to its
original depth ; the beſt of the ſoil being collected into heaps on the brink of the ditch for
the uſe of the farmer, in bottoming his yard or
his dung heaps, and the remainder laid to the
roots of the ſtubs, or formed into a bank behind them.   On the top of the bank a bruſh
hedge is ſet as a guard to the back ;—while
ſometimes the bottom of the ditch is *pointea*
(that is, narrowed to a point), or filled with
thorns or other buſhes,—as a guard to the face
of the young hedge.

The laſt, however, is ſeldom done, nor often requiſite ; for the Norfolk huſbandmen are
pretty obſervant in cutting thoſe hedges, in
any given year, which face their wheat in that
year ; by which means the young hedge acquires four or five years growth before the
incloſure, it is expoſed to, becomes a ſpring
or ſummer paſture.

This is the uſual treatment of old *rough*
hedges in which pollards and ſtubwood abound,
and which conſtitute the principal part of the
hedges of Eaſt Norfolk.

There

There are, however, many *planted* hedges;
fome of them very old: of thefe, a twofold
treatment prevails: namely, that above-de-
fcribed; and another, lefs eligible, called
" buckftalling;" which is cutting off the
hedgewood, about two feet above the top of
the bank, and " out-holling," that is, fcouring
out the ditch for manure; without returning any
part of the foil to the roots of the hedgewood. But by a repetition of thefe bad practices, the hedges, fituated as they are in Norfolk, near the top of an artificial bank, with a
deep ditch beneath them, are at length left
deftitute of mould to nourifh and fupport
them, dwindling away, ftub after ftub, until
they are no longer adequate as fences.

The practice of *plafhing*, or laying hedges,
is, in a great degree, unknown in this Diftrict.
—Workmen, from countries where this is a
favorite and common practice, have been
employed by gentlemen in this Diftrict; but
the fuccefs has been fuch as has rendered thofe
to whom it has become known, inveterate enemies to the practice.

The unpardonable cuftom of hacking off
the fide boughs of tall hedges, leaving the tops

H 3   to

to overhang the young fhoots, is here too prevalent. But fuflering the foil to be wafhed
away from the roots, is not more deftructive
to a hedge than is this vile practice.

If " kid" and " oven fuel" be wanted, let a
hedge which is fully grown be felled to the
ftub. There is fcarcely a farm in the Diftrict
which is not more or lefs " wood-bound;" that
is, injured by overgrown hedges; which are,
year after year, receiving irreparable damage
for want of cutting; while the undergrown
ones are damaged by a lefs pardonable treatment.

The tenant's motive is founded in felf-inte-
reft: he gets fuel and " manner," without any
contingent expence or trouble ;—and whether
the hedge endure, henceforward, for one or
for two centuries, is not an object to him.—
But as, at the expiration of his leafe, his farm
will be worth more or lefs, according to the
ftate of its fences, it ought to be the efpecial
care of the landlord, or of his agent, to fee that
they are properly treated,

V. THE METHOD OF RAISING NEW HEDGES
In Norfolk is a cheap one; and may be practifed

tifed in any country where the foil is free from
ftones and other obftructions of the fpade.

The hedgeling is defended on one fide by a
deep ditch, while the other fide is fufficiently
guarded by the excavated mould formed into
a mound, and crefted with a ftout brufh hedge;
in the fetting of which the Norfolk labourers,
from conftant practice, are very proficient.

It is a ftriking, and indeed an interefting fact,
that hedges in Norfolk are raifed with good
fuccefs, although neither poft, rail, ftake nor
edder be made ufe of in defending them.—
And it may be a moot point, whether a want
of underwood has given rife to this, as a practice of neceffity; or whether the practice, by
rendering coppices lefs valuable, has been a
means of doing away, fo completely, the
woodinefs of this Diftrict.

But notwithftanding much praife is due to
the Norfolk method of defending young
hedges, the mode of planting, here in common
ufe, is very reprehenfible. Inftead of the
quickfets—provincially, "layer"—being planted in or near the foil which is to fupport it, they
are laid in near the top of the bank—perhaps, two feet above the natural level of the

H 4   adjoining

adjoining inclofure—and probably five feet
above the bottom of the ditch: nor are they,
there, planted with their roots downward, in
the manner which nature dictates; but with
their heads pointing into the ditch: and, to
complete the abfurdity of the bufinefs, the
workman, in dreffing the face of the bank, frequently draws the back of his fpade down-
wards over the tops of the plants, preffing
them, of courfe, flat to the face, in which they
not unfrequently ftick! yet, he fays, he thereby does no harm: and it is poffible he may be
right; but, to a perfon who has feen any other
method of proceeding, he appears to be doing
very wrong.

Neverthelefs, it is furprizing to fee the progrefs which quick, thus planted, will fometimes
make the firft two or three years after planting: and this, probably, is the falfe light by
which the advocates for the method are led
away. The top of the bank is loofe *made ground*,
and the upright brufh hedge, by collecting
driving rains, fupplies it amply with moifture.
But the fame rains not unfrequently affift in
wafhing down the face of the bank, together
with the quick, into the bottom of the ditch.

Even

Even the ordinary mouldering of the bank, by
frosts and moderate rains, leaves, in the courfe
of a few years, the roots entirely expofed.—
Should the plants preferve their upright pofture, they foon lofe their vigour; but it is no
uncommon thing to fee them hanging, perhaps by one fibre, with their heads downward
againft the face of the bank. Confequently,
hedges which have been planted in this manner are full of dead gaps; and the plants which
have furvived and have got down to the natural
foil, are, by the crowns of their roots being
conftantly expofed, ftinted and unhealthy.—
Whoever will be at the trouble of making the
obfervation, will find, that the full-ftemmed
luxuriant hedges, which occur, more or lefs,
in every part of the Diftrict, (the Norfolk foil
being naturally affected by the hawthorn) but
more particularly in the Fleg Hundreds, have
been planted at or near the foot of the bank.

The reafon why a hedge planted low *in the
face* of the bank, does not flourifh for a few
years after planting is obvious: the bank being
fteep, and without a break from top to bottom,
it fhoots off the rain water, which falls againft
it, into the ditch; while that collected by the

dead

dead hedge, above, is not fufficient to moiften it to the bottom; which is, of courfe, deprived of the benefit of rain water. Befides this want of moifture, the fuperincumbent weight of the bank is inimical to the tender fibrils of the young plants; and their progrefs, fo long as they remain confined under the bank, and cramped with its preffure, is of courfe flow.

But this difficulty once overcome; the roots having once reached through the bank, and got poffeffion of the adjoining inclofure; the plants flourifh amain; while their principal roots being firmly and cooly fituated, they continue to flourifh, even in defiance of "buck-ftalling" and "out-hoiling."

It is not my defire to cenfure the practices of Norfolk hufbandmen; much lefs my intention to aim generally, at their inftruction: I rather hope to diffeminate over the Ifland the excellencies of their management: neverthelefs, Norfolk, as every other Diftrict I have yet vifited, has its prejudices, and its want of *perfection*, in particular departments of management. It may however be faid, and I believe with ftrict juftice, that no Diftrict has *fewer*
imperfections

imperfections than Norfolk; and what is fingularly to the credit of the Norfolk hufbandmen, their perfeverance in practifing the method of planting hedges above defcribed, may
perhaps be called their only *rooted* prejudice.

The reafon why quick, recently planted at
the foot, *and in the face,* of a tall bank, is
checked in its growth, for the firft two or three
years, is not more obvious than the method of
preventing it. If inftead of laying-in the
plants in the immediate face of an unbroken
bank, they were to be planted on the back
part of an *offset,* or break in the bank, the evil
effects abovementioned would be removed:
for by this fimple alteration in the formation of
the bank, the young plants become fupplied,
at once, with every thing neceffary to their
fupport; namely, moifture, air, and loofe
earth for the infant roots to ftrike in.

This is not merely a theoretic plan: it is in
common practice in many parts of the kingdom; and I have myfelf practifed it, in three
different and diftant parts of it, with fuccefs.

In Norfolk however, where hares are vermin, fome caution is neceffary: the fhelf
fhould not be made too wide; and fhould, while
the

the plants are young, be kept ftuck with bufhes, to prevent the hares from running along it.

The fize of the ditch is from three to five feet wide—and two to three and half feet deep; the medium, four feet wide and three feet deep, with a bank three feet high, forming what is called " a fix-foot dick." For an out-fide fence againft a common or a road, five feet wide and feven feet high, (meafuring from the bottom of the ditch to the top of the bank when frefh-made) is a more fuitable fence.

The price of a common fix-foot ditch is fourteen pence a rod (of feven yards), or one fhilling a rod, and beer, for making the ditch, planting the layer, adjufting the bank, and fetting the hedge.

The mean diftance of planting quick is about fix inches: the calculation is a hundred to three rods; the price fourpence to fixpence a hundred.

Thus, *the whcle expence* of planting a quick hedge in Norfolk is not twopence halfpenny a yard; while in many parts of the kingdom, where two rows of pofts and rails are in common ufe, eightpence to one fhilling a yard is the ufual expenditure.

At

At prefent, it is a practice, though perhaps not of long ftanding, to fow *furze feed* upon the top of the bank, as a guard fucceffive to the brufh hedge, and as a fource of kid and fuel.   The common way is to fow it *upon* the back, at the foot of the dead hedge: this, however, is injudicious ; for the furze being of a fpreading nature it is liable, after the hedge is gone to decay, to overrun the quick.   Many fine young hedges I have feen materially harmed through an injudicious management of the furze hedge; which ought to ftand *on the back*, not upon the top, of the bank ; as in this fituation it is a better guard to the bank (which is liable to be fcraped down by cattle and fheep), and lefs injurious to the hedge it is intended to defend.   About two thirds of the diftance between the foot of the bank and the foot of the brufh hedge ; namely, one third of that fpace from the foot of the hedge ; is a good fituation.   But fee MIN. 104. on this fubject.

I met with one inftance, and that in the practice of one of the firft men in the county, . of furze feed being fown on what is called the

" out-

" out-holl," namely, the outer brink of the ditch.

This is a good guard to the face of the hedge : and, if the fide towards the inclofure be kept cut, to prevent their fpreading into it, furzes, growing in this fituation, become a fupply of fuel, without being an incumbrance ; a ditch being always confidered as irretrievable wafte ; and this is the firft inftance I have met with of its being rendered valuable by being *cropped*. If inftead of fowing the furze feed on the brink, it were drilled on the flope of the ditch, there would be lefs danger of the plants encumbering the adjoining inclofure.

A principal inconveniency of the Norfolk mound fence is the mouldering of the back of the bank, for the firft two or three years after making or repairing; before it gets grafled over.

To obviate this I have had *grafs feeds* fown, after the bank was raifed, but before it was finifhed, and the feeds dreffed in with the back of the fpade, in the finifhing operation of the bank : the fuccefs has been beyond expectation : in a few weeks the bank becomes green, and

and the firſt year furniſhes a ſupply of uſeful
herbage; inſtead of being, as it uſually is, a
nurſery of wingſeeded weeds. The back of the
bank in this caſe ſhould not be made too upright. The beſt ſeeds are thoſe of white clover (among which thoſe of ray graſs or other
graſſes may be mixed); for this plant, by running upon the ſurface, and ſtriking root at the
joints, ſoon forms the requiſite matt of herbage.

VI. REPLANTING WORNOUT HEDGES. It will
be doing juſtice to the Norfolk management
to mention a practice, which at preſent prevails, of grubbing up old wornout hedges,
and planting new ones in their ſtead.

In this caſe the old hedge is (or ought to be)
thrown down in autumn—that the ſoil may be
thoroughly ſoaked and tempered with the winter's rains and froſts:—early in ſpring the foot
of the bank ſhould be formed, and, in due ſeaſon, the layer put in, and the fence completed.

By this means a diſgraceful nuiſance is removed, and a new ſtraight hedge obtained;
and this at a ſmall additional expence.—The
roots alone, if the old hedge be full of large
ſtubs, and loaded with ſtems,—will pay for
grubbing:

abundantly in the Norfolk foil; some few barren spots excepted; in which situations *furze* is
the principal fence. *Crabtree* is sometimes,
though seldom, planted; but I have seen it
make a rapid progress upon very poor soil; and
for such it would, I apprehend, be found preferable to the hawthorn. *Holly* abounds in old
hedges; growing very luxuriantly, and forming
an admirable shelter for cattle in winter; besides giving, in that bleak season, a chearfulness
and fancied shelter to the face of the country.

IX. Upon some estates it is the practice to
put in, when a new hedge is planted, a holly at
every rod, and an OAK PLANT at every two or
three rods, among the whitethorn layer.

This is an excellent practice; provided the
young oaks be trained to a proper height before they be suffered to form their heads. For,
in this case, they will become a valuable source
of timber, without injuring, in any material
degree, the inclosures they grow between. It
is the roots of the ash and elm, and the tops of
low pollards, and tall overgrown hedgewoods,
which are injurious to the farmer. A timber
oak, of fifteen to twenty feet stem, does very

little if any injury either to the crop, or the hedge growing under it.

But if, on the contrary, the oaklings, thus planted, be suffered to rise with more than one stem, as stubwood; or, rising singly (which is seldom the case in a young hedge), they be permitted to form their heads at eight or ten feet high, with flat wide-spreading tops,—they lose their intended value, and become nuisances, not only to the adjoining inclosures, but to the hedge in which they grow.—Eligible, therefore, as it is to plant young oaks among hedgewood, the advantage to be obtained from it rests wholly on the after-management.

For reasons why a tenant should not be suffered to *prune timber trees*, see MIN. 5.

For reflections on the time of cutting hedges, see MIN. 34.

For a proposed method of *preventing tenants from destroying hedges*, see MIN. 42.

For observations on *ditches against the sides of hills*, see MIN. 45.

For observations on *ivied ditchbanks*, see MIN. 63.

For

For obfervations on *thinning timbers*, and on *twin timbers*, fee MIN. 85.

For obfervations on *renewing* wornout hedges, fee MIN. 87.

For an inftance of a fufficient *furze bedge*, fee MIN. 88.

For general obfervations on *timbers and pollards* in hedges, fee MIN. 90.

For an inftance of *ditches wafhed down* by rain, fee MIN. 103.

For the method of *fowing furze feed*, with general obfervations on *furze bedges*, fee MIN. 104.

For the management of hedges in Fleg, fee MIN. 106.

For reflections on the *Midfummer fhoot*, fee MIN. 130.

15.

I N C L O S U R E S.

THIS DIVISION of the county being principally inclosed—some heaths and a few common-fields towards the north coast excepted—instances of INCLOSURE seldom occur. Two instances, however, have fallen so far under my notice, as to enable me to convey a general idea of the principles on which they were conducted.

One of them took place in the northern part of the District. The subjects of inclosure were a heathy waste of several hundred acres, of a tolerably good soil—(but, being overgrown with furze, heath, brakes, and other incumbrances, afforded little profit either to individuals or the community); together with two or three hundred acres of common-field land

This inclosure was prosecuted on the same liberal principles which raised the HOLKHAM estate,

eflate, and other eftates in Weft Norfolk, to
their prefent ftate of productivenefs. But as
the particulars which I procured, refpecting it,
will appear in a Minute at the clofe of the fecond volume, it is unneceffary to mention
them here.   ⸢

The other took place (or was intended to
take place) in a more fouthern part of the
Diftrict: the fubject, part of an extenfive and
chiefly barren heath, belonging to *feveral* fur-
rounding *parifhes*, and fituated *diftant from
manures*. But here I am debarred, by motives
which I flatter myfelf are a fufficient excufe for
my filence, from entering into further particulars; and my only reafon for introducing
the article INCLOSURES into the prefent volume
was, to gain an opportunity of inferring, from
obfervations made in this Diftrict, that very
much depends, not only on the MANAGE-
MENT, but on the SUBJECT, or fite, of inclofure; and that lucrative and laudable as inclofures in general are, or might be rendered,
it behoves men of landed property, and all
men concerned in thefe important tranfac-
tions, to ftudy with fufficient attention the

I 3   NATURAL

NATURAL ABILITY of the object in view, and to raife their eftimate with circumfpection, on PRINCIPLES OF MANAGEMENT fufficiently enlarged, to guard againft mifcarriages, and fecure, with a degree of moral certainty, a PERMANENT IMPROVEMENT.

For fome account of the *Felbrigg* inclofure, fee MIN. 137.

16. PLANT-

16,

PLANTING.

PLANTING is not only laudable as an art,
at present of the highest importance to this
island, but pleasurable as an amusement.

In Norfolk, I had neither leisure nor opportunity of extending, on a large scale, my *practice* in this art; but, as far as *observation* could
inform me, I had every advantage. A person
who had been regularly bred up as a nursery-
man, and who was a credit to the art he professed, gave me every opportunity of making
myself fully acquainted with the business of the
nursery, and the *manual operations* of planting:
while a suite of plantations, of various ages,
and in various *states*, passing daily under my
eye, afforded me an opportunity, equally for-

I 4   tunate,

tunate, of making my obfervations on what may
be termed the *theory* of planting.

But my mind being fufficiently employed on
the fubjects of ESTATE AGENCY and HUSBAN-
DRY, I did not attempt, in Norfolk, to digeft
my ideas upon PLANTING.   I was fatisfied with
having gained a general knowledge of the fubject, and with having impreffed on my memory a few leading principles.

HEDGEPLANTING, and the management of
HEDGEROW TIMBER, I confidered as infeparable departments of the management of eftates
(fo nearly are planting and eftate agency allied);
and therefore ftudied them with unremitted attention.   I was alfo led, in a few inftances, from
the eftate to the plantation, as will appear by
Minutes made at the time of practice; and
was alfo induced to minute a few ftriking incidents which occurred to my obfervation.

But THE PROPAGATION OF WOODLANDS,
merely as fuch, not being a practice of the
Diftrict, I had few opportunities of making
obfervations on that important fubject.   Or-
namental plantations, about the refidencies of
men of fortune, are here, as in other Diftricts,
                                        fafhionable:

fashionable : not, however, as objects of ornament merely, but likewise as nurferies of game.

 But it being my intention to confine myfelf, in this work, to utility, rather than to treat either of ornaments or amufements, I will, under this head, only beg leave to recommend to the proprietors of landed eftates in Eaft Norfolk to propagate COPPICE WOODS on the fpringy margins of meadows, and on thofe incorrigible fwamps which occur in almoft every eftate ; and to remove the woody hedge-rows, fo difgraceful to Norfolk as an arable country : raifing, in the new-planted hedges, OAK TIMBERS at fuitable diftances ; training them up to fuch height as will render the timber of the greateft value, and do the land they grow in the leaft poffible injury. I will alfo beg leave to intimate that the fpirit which, at prefent, very properly prevails of extirpating ASH TIMBER from hedgerows, will, in all human probability, be productive of a fcarcity, in time to come, of that neceffary material in rural affairs : and it is equally probable, that whoever, at this time, propagates GROVES OF ASH, in angles and vacant corners, will be increafing, at a fmall expence, the value of his eftate,

and

and be providing, at the fame time, a *neceffary
of life* for the rifing community.

It now only remains to mention the method
of SELLING and TAKING DOWN TIMBER, in
this Diftrict.

The prevailing practice is to fell it ftanding, at fo much a ton when fallen; meafuring
the *timber*, down to fix inches timber girt; the
topwood and the *bark* (of oak) becoming the
property of the purchafer; who is ufually at
the expence of taking it down.

It is likewife cuftomary for the purchafer
to difpofe of the bark (of oak), and fometimes
the topwood, by the fame admeafurement;
the prices of both varying according to the
proportion which the tops of the trees, under
fale, bear to their ftems.

The price of *oak timber*, in 1782, was three
guineas to three pound fifteen fhillings a ton,
of forty feet: the price of *oak bark*, from ten
to twelve fhillings: and of *topwood*, from
feven to twelve fhillings, each load of timber.
The price of naked oak timber, in the rough,
was fifteen to twentypence a foot.

The price of *afh timber*, ftanding, was forty to
fifty fhillings a ton: in the ftick, ninepence to
one fhilling a foot.

The

The *elm* of Norfolk is of little value; for before it acquires a fize to be ufeful, it begins to decay at the heart;—perhaps, owing to the lightnefs of the foil.

The *afh* on the drier lighter foils appears ftunted and fhort; but in, and near, the meadows and fwamps, it is of a firm growth, and a good quality.

The *beech* is very rare in this Diftrict; neverthelefs, I have feen it, upon a fubftratum of marl, of a beautiful growth, and confiderable fize.

The method of TAKING DOWN timber, in Norfolk, is uniform, and, perhaps, peculiar to the country. It is called, very aptly, *grub-felling*: the operation partaking both of grubbing and of felling with the axe,—in the common way aboveground; a method which is wafteful of timber. The Norfolk woodman, therefore, fells below the furface of the ground; by cutting off the horizontal roots clofe to the ftem; which, inftead of fhortening, he, in effect, lengthens, by adding to it a conical point, cut out of the crown of the root: fo that by this way of proceeding, a greater length of timber is obtained, than by,

firft,

firſt, grubbing, and, afterward, cutting off the butt with a ſaw. Grubfelling is, no doubt, the moſt eligible way of taking down hedge-row timber; and this accounts for its being the eſtabliſhed practice in Norfolk.

For an inſtance of the circumſpection requi-ſite in *pruning hedgerow timbers*, ſee MIN. 5.

For an inſtance of *topping young oak plants*, in a neglected nurſery ground, with a common ſpade, ſee MIN. 36.

For an inſtance of ſucceſs in *tranſplanting large oaks*, ſee MIN. 37.

For general obſervations on the proper ſoil and ſituation for the *aſh*, ſee MIN. 38.

For an idea relative to *changing the crop* of timber in a given ſituation, ſee MIN. 81.

For obſervations on *thinning hedgerow tim-bers*, and on *twin timbers*, ſee MIN. 85.

For general obſervations on the treatment of *timbers and pollards in hedges*, ſee MIN. 90.

For an inſtance of *thinning a tall mixed plan-tation*, with obſervations on different *ſpecies* of timber trees, and with reflections on the *after-management* of plantations in general, ſee MIN. 95.

For obſervations on the *Midſummer ſhoot*, ſee MIN. 130.

GENERAL

17.

GENERAL MANAGEMENT

OF

FARMS.

THE PRINCIPAL OBJECTS of the
Eaſt Norfolk huſbandry are,

BULLOCKS,
BARLEY,
WHEAT ;

the other productions of the Diſtrict being in a
great meaſure ſubordinate to theſe three; from
which, chiefly, the farmer expects to pay his
rent and ſupport his family.

The bullocks are fatted chiefly on

TURNEPS,

and ſometimes finiſhed with

RAY GRASS, and
CLOVER :

which laſt are alſo raiſed for horſes, ſtore-
cattle, and the dairy.

OATS,

OATS,

too, are raifed in fmall quantities for horfe-corn; and

BUCK *,

in great abundance, for pigs and poultry. Some few

PEAS

are alfo grown for fwine (or are bought up by the millers, to improve the *colour* of their wheat-flour) ;—and fome, but very few,

VETCHES,

for foiling horfes.

WELD,

HEMP †,

HOPS, and

COLE SEED,

(the laft more particularly in Fleg) are occa-fionally raifed, but in inconfiderable quantities.

---

* BUCK—*polygonum fagopyrum*—buck wheat, or *brank*; its common name in the fouthern hundreds of Eaft Nor-folk; but in *this* part of the county its only name is BUCK: indeed the addition *wheat* (probably a corrup-tion of the Dutch *weet*) is abfurd, and altogether im-proper.

† Some fmall quantities are grown upon the eaftern coaft.

SHEEP

SHEEP

can scarcely be enumerated among the objects of the East Norfolk husbandry; and

Cows

are kept chiefly for the purpose of breeding,
and the use of the family.

SWINE and
POULTRY

are well attended to; and, in the southern
parts of the District, are carried, in great quantities, to the Norwich and Yarmouth markets.

RABBITS,

though some few warrens occur in East Norfolk, are not a staple production.

But before the particular practices observed,
and the processes made use of, in obtaining, separately, these several PRODUCTIONS, can, with
any degree of propriety, be described;—it
will be necessary, first, to premise such GENE-
RAL PROCESSES, and departments of management, as do not pertain, especially, to any
individual OBJECT.

THE GENERAL SUBJECTS necessary to be
premised on the present occasion, are,

The prevailing method of LAYING OUT
FARMS, in Norfolk.

The

THE SUCCESSION OF ARABLE CROPS, in this Diſtrict.

THE SOIL PROCESS;—or the Norfolk method of putting the ſoil into a proper ſtate of cultivation.

THE MANURE PROCESS;—or the general application, and method of applying, manures in Norfolk.

THE SEED PROCESS;—or general obſervations on the different modes of ſowing.

THE VEGETATING PROCESS;—or the ſummer care, protection, and management of crops, in general, from ſeed-time to harveſt.

THE HARVEST PROCESS — not the proceſs of harveſting any one particular crop; but the general buſineſs of harveſt.

THE FARMYARD MANAGEMENT; not a detail of the barn management and conſumption of one ſeparate ſpecies of crop, nor the winter treatment of any one particular ſpecies of liveſtock; but a deſcription of ſuch general buſineſs of the barn, and the farmyard, as cannot with the ſmalleſt degree of propriety be given under any one ſpecies,—either of ſtock, or crop.

For

For obſervations on the Norfolk farmers partiality to arable land, ſee Min. 49.

For further obſervations on this ſubject, and of their neglect of graſsland, ſee Min. 51.

For an evidence that the ſtock of a farm ought to be adapted to the given ſoil, ſee Min. 75.

For an evidence of the cheapneſs of the Norfolk practice of huſbandry, ſee Min. 98.

For the general management of the Fleg Hundreds, ſee Min. 106.

For an evidence of the excellency of the arable management of Norfolk, ſee Min. 112.

For an evidence of its being adapted to a dry ſoil, ſee Min. 114.

For the general management in Blowfield Hundred, ſee Min. 118.

18.

LAYING-OUT FARMS.

MANY of the prefent farms, efpecially thofe of confiderable fize, have formerly lain to perhaps two, three, or more feparate meffuages; each, perhaps, occupied by its refpective owner: this, and the intermixture of property already fpoken of, accounts for that abundance of petty inclofures,—or "pightles"—fo difgraceful to Eaft Norfolk as an arable country.

It is, however, the prevailing fafhion at prefent, when adjoining pightles belong to the fame proprietor, or when they can, by exchanges, be brought into the fame hands, to erafe the intermediate fences, and lay them into inclofures proportioned to the fize of the farm to which they belong.

This, namely proportioning the fize of the fields to that of the fann, is a matter to which

Norfolk

Norfolk husbandmen, at prefent, are very attentive. The fingular fyftem of hufbandry practifed in this Diftrict calls for a greater number of divifions than are necefiary in moft other places. For although an Eaft Norfolk farmer divides his farm into what he calls " fix fhifts," to receive his principal crops in rotation, he does not wifh for fewer than nineteen or twenty arable divifions, in order that he may have an opportunity of diftributing his turnep crop over different parts of his farm.

For fimilar reafons he does not clafs, but intermixes, his other arable crops.

This intermixture of crops renders driftways necefiary ;—and they are nowhere more numerous than in Norfolk.

Another important matter to which Norfolk hufbandmen are attentive in laying-out their farms, is that of endeavouring to lay their " furlongs" north-and-fouth, that the fun may have an equal influence on either fide the narrow ridges, upon which their wheat is almoft univerfally raifed.

19.

SUCCESSION.

IN NORFOLK, as in other arable countries, hufbandmen vary more or lefs in the fucceffion of crops and fallows to each other.— But if we confine ourfelves to *this* Diftrict; namely, the north-eaft quarter of the county; we may venture to affert, without hazard, that no other Diftrict of equal extent in the kingdom is fo invariable in this refpect; common-field Diftricts excepted.

It is highly probable, that a principal part of the lands of this Diftrict have been kept invariably, for at leaft a century paft, under the following courfe of cultivation:

      Wheat,
      Barley,
      Turneps,
      Barley,
      Clover,
      Ray grafs, broken up about Midfummer, and fallowed for wheat, in rotation.

Thus,

Thus, fuppofing a farm to be laid-out, with nineteen or twenty arable divifions, of nearly equal fize, and thefe to be brought into fix regular fhifts, each fhift would confift of three pieces; with a piece or two in referve, at liberty to be cropped with oats, peas, tares, buck; or to receive a thorough cleanfing by a whole-year's fallow.

This courfe of culture is well adapted to the foil of this Diftrict, which is much more productive of barley than of wheat; and is in every other refpect, as will hereafter appear, admirably adapted to that excellent fyftem of management of which it is the bafis.

The foil of the fouthern parts of the Diftrict being ftronger and deeper than that upon which the foregoing courfe of crops is prevalent, it is better fuited to wheat; and there the round of

> Wheat,
> Turneps,
> Barley,
> Clover,

is common; though not in univerfal practice.

This difference in foil and management renders it neceffary to confider the fouthern

K 3 Hun-

Hundreds of Fleg, South-Walsham, and Blow-field, as appendages, rather than as parts, of the District most immediately under description: which is furnished with a less genial soil; namely, that shallow, and somewhat lightish, sandy loam, which may be called the common covering of the county; broken, however, in some places, by a richer, stronger, deeper soil; and in others, by barren heaths and unproductive sands; from which even the Hundreds of Erpingham, Turnstead, and Happing, are not entirely free; though, perhaps, they enjoy a greater uniformity of soil than any other District of equal extent in the county.

This, therefore, is the site best adapted to the study of the system of management which has raised the name of Norfolk husbandmen, and which is still preserved, inviolate, in this secluded District. For a shallow sandy loam, no matter whether it lie in Norfolk or in any other part of the kingdom, there cannot, perhaps, be devised a better course of culture; or, taken all in all, a better system of management, than that which is here in universal practice *.

* If any improvement of the present system can be made, it would perhaps be by adopting the practice of a judicious

But excellent as this succession of crops undoubtedly is, it cannot be invariably kept up;
for even a Norfolk husbandman cannot command a crop of turneps or a crop of clover;
and when either of these fail, the regularity of
the succession is of course broken into.

If his turneps disappoint him, he either lets
his land lie fallow through the winter, and sows
it with barley, in course, in the spring; or
more frequently, though less judiciously, sows
it with wheat in autumn; sometimes, though
not always, sowing it with clover and ray grass
in the spring; by this means regaining his
regular course.

If the clover miss, the remedy is more difficult; and no general rule is in this case observed. Sometimes a crop of peas is taken the first
year; and the next, buck plowed under: or
perhaps a crop of oats are taken the first year,
and over these clover sown for the second: in

cious husbandman in the northern part of the District (Mr.
Edmund Bird, of Plumstead); who divides his farm into
seven, instead of six, shifts; his course of *crops* are the
same as those of his neighbours; his seventh shift being
a whole-year's *fallow* for wheat.

　　　　　　either

either of thefe cafes, the foil comes round for wheat the third year, in due fucceffion.

It has already appeared in the HEADS OF A LEASE, page 75, that the Norfolk farmers are reftricted from taking more than two crops of corn fucceffively. At the clofe of a leafe this reftriction may fometimes have a good effect; for ill-blood between landlord and tenant too frequently leads a farmer to do what he knows will, in the end, be injurious both to himfelf and his farm. The crime of taking more than two crops of corn fucceffively is, however, held, by farmers in general, in an odious light, and is never practifed by a good farmer, unlefs " to bring into courfe" a fmall patch, with fome adjoining piece;—or to regulate his fhifts.

20. SOIL

20.

SOIL PROCESS.

IN THIS important department of husbandry the Norfolk farmers are proficients.—It is observable, however, that Norfolk being an old-cultivated country, and having been, century after century, kept under a course of arable management, the difficulties of breaking-up rough waste lands, and old leys, are, at present, unknown; the whole business of the soil process being, now, the regular routine of removing those foulnesses, which all arable lands are liable to; and in putting the soil into a fit state for the reception of the seed.

But these operations, simple as they may seem to unpractical observers, require much skill and judgment; for on a proper conduct in this department depends, considerably, the profit or loss of an arable farm. And as the Norfolk husbandmen appear to me to be masters in this art, I will endeavour to convey to my readers, in an ample manner, their conduct in this particular;

cular; in doing which, it will be proper to
confider the following articles feparately:

1. Plowing,   4. Cleanfing,
2. Harrowing,   5. Laying-up,
3. Rolling,   6. Draining;

and, previoufly, to give fome account of the
fingular practice of this country, with refpect
to the hours of work obferved in every department of the foil procefs.

The univerfal practice, I believe throughout
the county, is to go what is called "two journies." In winter, when days are fhort, the
teams go out as foon as it is light, and return
home at twelve o'clock to dinner:—go out
again at one, and remain in the field until dark.
In longer days, the cuftom varies:—the moft
general practice is to go out at feven in the
morning;—return at noon:—go out again at
two;—and return at feven in the evening.—
Ten hours; namely, five hours each journey;
—are the longeft hours of work; except in
the hurry of barley feedtime, when thefe hours
may fometimes be exceeded.

The length of day is, therefore, not exceffive; but the work performed in fo fhort a
time is extraordinary. The Norfolk plowmen

men always do as much—in general, a great
deal more—in one journey, that is in five
hours, -than plowmen in general do in eight
hours; which, in moſt parts of the kingdom,
is the length of the plowman's day.

This faſt, however, is no longer extraordinary, when we obſerve their paces, reſpec-
tively. Plowteams, in general, travel at the
rate of one to two miles an hour; whereas, in
Norfolk, they ſtep out at not leſs than three to
four miles an hour; and the ſame, or a greater
agility, is preſerved in the other departments.

I. PLOWING.—Every thing is plowed with
two horſes, abreaſt, driven and guided by the
plowman (ſee IMPLEMENTS); and the common
day's work, except in wheat ſeedtime is two
acres! a faſt, this, which nothing but actual
obſervation could have taught me to believe.

The Norfolk huſbandmen pay due attention
to the *ſtate of the ſoil* to be plowed, being careful not to plow it too wet *, nor too dry; the

* The Norfolk plowmen have a ſingular expedient to
prevent the ſoil when moiſt from turning up in whole
gloſſy furrows, which they term "ſcoring;" to prevent
which they tie a piece of ſtrong rope-yarn round the plate
or mouldboard; which, by this means, is prevented from
acting as a trowel upon the ſoil.

latter

latter moft efpecially: not only becaufe their plow and team are ill calculated for ftubborn work; but left, in breaking up the foil at a time when it is too dry to be cut clean with the fhare, it fhould rife in clods, and thereby difturb the " pan;" which, upon every occafion, is held facred (fee Soil).

Inftances of the mifchiefs of *deep plowing* are related: one of them by an old, and moft judicious hufbandman, to whofe opinion the greateft deference and attention is due *. His men having, in his abfence, plowed part of a clofe when it was too dry, it broke up in large thick clods; the pan, which adhered to the foil, being of courfe brought up to the furface. He immediately forefaw the effect which, I have not a doubt, followed. This patch, from no other apparent circumftance whatever, could not, with all his fkill and induftry, be brought to bear a crop of any kind equal to that of the reft of the clofe, for fix or feven years afterward. The crops on this part were uniformly, and obvioufly, not only foul, but bad; and this, notwithftanding an extraordi-

* Mr. Arthur Bayfield, of Antingham.

nary

NORFOLK.

from time to time, beſtowed upon it.

From this and other inſtances of a ſimilar
kind, as well as from general obſervation, I am
convinced that to plow beneath the wonted
depth, would, under the ſingular circumſtances
of the Norfolk ſoil, be injudicious management;—unleſs ſome ready method could be
hit upon of forming, at a greater depth, a freſh
pan.

The methods of plowing are various.—In
making fallows, the prevailing practice of
plowing fleet and "full pitch," alternately, is
very judicious: it not only breaks and mixes
the ſoil more readily than the common practice of plowing always the ſame, or nearly the
ſame depth; but, in the firſt two plowings, it
renders the operations more eaſy: the firſt, being thin, goes lighter off the ſhare; and the
ſecond being always (except for turneps) a
croſs-plowing, the ſhare has freſh firm ground
to lay hold of, by which means the plow is
kept ſteady to its work.

To increaſe this advantage it is common, on
very thin ſoils, to break up fallows by "rice-
balking," or by "ſlob-furrowing;" which are
nearly

nearly the fame operation performed in different ways.

In rice-balking, the " flag " * is always turned toward the unplowed ground, the edge of
the coulter paffing clofe to the edge of the flag
laft turned: whereas, in flob-furrowing, the flag
is turned toward the plowed ground, the coulter paffing fifteen or fixteen inches from the laft
plow-furrow ;—into which, in this cafe, the
edge of the flag hangs ;—and, in both cafes, a
flip of unplowed foil, of a width nearly equal
to that of the flag, is buried.

Thefe methods of plowing are not peculiar
to Norfolk ; but I know no Diftrict in which
they are fo commonly practifed by farmers in
general as they are in this county.   The firft
is moft in ufe: it is the neater, and, perhaps for
the Norfolk foil, the more eligible operation.

Another method of plowing practifed in
Norfolk, but not peculiar to it, is " two-fur-
rowing :"—trench plowing—double plowing.
This is done with two plows, one following the
other in the fame place : it is, in the fhallow
foil of this Diftrict, a difficult operation ; but
the wheels and the broad fhare of the Norfolk
plow render it fingularly well adapted to this

* The provincial term for the furrow turned.

busine fs.

bufinefs. The foil, perhaps not more than four
or five inches deep, is to be divided into two
thin flices, the under one being to be taken up
thick enough to bury the firft, without bringing
up at the fame time any part of the fubftratum
or pan: and this I have feen done with great
exactnefs.

The price of plowing, with a plain, clean furrow, is two fhillings and fixpence an acre! which
is the current price of the country, and the rate
which is, I believe, almoft invariably adopted
by referees between out-going and in-coming
tenants.   This interefting fact alone, accounts
for the comparative high price of land in Norfolk.   In many parts of the kingdom, ten fhillings an acre is a price of plowing, equally
current.   How much, then, it behoves gentlemen of landed property to introduce upon
their eftates the practice of PLOWING WITH
TWO HORSES, AND OOING TWO JOURNIES A
DAY,—where it is practicable ; and where it is
not, to endeavour, by other means, TO LOWER
THE EXPENCE OF PLOWING ; and thus by introducing a real improvement, add a permanent
increafe to their rent-rolls.

II. HARROWING.—In making fallows, it is
cuftomary to harrow prefently before each plowing ;

ing; the operation being too frequently deferred so long, that the seeds of weeds, set at liberty by the harrows, have not time to vegetate, before they are again turned under the soil, and placed out of the sphere of vegetation.

This injudicious management is not however universal, good farmers making a point of letting their fallows lie a sufficient length of time between the harrowing and the succeeding stirring.

One admirable practice peculiar, I believe, to Norfolk, is that of making the horses trot at harrow: it being a custom which is prevalent throughout almost every department of this operation, to walk the horses against the rise, if any, and trot them back again in the same place. This excellent practice not only rids work and disengages the root weeds from the harrow tines, as well as from the soil, leaving them loose on the surface; but levels the land, in a manner which would be difficult to describe, and which observation, alone, can render evident.

The day's work of a pair of horses, walking one way and trotting the other, the harrows overlapping so as to give the ground a full double tine, is laid at about seven acres.

III. ROLLING.

III. ROLLING.—Very little general matter falls under this head. One circumstance, however, requires to be mentioned.

The roller, notwithstanding the lightness of the soil, and its proneness to be injured by dry weather, is never used in Norfolk for the purpose of compression. I never saw one used by a farmer either upon fallow or upon a lay; not even upon the first year of a clover lay to smooth the surface for the sithe.

The only uses to which I have seen a roller put, in this District, are that of smoothing the surface before sowing, to prevent the seed from running down too low, and that of smoothing it afterwards as a preparation for the sithe * : and even *this* operation is performed with a roller not more perhaps than seven or eight inches in diameter! a circumstance which I confess I am no way able to account for: nevertheless, it would be rashness to condemn an established practice, unless I could, from my own experience, or from adequate observation on the experience of others, prove it to be ineligible.

* And sometimes wheat is rolled in autumn. See WHEAT.

I can-

I cannot, however, refrain in this instance
from recommending to the Norfolk husbandmen to try, by accurate and repeated experiments, whether the rolling of fallows, lays,
corn-crops, and meadows, with a heavy roller,
would, or would not, be eligible management,
on the Norfolk soil.

IV. CLEANSING PLOWLAND.—The Nor-
folk method of cleaning fallows from "quicks"
and other root weeds, is, when they are dif-
engaged from the soil, to draw them into "ringes"—rows—with the same harrows with which
they were disengaged (neither horse nor hand-
rakes being ever used in the operation). In this
case, the horses, walking slowly, are driven
with reins, the driver following the harrows,
and lifting them up, at stated distances. The
"quicks" are then shook into heaps with forks,
and either burnt in the close, or carried off to
digest in large heaps, as the weather suits, or
the judgment of the farmer may determine.

If it be right, in making a fallow, to burn or
carry off the roots of couch or other grasses,
this is perhaps as simple a process as can be
used for the purpose.

It

It is a general idea that marl helps to cleanse the foil from quicks.

V. LAYING-UP PLOWLAND.—For wheat, the foil is ufually gathered up into very narrow ridges: but for every other crop it is laid into wide flat "warps," or beds of about ten paces wide; without any regard being had to the nature of the fubfoil: which, notwithftanding it is, in general, fufficiently abforbent to admit of this practice, is fometimes too retentive, and cold, to admit of it with propriety.

This kind of land, however, feldom occurs in Norfolk; and this circumftance may be a good reafon why a Norfolk farmer is fo truly helplefs on a wet cold-bottomed foil*; and may account, in fome meafure, for his generally failing in his attempts to farm on any other foil than that of his own country.

The idea of gathering the foil into ridges, and finking crofs furrows for the purpofe of getting rid of the furface water, is unknown to him: if the fubfoil is not thirfty enough to drink up the rain water as faft as it falls, it lies upon the warps, or makes its way acrofs them in a channel of its own.

* For a ftriking inftance, fee MIN. 114.

This,

This, however, even fuppofing the practice to be without exceptions, is no heavy charge againft the Norfolk hufbandmen, confidered merely as fuch ; for the Norfolk foil in general is fufficiently abforbent to require neither ridge nor furrow.

But there are patches, efpecially on the fides of the fwells, and on the margins of the meadows, which are too retentive to admit of fuch management; and there are *fome few* hufbandmen, who are fufficiently attentive to furface-drains for carrying off the fuperfluous rain water ; or, if that be found infufficient, have recourfe to

VI. UNDERDRAINING.—This, however, is a practice which is not of long ftanding in the Diftrict; but may, I make no doubt, be found highly ufeful to many parts of it.

Underdraining has, hitherto, been chiefly, I believe, done with wood; there being no ftones in the Diftrict; except a few fmall flints gathered off the land ; and except fea ftones upon the coaft ;—either of which would, if properly ufed, be preferable to wood.

For

For an inftance, and the method, of under-draining with wood, fee Min. 2.

For a particular foil procefs for barley and turneps, on a very thin light foil, fee Min. 57.

For an evidence of the excellency of the Norfolk foil procefs, fee Min. 98.

. For an inftance of injudicious management of a wet foil, fee Min. 114.

For further obfervations on fallows, fee the heads buck, turneps, barley, wheat.

21.

MANURE PROCESS.

THE PRINCIPAL MANURES set on upon the lands of this District appear, in page 15, to be,

1. Marl, clays, and other earths.
2. Dung, and composts formed with it.
3. Lime.
4. Soot.
5. Rapecake;
6. Malt dust.

I. MARLING. Marl has been so long in use in *this* District, that there are few farms without marl pits upon, or near them ; so that *searching for marl* is at present seldom requisite, and the art of discovering it not much studied. The herb coltsfoot *(tussilago farfara)* abounding on the soil, is considered as an indication of a jam of marl being situated near the surface. But, whether this is, or is not, an infallible guide,—time and accidents or intentional researches have not failed to discover

beds

beds of marl in almoſt every eſtate, and, in
ſome places, on almoſt every farm, ſituated
ſufficiently near the ſurface to be worked with
advantage.

Of the *quality of marls*, as has been already
obſerved, the Norfolk farmers are, in a great
meaſure, uninformed. That which falls moſt
readily, and " gets to work" the ſooneſt, is
in the beſt eſteem ; but, in general, the quantity of " uncallow" (namely, the coping, or
covering of earth, which lies upon the head,
or jam) is more attended to than the intrinſic
quality of the marl.

The *depth of uncallow* is generally very un-
equal : perhaps, on the ſame jam of marl it
will vary from one or two, to ſix or eight, feet
deep, the ſurface of the jam uſually riſing into
inequalities, termed heads.

The *depth of the jam* is equally uncertain : I
have ſeen one worked twenty feet deep ; but
in general, I believe, ten or twelve feet may
be reckoned a middling depth.

The *bottom of the jam*, being generally a
white abſorbent ſand, no pump or artificial
drain is requiſite to free a Norfolk marl pit
from water, which no ſooner touches the ſand

than it vanifhes, as through the grate of an open drain.

In *working a marl pit*, the top foil is thrown back for manure—the remainder of the uncallow thrown to the bottom of the pit, and levelled for the carts to ftand upon. When the jam is low, the marl is thrown immediately from it into the carts; but if it be too high for this operation, piles are driven in a row a few feet from the face of the jam; and, as foon as a crack is formed, water is poured into it, more efpecially when the marl is dry and ftubborn; and by this means many loads are thrown down at once; either to the bottom of the pit, or to a platform, level with the body of the cart; into which the marl, in this cafe, is thrown with great eafe. Taking up the bottom of the jam is the moft difficult part of the operation; the marl being firft to be caft upward to the bafe of the pit, and afterwards to be thrown into the carts. But by thus bringing up the bottom, two valuable things are obtained;—a drain for the water, and a moft convenient receptacle for the next line of uncallow.

The .

The *labour* beftowed on marl previous to its being put into the cart, whether it be incurred by throwing down, loofening by pecks, crows, &c. or fetching up the bottom, is termed "cafting"—the act of throwing it into the cart being called "filling."—The price of cafting is threepence to fixpence a load, according to the circumftances of the pit (the uncallowing being generally done by the day); and the price for filling twopence to twopence halfpenny, according to the fize of the loads carried. I have known threepence a load given for filling and fpreading large loads : the price of fpreading, alone, is about one fhilling an acre. The number of loads carried out in a day by one team, varies, of courfe, with the diftance to be carried : when the pit happens to lie in or contiguous to the ground to be marled, thirty loads have been carried ;—but five-and-twenty is, I believe, confidered as a good day's work.

The *quantity* fet upon an acre is equally various; depending upon two things:—upon the judgement of the perfon who marls ; and upon whether the land has, or has not, been marled heretofore.

It

It is known, from common experience, that land which has been recently marled receives no apparent benefit from a second dressing of the same manure : but it is equally well known that, after some length of time has elapsed, a repetition of marling will generally answer.

It is a notion, pretty generally adopted, that, in this case, the quantity ought to be greater than it was the first or preceding time : and it being formerly the practice to set on a great quantity at once,—seldom, perhaps, less than forty loads an acre,—this notion has, probably, deterred many persons from doing that which would have been serviceable to themselves and their country.

But there is not, I believe, any general rule known, respecting either time or quantity : I have had frequent opportunities of making observations on a farm which affords a striking instance on this subject. Two or three different tenants had failed successively on this farm ; though by no means high rented. The greatest part of it had, within the memory of man, been marled with not less, in all human probability, than forty loads an acre ; and the tenants who failed despaired of reaping any benefit from a second marling after so short

an

an interval of time; but this farm falling into
the hands of a more judicious tenant, he has, by
marling, (and by other acts of good management) accumulated, in little more than twenty
years, a farmer's fortune; during which time
he has marled upwards of one hundred acres;
and, has found, from long experience, that
twenty-five loads an acre is, notwithstanding
the recent marling, a sufficient quantity,

I do not mean to intimate that the same management would every where produce the same
effect; but I will venture to say, that no man
having marl upon his premises, ought to neglect to try its effect, by accurate and repeated
experiments, upon every piece of land in his
possession,—without being led away by any
received notion,—or general rule.

The quantity set on, upon land which is not
known to have been marled, or out of which
the marl is worn, is, at present, less than formerly.

In the southern Hundreds, to which marl is
obliged to be fetched a great distance, ten or
twelve loads are considered as a dressing; six
or eight are frequently set on.

In the more central and northern parts of
the District, where marl is common on almost
every

every farm, twenty to thirty loads an acre are generally allowed,—and sometimes forty loads.

When it is known, from experience, or taken for granted without proof, that land, either through a recent marling or other caufe, is not improveable by marl alone, a fmall quantity is frequently mixed up with dung; either by bottoming the farm yard, or the muck-heaps, with it; or by mixing it layer for layer with the dung in the heaps. In either cafe, they are afterward turned up, and thereby mixed more intimately together.—With this preparation, marl has been found to anfwer, where, in its natural ftate, it had no effect.

The fymptom, or indication, of a piece of land requiring to be marled, is taken from the plants which prevail upon it.—" Buddle" (*chryfanthemum fegetum*—corn marigold) is confidered as a certain intimation that the land it abounds upon requires to be marled.— " Smartweed" (*polygonum Pennfylvanicum*— pale-flowered perficaria) is likewife an obfervable fymptom. It is, I believe, an undoubted fact, that marl, in a manner, extirpates thefe plants from the foil;—and that " quicks" (*triticum repens*) are confiderably checked by it.

With

With refpéct to the *crop*, for which marl is
fet on, there is no general rule : it is fometimes
fet on for turneps, fometimes for barley, and
frequently upon the fecond year's lay for
wheat; which laft is, perhaps, the beft management.

The *expence of marling* varies with the quantity fet on, the diftance to be carried, and the
ftate of the pit.—Suppofe twenty-five loads an
acre to be fet on, the diftance from a quarter to
half a mile, and the expence of cafting threepence a load; and that a team draws out and
fets on the twenty-five loads in two days :

25 loads, at 6*d.* for cafting, filling, *£. s. d.*
   and fpreading -   -. 0 12 6
Two days work of a team, at 10*s.* 1 0 0
Uncallowing, and extra wear and
   tear of implements and tools 0 7 6
                           ————
                      £. 2 0 0

II. Dunging.   *The method of raising* dung
upon the premifes will appear under FARM-
YARD MANAGEMENT.

The *application* of dung is, in the ordinary
practice of the Diftrict, to the TURNEP and the
WHEAT crops.

                               For

For TURNEPS, the " ſtable muck" is uſually
carried out, from time to time, as it accumu-
lates, or as the weather anſwers, in winter; ahd
the " par muck," wanted for this crop, early in
the ſpring; and piled up in heaps in or near
the intended turnep cloſes; a bottom being
previouſly formed of marl, or " manner,"
about a foot thick, and neated up into a long-
ſquare bed to ſet the pile upon.

The method of carrying out farm-yard dung,
"when a farmer wants to get buſineſs forward,"
is generally this: Two fillers, a driver, and an
unloader, with ſix horſes and three carts, are a
ſet, for a ſhort diſtance: one of the carts being
always in the yard—one on the road—and one
at the dung-heap; it being a univerſal practice, which prevails throughout the Diſtrict, to
ſet the carts by the ſide of the heap and un-
load them with forks.

The crime of drawing the load upon the
heap is rarely committed in Norfolk. On the
contrary, every lump is carefully broken, and
the whole piled up light and even, with almoſt
as much care and attention as farmers, in ſome
places, beſtow upon their hayricks.

                                              The

The ordinary day's work of the set above-mentioned is twenty-five loads; if the distance be very short, thirty loads are frequently carried out: in this case, however, an additional boy is required to assist in levelling and forming the heap.

The filling is generally done by the load;—another admirable practice: the price one penny a load; a striking instance of the low wages and hard work of this country.

This practice ought to be copied in every country; for it would, in most places, be cheaper to pay even threepence a load, than to have the dung cart filled by the day; in which case, the team is ever standing idle until the load be made up: whereas, when the filling is done by the load, that seldom happens. This accounts sufficiently for the extraordinary number of loads carried in a day, in Norfolk.

For WHEAT, the remainder of the par-yard muck is generally, in the spring, after the cattle are turned out to grass, turned up into piles in the yards, where it remains until the soil be prepared to receive it;—the piles being, by good farmers, re-turned in the summer;

mer; an operation, however, which is too frequently neglected.

Or, inſtead of turning the piles in the yard,
they are ſometimes carried, at leiſure times in
ſummer, on to the land, and there piled afreſh:
in either caſe, the compoſt, by the time it be
wanted to be ſet on, is thoroughly mixed and
digeſted.

The method of ſetting on dung is ſimilar to that
of carrying it out: and from twenty-five to
thirty loads are conſidered as a day's work for
one team and two fillers: all ſet on in hillocks.

The *quantity* ſet upon an acre is, of courſe,
proportioned to the quantity of land to be manured, and the quantity of dung to be ſet on:
ten loads of good ſpit dung, or twelve to fifteen
loads of compoſt, is, perhaps, the *medial* quantity ſet upon an acre, for *turneps:*—for *wheat*
a ſmaller quantity, and generally of a worſe
quality, is uſually allowed.

Some few farmers manure their *clover lays,*
but this is by no means common; the application of dung being, as has been ſaid, in a manner wholly to the turnep and wheat crops.

It may alſo be ſaid, in general terms, that all
the dung ſpread upon this Diſtrict is *plowed*
in;

in: WHEAT is fometimes *top-dreffed* with it; but I have met with few inftances of that fpecies of management.

III. LIMING.   It has already been obferved under BUILDINGS AND REPAIRS, page 91. that the lime of this Diftrict is burnt entirely from marl, with fea coal, in drawing kilns: at leaft I never obferved a ftanding kiln *.

The price varies, in a fmall degree, in different parts of the Diftrict: nine fhillings a chaldron of thirtytwo bufhels is a medium price.   See note, page 91.

. Lime, however, cannot, as has been before obferved, be confidered as a common manure in this Diftrict ; and while men will continue to draw general conclufions, from particular incidents or experiments, in matters of agriculture, more efpecially on the effects of this myfterious manure, they will ever be of different opinions.   Until the operation of lime upon foils, and vegetables, be better known than it is at prefent, it is in vain to *reafon* about it.

* Namely, a kiln which is filled, and burnt out, without drawing off any of the lime while burning.

If, by accurate and repeated experiments, a given lime be found to have no profitable effect upon a given foil, it would be abfurd to continue to lay that particular lime upon that particular foil. On the contrary, if, by a fimilar courfe of experiments, a given lime be found to act profitably upon a given foil, it would be equally abfurd to let any *argument*, howfoever plaufible, prevent a man from reaping the advantage which fo fortunate a circumftance has thrown in his way.

There may be foils in Norfolk upon which the Norfolk lime would have no beneficial effect; but that there are fome upon which it has a beneficial effect, I am certain; not only from my own experience, but from the practice of fome of the beft farmers in the Diftrict; and this, too, upon lands which have been heretofore marled.

If by lime, or any other foffil or extraneous manure, a Norfolk farmer could fecure a crop of wheat without dung, the advantage would be very great. The whole fyftem of the Norfolk management hinges on the turnep crop; and this depends, in a great meafure, on the quantity of dung. No dung,—no turneps,—no bullocks,—

bullocks,—no barley,—no clover,—nor teathe upon the second year's lay for wheat.

How much then it behoves the Norfolk husbandmen, and turnep farmers in general, to treafure up dung for the turnep crop. The lofs of a crop of wheat is only a fingle lofs, and its effects momentary and certain ; whereas the lofs of the turnep crop deranges the whole farm, and its effects may be felt to the end of a leafe.

If it be found, from adequate experience, that lime is infufficient to anfwer the defired purpofe ; and if it be found neceffary to right management that a certain quantity of wheat fhould be every year grown ; other factitious or extraneous manures might, by a continued fearch and a proper fpirit of induftry, be obtained. '

The general *method of applying* lime . is to let it fall in large heaps, and to fpread it out of carts upon fallowed ground, either for wheat or for barley..

The quantity ufually fet on—about three chaldrons an acre.

IV. Sowing soot. Near towns foot is ufed as a topdreffing for wheat, in February or March.

      The

The time of sowing is confidered as very material. If it be fown early, and the froft catch it, its ftrength is thereby lowered: if late, and no rain falls to wafh it in, it is thought to be rather injurious than beneficial to the crop of wheat. And it is not, in any cafe, found of much, if any, fervice to the fucceeding crop of barley.

The method of sowing it is extremely fimple ; and, in the only inftance I faw the fowing of foot practifed, here, was very complete.

A favourable opportunity being embraced, when the wind blew gently, and in the fame direction, or nearly in the fame direction, as the lands or ridges lie,—the waggon which brought it from Norwich, and which, until the opportunity offered, had ftood fafe under cover, was drawn, in a furrow, againft the wind ; while a man, ftanding on the outfide of the waggon, fpread the foot, with a fhovel, feveral yards wide, on either fide of him ; the height of his fituation at once enabling him to fpread it wide, and even. As he reached the windward end of the lands, the team wheeled round under the hedges, and took a frefh width.

The

The quantity set on was forty bushels an acre.

V. MANURING WITH RAPECAKE.—Rape-cake is not a common manure in *this* District: but it is used by some very good husbandmen, towards the north coast: particularly by the judicious manager mentioned, in this section, under the article MARLING *; who has not only marled one hundred acres of land, which men of less judgment than himself considered as unimprovable by marl; but has, in the course of about twenty years, laid out eight hundred pounds in rapecake: and his success is a striking evidence in favour of the doctrine above held forth; namely, that of applying the dung wholly to the turnep crop, and dressing for wheat with some other manure.

He fetches the cake seven or eight miles, from Cromer or Blakeney; where it costs him from forty shillings to three pounds a ton; with which he dresses three acres. Being previously ground, or broken into small pieces, it is sown, by hand, out of a common seedbox, upon the last plowing but one of a summer fallow, for wheat.

* Mr. Edmund Bird, of Plumstead.

VI. Maltdust.—This is the moſt general adventitious manure of the Diſtrict;
every malt-houſe furniſhing more or leſs of
it; but the quantity, even upon the whole,
being ſmall, it can only be of advantage to a -
few individuals.

For obſervations on marling, in South-
Walſham Hundred, ſee Min. 55.

For a propoſed melioration of the ſoil by an
improvement in the ſoil proceſs, ſee Min. 77.

For obſervations on " claying," in Fleg, ſee
Min. 106.

For experiment on the time of manuring
graſsland, ſee Min. 127.

For the expence of marling by means of
water carriage, ſee Min. 136.

22.

THE SEED PROCESS.

I. BROADCAST may be faid to be the only method of fowing in this Diftrict :—and the plow (with fome few exceptions) the only implement ufed in covering the feed.

II. Drilling, notwithftanding the foil is fo peculiarly adapted to this operation, is en- tirely unpractifed. The only exception to random-fowing is,

III. Dibbling—provincially, "dabbing."— It is performed in two ways; namely, by hand dibbles, and by *dibbling rollers*: the lat- ter however being in the hands of very few, and being, I believe, ufed for wheat only, they will be mentioned more particularly under that article. But *hand dibbles* are ufed for peas as well as for wheat. Indeed, in this Diftrict, they are more in ufe for the former

M 4   than

than for the latter; the dibbling of which cannot be said to have yet gained a footing in it: nor, perhaps, are the shallow foils of *this* part of the District adapted to the practice, how excellent foever it may be upon deeper richer foils. Nevertheless, the practice being peculiar to Norfolk, (and the part of Suffolk adjoining to Norfolk) I embraced every opportunity of gaining what information I could refpecting it, and was fingularly fuccefsful in my enquiries; the refults of which appearing fully in Minutes made at the time of enquiry, I forbear faying any thing further upon the fubject in this place.

IV. STATE OF THE SOIL.—The hufbandmen of Norfolk, notwithftanding the natural dryness and lightnefs of their foil, are particularly careful not to fow fpring crops when the foil is what they call " cold and heavy."—When they are under the neceffity of fowing under this predicament, they endeavour to fow above and harrow in the feeds;—whereas, if the feafon be tolerable, it is a prevailing practice to plow-in almoft all kinds of grain. When the foil is feen to fmoke after a fhower at fun-
rife,

rife, it is confidered to be in a defirable ftate for femination.

For the refult of experiments with Mr. Duckett's Drill, fee MIN. 19.

For obfervations on dibbling, fee MIN, 23, 26, 28.

For reflections on regulating the time of fowing by the *feafon* rather than by the *fun*, fee MIN. 125.

23. VEGE-

23.

VEGETATING PROCESS.

I. IT HAS already been obferved, that ROLLING crops is feldom practifed in this country; unlefs to fmooth the furface, in a flight degree, as a preparation for the fithe.

II. HOING is ftill lefs in practice; except for TURNEPS, and fometimes for the furrows of WHEAT,

III. HANDWEEDING is, however, carefully attended to by farmers in general; and is, generally, performed by the acre :—a practice I have not met with elfewhere; though moft eligible to be adopted in every Diftrict : a farmer has not a more difagreeable tafk than that of attending to weeders by the day. The price is, of courfe, proportioned to the foulnefs of the crop to be weeded :—from fixpence to five fhillings an acre is given.

IV.

IV. Stonepicking clover-lay is also generally done by the acre :—the price twopence to threepence an acre ; the quantity of stones being in general small.

V. The method of frightening rooks, in practice here, especially when they take to patches of corn which are lodged before harvest, is simply to stick up a tall bough in the part infested : if a gun be fired near the place, before the bough be set up, this simple expedient seldom fails of being effectual.

If rooks make an attack after seedtime, or when they take, generally, to the crop before harvest, a boy is set to scare them ; they being seldom attempted to be shot at in Norfolk ; where a notion prevails, and is perhaps well founded, that rooks are essentially useful to the farmer, in picking up worms and grubs; especially the grub of the cock-chaffer, which, it is believed, is frequently injurious to the meadows and marshes of this country.

VI. But whether rooks are, or are not, upon the whole, hurtful to the farmer, there are, in Norfolk, three species of animals, which, on a
certainty,

certainty, are injurious to him: thefe are
HARES, PHEASANTS, and SPARROWS: the laft
of which are not lefs difgraceful to the farmers
themfelves, than the two former are to their
landlords; and it would be very difficult to fay,
which of the three would, to a well wifher to
hufbandry, and a ftranger in the country, appear the moft difgufting fight. I confefs, that
having preconceived fome idea of the mifchiefs that muft neceffarily arife from an inordinate quantity of game, the clouds of fparrows which are fuffered to prey upon the produce of this country, were to me the greater
caufe of furprife.

But fhameful as is the wafte arifing from
fparrows, it is inconfiderable, when compared
with the devaftation which is caufed by hares
and pheafants, *in the neighbourhoods of kept
covers.*

THE TURNEP CROP, the main ftem of the
Norfolk hufbandry, falls a facrifice to *hares.*—
The quantity they *eat* is confiderable, but
fmall in comparifon with the *wafte* they create.
Before a hare will make her meal off turneps,
fhe will tafte, perhaps, ten, without meeting
with one to her tooth. Her method of tafting,
is

is to peel off a piece of rind, about the fize of
a fhilling, upon the top of the turnep; in order
that fhe may, with nicer judgment, make her
eſſay upon the pulp: in doing this, a receptacle is formed for the rain, and a wound of
courfe made for the froft to operate upon: the
part prefently becomes putrid; in a few weeks
a general mortification takes place; and the
turnep thus partially bitten, is, as a *food*, entirely
loſt to the farmer, and to the community.

THE WHEAT CROP ſuffers principally from
pheafants: they begin with it the moment it is
fown, and prey upon it fo long as it remains in
the field; frequently follow it into the rickyard; and, in fevere weather, into the barn-
yard: nay, I have known them, not fatisfied
with robbing the pigs and poultry, make their
entry into the barn itfelf; where they have been
found, by the farmer or his labourers, feeding
in numbers upon the barn floor. Thefe de-
predations are not confined to wheat; but are
of courfe extended to other crops.

THE BARLEY CROP ſuffers principally from
bares; but upon this their mifchiefs are not fo
general as upon the turnep-crop. So long as
the barley keeps young and fucculent, they
feed

feed promifcuoufly; but when it begins to run
up to ftem, they confine themfelves (if the
piece be too large to keep the whole of it under) to particular parts; which, by being kept
continually cropt as it fhoots, affords them a
frefh bite through the fummer; fo that towards
the time of harveft, when the crop begins to
change, patches of half an acre or an acre, ftill
in a graffy ftate, become confpicuoufly fcattered over the piece.

Whether the crop be of barley or of wheat,
it receives, throughout, material injury by the
tracks made acrofs it.

CLOVER, alfo, receives injury from *hares*, by
the young heads being eaten down to the
crown in winter, and by the crop being checked in the fpring; thereby fuffering the drought
to get poffeffion of the foil. But the clover
crop receives ftill greater injury from *pheafants*;
which are not content with the foliage, but
feed on the vitals of the plant; pecking out its
" heart," as it is emphatically called: namely,
the center of the crown of the root.

It is, indeed, an opinion among farmers, who
are unfortunately fixed near kept covers,
that

that the pheafants do more injury to their clovers, than they do either to their turneps or
their barley; or, fome are of opinion, even to
the wheat crop; for the lofs of the clover by
pheafants, deranges their farm in a fimilar,
though not in fo fenfible a manner, as the lofs
of their turneps by hares; whereas the lofs of
the wheat, though great in the firft inftance, is
lefs injurious in its confequences.

To a perfon who has not been eyewitnefs to
the deftruction which accompanies an inordinate quantity of game, the quantity of damage
is in a manner inconceivable.

Let us fuppofe that a fuite of kept covers
give protection to five hundred brace of hares:
one hundred and fifty brace, it is confidently
afferted, have been counted, at one time, on one
fide of a fingle cover. I have myfelf feen
from fifty to an hundred brace under the eye
at once.

Let us further fuppofe that five hares de-
vour, or deftroy, as much food as one of the
fmall heath fheep of this country: this, if we
may depend on an accurate experiment made
on the quantity of turnep eaten by one of thefe

gluttonous

gluttonous animals in a state of confinement,
is, as the former, a reasonable supposition.

Any man, conversant in rural affairs, can
form some idea of the havock which two hundred wild heath sheep, turned loose into a
fenceless corn country, must necessarily make
among the crops. But if, in addition to these,
a thousand head of poultry were at the same
time let loose, it would be no difficult matter
for any man to conceive a pretty strong idea
of the consequences.

From what I have myself seen, and from
what I learnt from those whom woful experience has taught, I am led to believe, that
there are not less than one thousand acres of
turneps, one thousand acres of clover, one
thousand acres of barley, and one thousand
acres of wheat, annually destroyed, or materially injured, in this county, by hares and
pheasants.

My calculation is this:—Norfolk contains,
as nearly as this calculation requires, one mil-
lion acres of land. Suppose that half the county consists of marshes, meadows, sheep walks,
and other grasslands, heaths, commons, woodlands,

lands, roads, and hedgerows, there remains five hundred thoufand acres of arable land.

This however is, I believe, too fmall a proportion; we will therefore, to eafe the calculation, and to render it, perhaps, more accurate, eftimate the quantity of arable land at fix hundred thoufand acres; which being divided agreeably to the courfe of hufbandry moft prevalent throughout the county, affords, annually, one hundred thoufand acres of wheat, two hundred thoufand acres of barley, one hundred thoufand acres of clover, and from fifty to one hundred thoufand acres of turneps.

I am clearly of opinion, that a quantity equal to one acre in a hundred acres of wheat, to one acre in two hundred of barley, to one acre in a hundred acres of clover, and to more than one acre in a hundred acres of turneps, is wholly deftroyed or irreparably injured by hares and pheafants.

I do not mean that a thoufand diftinct acres of any of thefe crops can be picked out; but that there is, upon the whole, a deftruction adequate to the produce, on a par, of a thoufand acres.

	£.	s.	d.
1000 acres of wheat, worth on a par of crops, in a par of years, 6l.	6,000	o	o
1000 acres of barley, at 4l. 10s.	4,500	o	o
1000 acres of clover, and the consequential damages	5,000	o	o
750 acres of turneps, and the consequential damages, at 10l.	7,500	o	o
	£. 23,000	o	o

If we view this inordinate quantity of game in a moral light, its evil consequences, whether we confider them in a private or a public view, are still greater.

There are an hundred, perhaps five hundred, men in this county whofe principal dependence, for their own and their family's fupport, is on poaching. The coaltrade and fifheries are not more certain nurferies of feamen than kept covers are of poachers. An exceffive quantity of game is not more certainly deftructive of the crops they have accefs to, than it is inevitably productive of idlenefs and difhonefty among the laborers of the neighbourhood. Two or three fhillings for a pheafant, the ufual price, I underftand, given by the wholefale   .

dealers

dealers in Norwich, is a temptation, to a man who is not strictly honest and industrious, too powerful to be withstood.

For a while he goes on in security : but his ways and his haunts being at length discovered, he is taken ; and, if not knocked on the head in his scuffle with the keepers, sent to gaol.

Having lain here his wonted time, he sallies forth again, not only a more desperate poacher, but an incorrigible rogue, fit for any thing.

Having been two or three times taken, and having lain upon the whole, perhaps, twelve months in gaol ; having learnt to live by night, and to idle and sleep away the day ; he cannot reverse his way of life ; and he is become too notorious to carry on, any longer, his trade of poaching.

His case now becomes desperate ; and if he is not fortunate enough to get into a gang of smugglers, he takes, of course, to house-breaking, or some other highway to the gallows.

Nor is this the sum of mischief:—A gentleman who preserves an inordinate quantity of game upon his estate, is, in the nature of things, perpetually in hot water, with the yeomanry and

minor

minor gentlemen of his neighbourhood. And
for what advantage? A mere childish gratification—a toy.—The child has its bird of
pith, the schoolboy his daws and magpies, la-
dies their aviaries, and gentlemen their kept
covers;—merely for the sake of shewing off
the pretty creatures; or of saying that they
have got them in their possession.

In point of real diversion, kept covers are
utter enemies. What hounds can hunt in covers with a thousand hares in them? And the
diversion of shooting pheasants in a kept cover,
is just equivalent to that of shooting small-
birds in a rickyard, or poultry at a barndoor.

These observations do not arise from an anti-
pathy to rural diversions, nor, I flatter myself,
from an overweening fondness for rural economy. I have professed myself upon a former
occasion, and still profess myself, a friend to
both; and as such I beg leave to intimate to
gentlemen of large estates, that if, instead of
laying waste the lands immediately round their
residences, they would scatter small covers over
different parts of their estates; more especially
by the sides of rivulets in which water-cresses
abound; and if, instead of employing in the
shooting-

shooting-seafon half-a-dozen keepers night and day, at a great expence to themfelves, and to the certain injury of the health of thofe whom they employ, in this hazardous and difgraceful bufinefs, they would permit fuch of their tenants, as chofe to take out licences, to fport upon their refpective farms, and the unprotected farms in their neighbourhoods; I am clearly of opinion, I am pofitive, they would have a fufficiency of game, an increafe of diverfion, an increafe of income, and, what is of much more value to a man whom fortune has placed above dependency, an increafe of refpectability and perfonal happinefs.

To fay that the game laws are difgraceful to the laws of this country, would only be repeating what has been faid a hundred times, and by the firft characters in it; neverthelefs, they ftill remain an abfurdity in Englifh jurifprudence *.

* At prefent, a merchant or monied man, let him be worth an hundred thoufand pounds, and let him have an hundred men of landed property ready to give him permiffion to fport over their eftates and manors, he cannot do it without being guilty of a breach of the laws of his country. Nay, this man, nor any man, though he be poffeffed of the clear fee-fimple of a landed eftate of 99l. a year, remains in the fame predicament. Whilft another

N 3 man,

The legiſlature having lately thought fit to make rural diverſions an object of taxation, it might now be impolitic to make game altogether what it ought to be—private property. Neverthelefs it ſtill ſtrikes me, as it did long before the licences for ſporting were inſtituted, that game might be rendered a public and private good.

Wherever perſonal property is aſcertained, there, alſo, let a private property in game take place ; the property being inveſted in the proprietor of the land, not in the occupier of it ; and let every proprietor, great or ſmall, have a full and uncontroulable right to the game he can *find* upon his eſtate.

But the moment he ſteps off his own land, whether onto the private property of another, or into a foreſt or mixed property, though full permiſſion be firſt had from the proprietor or keeper, let him become liable to fine or impriſonment ; provided he do not annually pay, towards the ſupport of the ſtate, five guineas, or ſome greater ſum.

man, perhaps not worth a ſhilling, but becauſe he has in his poſſeſſion an eſtate of one hundred a year, though mortgaged for twice its value, is entitled to the privilege of ranging with impunity.

Let

Let this five guineas, or greater fum, qualify him fully to fport on forefts, waftes, and all undivided property, *without leave* from any perfon whatever; as well as to fport, *with permif-*. *fion*, over any man's private eftate.

But, notwithftanding his qualification, let him, for ftarting game, without permiffion, upon private property, *with intent to kill*, be guilty of an act of larceny or felony, and, as a larcenor or felon, let him be punifhed by the ordinary laws of his country.

Objections might be raifed to this plan; but not one, I will venture to fay, which might not readily be obviated.

24.

HARVEST PROCESS.

THE WHOLE busineſs of harveſt is done by harveſtmen; no part of it, generally ſpeaking, being done by the acre.

The price of a harveſtman is thirtyfive to forty ſhillings for the harveſt, be it long or ſhort, with his full board ſo long as harveſt work continues.

This is, in any year, a diſagreeable circumſtance; and, in a long harveſt, extremely tedious: in the backward harveſt of 1782 ſome farmers boarded their harveſtmen ſeven weeks, two or three of which, perhaps, they lay in a great meaſure idle.

What renders the expence exceſſive, is not altogether the number of appetites to be palled, but the extravagant manner in which they are, by cuſtom, expected to be gratified. In liquor, however, the Norfolk labourers are leſs waſteful than are the labourers of ſome other places.

The

The difagreeablenefs of boarding apart (and
this might no doubt be avoided), the bufinefs of harveft goes off with fingular alacrity
in Norfolk. Every man turns his hand to
any work which is going forward, To whatever requires the quickeft difpatch, whether it
be reaping, mowing, cocking or carrying,
a farmer can direct his whole force; or fuch
part of it as he may judge neceffary : an advantage which cannot be had when reaping
and mowing are done by the acre; the reapers, more efpecially, being as ufelefs to a farmer in this refpect, as if they were not employed upon his farm.

What adds effentially to the difpatch, and
confequently to the pleafure, of harveft, is the
comparative alertnefs and activity of the Norfolk harveftmen ; who, from four in the morning until dark, their mealtimes excepted,
work, not as for their mafters, but as for themfelves.

While, however, I thus pay due praife to
the laborioufnefs of the Norfolk workmen,
truth obliges me to fay, that in many inftances
their work is done in a loofe, and, what in fome
places would be called, a flovenly manner.

But

But this is a natural, or at leaft a ufual, confequence of difpatch. A man who reaps, for
inftance, from half to three quarters of an acre
a day, cannot be expected to do his work fo
neatly, to lay his corn fo ftraight, and bind his
fheaves fo tightly, as he who only reaps one
third of an acre.

Were it not for this extraordinary difpatch,
I do not fee how the crops of the Diftrict could
be harvefted. There are, it is true, a few
men, from Suffolk, Cambridgefhire, &c.
hired annually at Norwich, and retained
for the harveft; but their number is inconfiderable, compared with the numbers which
are employed in other arable countries; where
they pafs from place to place, as the harveft
ripens : whereas here they are at the end of
their journey : an extenfive tract of arable
country on one fide, and the fea on the other.
The beft refource which this country has is in
its numerous manufacturers, fome few of whom
can, in neceffity, turn their hands to harveft-
work.

One cuftom of this country refpecting harveftmen is very reprehenfible. Their work is
confidered to be merely that of *harvefting* ;
and,

and, if the weather be such that this does not afford them full employment, they consider themselves as having, from ancient custom, a right to refuse to do every other kind of work. It is (I am sorry that truth obliges me to relate it) no unusual thing for parties of them to be playing at cards in a barn, while the turnep-crop is receiving irreparable injury for want of their assistance : a crime, in this country, which both master and men ought to be equally ashamed of ; and it certainly would be worth the farmers' while to give their men an advance of harvest wages, rather than to suffer so disgraceful a custom. Were it not for the manufacturers and other handicraftmen, the later-sown crops of turneps would suffer greatly during harvest. Some years, it is true, harvest-men have little leisure for turnep-hoeing ; but, in others, they have a great deal; and, in every year, a strong morning dew, or a flying shower at the time of carrying, afford apt opportunities for this necessary operation.

The practice of trotting with empty carriages has already been noticed : it is on no occasion more valuable than in harvest ; a custom among farmers of driving their own harvest carriages is not less excellent.

Loose

Loofe corn of every kind is univerfally trodden in the barn with horfes; and, what is perhaps fingular to Norfolk, horfes are fometimes
employed in treading large ricks.

Ricks, in general, however, are carried up
too narrow and too high to be trodden with
horfes; their roofs, more particularly, being
frequently drawn up to an unnecefTary and, indeed, ridiculous height; thereby incurring unnecefTary labour in topping-up, and an unnecefTary quantity of thatch and thatching.

The price of the laft, however, being in a
manner fixed at fix pence a yard in length, be
the roof high or low, deep or fhallow, the lofs
in this falls rather upon the thatcher than the
farmer.

For the minutiæ of the harveft procefs, fee
the feveral crops:—namely, WHEAT, BARLEY,
&c. &c.

25.

FARMYARD·MANAGEMENT.

THIS HEAD may be divided into, .
  1. Barn management ; and
  2. Straw-yard management.

I. BARN MANAGEMENT.—Every thing is thrashed by the coomb of four bushels; little or no thrashing being done by the day *.

It is observable, that notwithstanding the spaciousness of the Norfolk barn-floor, the labourers in general object to their thrashing two in a barn ; rather choosing to work singly :—this, perhaps, is principally owing to the particular method of thrashing with two on a floor; which is to turn their backs on each other ; working as separately as if they thrashed on separate floors; the method of standing face to face, and giving stroke for stroke, being seldom, if ever used.

Every thing is thrashed rough ; no straw bound ; even wheat straw is usually shook off the floor, loose, with a common pitching fork.

* For the prices, see LIST OF RATES.

The

The method of dreſſing corn, here, is ſingular, and, as an eſtabliſhed and invariable practice, is, I believe, peculiar to this country;
in which there is not, perhaps, a ſingle *wind
fan* of any conſtruction; and I never ſaw the
natural wind made uſe of in the dreſſing of
corn.

In Weſt Norfolk, there are ſome ſail fans;
but, in this Diſtrict, the invariable practice is
to ſeparate the corn from the chaff, by throwing it from one end of the floor toward the
other with a ſhovel.

In this operation, the prime grain, being
heavieſt, flies fartheſt; the light corn and
" coſhes" next: to theſe ſucceed the broken
ears and prime chaff; and to this the ſmall
chaff and duſt; which being thrown againſt a
gentle draught of air, when it can be had, is
generally carried back pretty plentifully towards the face of the thrower, who uſually
guards his eyes with a crape or other partial
covering.

To avoid the inconveniency of the duſt as
much as may be, and to ſeparate as clean as
poſſible the corn and chaff from the " colder,"
                                        namely,

namely, the ears, short straws, &c.—the rough
corn, after the straw is shook off and raked
out in the usual manner, is riddled through a
fine riddle upon a horse placed near the leeward door; by which means a principal part
of the dust, and, if the draught of wind be
strong, much of the worst of the chaff is got
rid of. This not only renders the casting more
agreeable, but lessens the quantity to be
thrown.

The art of throwing is a sleight which can
be learned from practice only. A light, hollow wooden shovel is the tool made use of in
this operation. This is about half filled with
corn; which, to make the cast more true and
certain, is shook into the center of the mouth
of the shovel. This is done by a single motion,
with the arms hanging straight down, as if
with an intention to estimate the weight of the
corn in the shovel. The equipoise being thus
got, the contents are delivered by a sweeping
motion of the arms and the body; scattering
the grain in a long, narrow heap, of a semi-
lunar form.

The chaff and the light grain being removed, the broken ears and "coshes," namely,

the

the heavy grains whofe chaff fticks to them, are feparated by a riddle and the wicker knee-fan.

If the head grain be not fufficiently cleanfed by one cafting, it is returned in a fimilar way to the other end of the floor.—Finally, the weed feeds and fmall corn are feparated in the ufual manner, by the fkreen ; and the head grain meafured up, in a way as fingular as that by which it is feparated.

In one part of the kingdom the bufhel is fil-led with a fhovel—in another with a fhoal—in a third with a fieve ; but here no tool whatever is made ufe of ; the bufhel itfelf being thruft into the heap, and then filled up and levelled fit for the ftriker with the hands alone ; under a thorough conviction that corn may be meafured lighter in this way than in any other way whatever.

All corn is fent to market in "coomb bags," and generally with four bufhels in each bag.

The *meafure* of Norfolk is about eight gal-lons and a half to the bufhel, and twentyone coombs to the laft: that is, one coomb, or one bufhel, in twenty is thrown in. This cuftom has probably been introduced by the corn-fac-tors,

tors, under a pretence of lofs of meafure in fend-
ing their corn to market. Be this as it may,
the allowance is made to the cornbuyers only:
for in dealings between farmer and farmer for
feed, &c. the " bare" meafure only is given.

It is a practice among Norfolk farmers, as
prevalent as it is judicious, not to ftore up dreffed corn; but either to let it remain in the ftraw,
or, if this be wanted, to keep it a few weeks in
the chaff, till a fair market offers; frequently
ftowing it away in a recefs cut out of the face
of the mow, for this purpofe.

II. STRAWYARD MANAGEMENT.—The Nor-
folk hufbandmen are, in general, very attentive
to feparating their ftock in the ftrawyard. For
this purpofe their "paryards" are *parted* into
fundry divifions with faggots, in the manner
already mentioned under the fubject REPAIRS.

One divifion is fet apart for the cows—another for the "buds" or yearlings,—fometimes
a third for the two-year-olds,—and, when turneps are brought into the yards, a fourth for
the bullocks.

By this judicious management the weak is
placed out of the power of the ftrong, and the

VOL. I.   O   colder

colder and best of the straw may be given to
such as require the best keep.

Sometimes the straw is given to the cattle in
" bins;" sometimes laid in heaps; and frequently for bullocks at turnep, it is scattered
loose about the yard.

Upon the whole, the Norfolk farmers may
be said to be wasteful of straw; more especially
at the beginning of the winter, when it is frequently thrown into the empty yard entirely
waste as to fodder: this, however, is not looked upon in so improvident a light in Norfolk as
in most other places; for here a notion of the
utility of having plenty of straw among dung,
prevails so strongly, that the straw which is *eaten*
by cattle is considered by some men, as being
in a manner wasted as to manure.

For further observations on this subject, see
Min. 73.

26. MARKETS.

26.

M A R K E T S.

NORFOLK, taken collectively, as a coun-
ty, is singularly well situated for markets: the
Norwich manufactory is productive of a regu-
lar internal consumption; while Yarmouth,
Lynn, the smaller ports, Smithfield and St.
Ives, take off the surplus produce.

SMITHFIELD is the grand market for cattle
and sheep, and the SEAPORTS for barley.—
Wheat is principally bought up by the MIL-
LERS, and the surplus of what is consumed in
the country sent to the LONDON MARKET, in
flour. Some wheat in grain is also sent to Bear-
Key.

With respect to veal, pork, lamb, and sometimes mutton, a singular practice prevails in
Norfolk; most especially at the NORWICH
market; which is supplied with the above
articles entirely by the farmers: who, for fifteen or twenty miles round, are most of them
· capable of dressing a calf, a lamb, or a sheep;

which, with poultry made ready for the spit,
are carried weekly by themselves, their wives,
their daughters, or their servants, to Norwich
market: which, whether for plenty or neatness,
is, I believe beyond all comparison, the first in
the kingdom.

These articles are brought to market in pan-
niers—provincially, "peds"—either on horseback, or in market carts (a conveniency which
few farmers are not possessed of) and placed in
rows in the "ped market;" a spacious trian-
gular area in the center of the city; the market
women sitting in a row on one side of the peds,
while the other side is left free for their custo-
mers.

Whether viewing the neatness of the market
women themselves, the delicacy of their wares,
or the cleverness which, through habit, many
of them are mistresses of in the disposal of
them, the Saturday's market of Norwich exhibits an agreeable sight.

It is not necessary to add to this account of
the ped market, that the business of a butcher
in Norwich is confined, in a great measure, to
beef and a little mutton. Indeed the trade of
a butcher is not, in any part of the county, a
good

good one; the principal farmers butchering their own meat; and the smaller ones who kill for the ped markets, living chiefly on the offal and the unfold joints.

The corn market of Norwich is likewise a very good one. But the busineſs being chiefly done at the Inns, is not *seen*. The river Yare, which is navigable from thence to Yarmouth, affords an eaſy conveyance of the ſurplus corn bought up, at Norwich, for the London market.

The principal market of *this* Diſtrict is that of NORTH WALSHAM ;—a very good one; great quantities of barley and wheat are bought up weekly, and the ſurplus of the home conſumption either ſent down the north river navigation to Yarmouth, and from thence ſhipped off for the London or other market; or is delivered by land carriage at CROMER or MUNSLEY, and there ſhipped off.

When the ports are open for exportation, great quantities of corn are ſent immediately from Norfolk to HOLLAND, and other FOREIGN MARKETS.

One general obſervation remains to be made reſpecting the markets of Norfolk: they are

in

in general AFTERNOON MARKETS; no bufinefs
being done, in the corn market at leaft, until
three or four o'clock in the afternoon. The
market of Norwich is, however, an exception
to this cuftom, and there may be other fore-
noon markets in the county.

Many conveniencies and advantages accrue
to the farmer from afternoon markets: he has
all the morning to himfelf: he dines with his
family; and fees his men at work, and his
teams out for their afternoon journey, before
he fets off for market.   His market expences
are curtailed, and a habit of lounging out a
whole day, idly, prevented.   The only inconveniency incurre! by afternoon markets, to a
farmer, is the *neceffity* of returning home in the
dark of winter's evenings: this, however, is
an inconveniency which farmers in general
who go to market at ten o'clock in the morning *voluntarily* difpenfe with.   The Innkeepers
may be faid to be the only fufferers by afternoon markets.

The FAIRS of Norfolk are not fo confiderable as they are in fome other counties; except
the fair of St. Faith's, which is one of the
largeft fairs in the kingdom.

But

But, as I made a point of attending some of the principal fairs, and of minuting the obfervations which ftruck me while they were frefh in the memory, I forbear faying any thing further refpecting them in this place; but refer to the Minutes themfelves; which I publifh the rather, as nothing gives a more lively and juft idea of what may be called the ECONOMY OF LIVESTOCK in a given Diftrict, than the bufinefs which paffes at the fairs of that Diftrict. Befides, fairs and markets are the great ftumblingblocks to gentlemen farmers; who, through want of *affability*, or want of *courage*, remain in general entirely ignorant of the bufinefs of fairs and markets; even when they have made confiderable progrefs in the bufinefs of the farm.—This is my only motive for giving the minutiæ of the Minutes as they ftand in my Minute-book; for on a fubject fo totally new as this is, I believe, to written agriculture, every incident becomes valuable; I mean to thofe, whom, in this particular, I moft efpecially wifh to inform.

For obfervations on St. Faith's fair (1781), fee MIN. 27.

For obfervations on Holt fair, fee MIN. 39.

For obfervations on Walfham corn-market, fee MIN. 80.

For obfervations on Aylefham fair, fee MIN. 94.

For obfervations on Norwich clover-feed market, fee MIN. 101.

For obfervations on Walfham fair, fee MIN. 105.

For obfervations on Worftead fair, fee MIN. 107.

For obfervations on Ingham fair, fee MIN. 112.

For general obfervations on Norfolk fairs, fee MIN. 112.

For obfervations on Cawfton fheepfhow, fee MIN. 123.

For obfervations on St. Faith's fair (1782), fee MIN. 134.

For fundry obfervations on Smithfield market, fee the article BULLOCKS.

27. WHEAT.

27.

W H E A T.

IN TAKING a fyftematic view of the culture of this crop, it will be proper to confider,

1. The fpecies of wheat ufually cultivated
   in Norfolk.
2. The foils on which it is ufually grown*.
3. The fucceffion; or the crop, &c. which
   wheat ufually fucceeds, in the management of Eaft Norfolk.
4. The foil procefs,
5. The manure procefs,
6. The feed procefs,   in practice for
7. The vegetating procefs, wheat in Nor-
8. The harveft procefs, folk.
9. The farmyard procefs,
10. The markets, for wheat.

I. THE SPECIES.—The long-eftablifhed
" ftock" of this country is the " Norfolk red,"
—which is faid to weigh heavier than any other

* The MANURES applied for WHEAT appear under
art. MANURE PROCESS.

wheat

wheat which has yet been introduced into the
county. Its appearance, however, is very
much againſt this aſſertion: it is a very long
bodied, thin grain, partaking more of the
ſhape of rye, than of well bodied wheat.

A favorite new ſpecies has lately been introduced, under the name of the " Kentiſh white
coſh." The grain is plump and red; but the
" coſh," or huſk, white; reſembling very
much the velvet wheat of Surrey and Kent.
The " caſt," or yield of this is allowed to be
greater than that of the " old red,"—and the
millers begin to like it nearly as well;—
though, on its firſt introduction, ſome fifteen or
twenty years ago, they were, or affected to be,
prejudiced againſt it.

A remarkable circumſtance is ſaid to take
place, reſpecting this ſpecies of wheat, when
ſown repeatedly in Norfolk. Though the coſh
be perfectly white on its introduction, and
though it be ſtudiouſly kept ſeparate from the
red coſh; yet, by being repeatedly ſown, year
after year, it loſes the fairneſs of its huſks;
which firſt become " pied," and, at length,
change entirely to a clear red, reſembling thoſe
of the old Norfolk ſtock. I have ſeen them in
their

their pied ftate, and have been affured by men
of obfervation, that they acquire this ftate,
though kept perfectly feparate from the red
cofh variety. If this be really a fact, it is a
ftriking evidence of the power of foils and
fituations, in eftablifhing what the botanifts
call *varieties*, in the vegetable kingdom.

II. THE SOIL.—In this, as in moft other
Diftricts, wheat is fown on almoft every fpecies
of foil. But the farmers here, as in other
places, too frequently find out, at harveft, that
a full crop of barley, or oats, would have paid
them better than half a crop of wheat.

In the northern parts of this Diftrict there
are many very light-land farms,—and fome in
the central parts of it—which pafs under the
denomination of barley farms: and on which
the occupiers judicioufly content themfelves
with a fmall proportion of wheat.

But the fouthern parts of the Diftrict, and
the fouth-eaft parts of the county in general,
enjoy a ftronger, richer foil, well adapted to
the propagation of wheat.

III. THE SUCCESSION.—In the regular courfe
of hufbandry, the wheat-crop fucceeds invariably

bly the *second year's lay*; but, as has been already intimated, the regular fucceffion is in a greater or fmaller degree broken into by farmers in general; and it fometimes happens that wheat is fown on the *first year's lay*—fometimes after *peas*, or after *buck harvefted* or *buck picwed under*, or *turneps*, or fometimes on a " right-out fummerly," or, *fummer fallow*. But it may be faid, without hazard, that three fourths, perhaps nine tenths, of the wheat fown in *this* part of the Diftrict, is fown on *the fecond year's lay*.

IV. SOIL PROCESS.—This varies with the nature and ftate of the foil,—the nature of the preceding crop,—the circumftance of the farm, and the fkill and judgment of the farmer.

1. The prevailing practice is to make a " backward fummerly"—a fort of *autumnal fallow*—of the SECOND YEAR'S LAY.

When pafturage is fcarce, the fecond year's lay is fometimes fown on the " flag;" that is, upon the unbroken furrow of *one plowing*; efpecially if the feed be intended to be dibbled in. But, for broadcaft fowing, neither the depth of the Norfolk foil (except in fome few

places)

places) nor the conftruction of the Norfolk plow, will admit, with any degree of proprie- ty, of this (in many parts of the kingdom) moft excellent practice.

THE BACKWARD SUMMERLY of the SECOND YEAR'S LAY, is made in different ways.

Some farmers plow only twice; rice-balk- ing the firft time very fleet. When the flag is rotten, they harrow acrofs and fet on the muck; and, the laft plowing, go a full depth; laying the foil in "warps," or wide flat beds, on which they fow the feed abovefurrow.— This, however, is confidered, as it really is for wheat, a flovenly practice.

Others plow three times: the firft fleet; the fecond a full pitch; the laft of a mean depth; with which laft plowing the feed is plowed in underfurrow. The foil is harrowed between the plowings, and the dung in this cafe fet upon the fecond harrowing, and plowed in with the feed.

But the practice of thofe who excel in their profeffion, and who are, in their neighbour- hood, looked up to as fuperior hufbandmen, is this:

His

His fecond year's lays having finifhed his
bullocks, and brought his ftock cattle, and
horfes, through the fore part of the fummer;
and his firft year's lays having been mown, and
ready to receive his ftock ; the farmer begins
to break up his " clland" for wheat, by rice-
balking them as fleet as poffible, fo as to carry
an even regular furrow; embracing the opportunity when the furface has been moiftened by a fummer fhower.

In this rice-balked ftate his fummerlies remain until the wane of harveft; when his corn
being chiefly in, and his horfes more at leifure,
he harrows, and afterwards plows his fummerlies acrofs the balks of the firft plowing;
bringing them up, this fecond plowing, the
full depth of the foil.

On this plowing he fpreads his manure,
harrows, and immediately "fcales" it in by
another fleet plowing.

This third plowing has feveral good effects :
it mixes, effectually, the foil and the manure,
—cuts off and pulverizes the upper furfaces of
the furrows of the fecond plowing; and by
doing this, moft effectually eradicates or fino-
thers fuch weeds as had efcaped the two former

mer earths; and, at the fame time, by ex-
cluding the air from the under parts of thofe
furrows, renders the whole as mellow and friable as a fummer fallow.

In this ftate it lies until feed-time; when it
is harrowed, rolled, fown, and gathered up
into ridges of fuch width as is agreeable to the
nature of the foil, or the fkill or fancy of the
farmer.

Thofe of fix furrows are the moft prevalent;
but there are very good farmers who lay their
wheat land into four-furrow, and others into
ten-furrow, ridges; which laft they execute in
a ftyle much fuperior to what might be expected from *wheel* plows.

But the fix-furrow work is that in which the
Norfolk plowmen excel. It is generally performed with three plows in this manner: the
firft fets out the ridge, the fecond takes the
middle bout, and the laft makes up the furrows. The beft plowman is of courfe put
laft, the fecond firft, and the worft takes the
middle bout. The firft plit is fometimes turned partially back by the fecond, by letting the
off-horfe go back *in* the firft made furrow; and
fometimes the firft furrow is left entirely open,

by

by letting the off horfe go back *out* of the firft
furrow. The laft way makes the ridges wider,
and rids more ground, but the firft ftirs the
ground better, and is thought to diftribute the
feed more evenly. The plowman who goes laft
and makes up the furrows, divides his horfes
by means of a long "horfetree," or middle
whipping; fo that each of them takes an outfide furrow, while he and his plow alone occupy the furrow he is making up. This anfwers
two good purpofes:—it gives the plowman a
free fight, and prevents the horfes from treading
the ridges. If the foil be wet and poachy,
fome judicious farmers divide the middle-
bout horfes in the fame manner.' The horfes
are of courfe rather aukward at the firft fetting-
off; but they foon become tractable, and much
more fteady than when they ftagger about, and
joftle each other, in the fame furrow. The
four-furrow ridges are plowed in a fimilar manner by two plows.

There are feveral advantages arife from this
method of laying-up narrow ridges. The
whole bufinefs is carried on in regular progrefſ-
fion. The feedfian begins on one fide of
the clofe, and ·fows towards the other with

as little interruption as he could do for one plow. For although two or three plows are employed in the fame piece, there are no fresh settings-out, nor any uneven work at laft; fave fuch as is neceffarily given by the figure of the field.— There is much time faved (more efpecially when wheel plows are ufed) in altering the plows; and the whole piece is equally well executed; each ridge being fet out, and each furrow made up, by the fame men.

The Norfolk plowmen, when plowing in wheat, carry very narrow furrows; fo that a fix-furrow ridge, fet out by letting the off-horfe return *in* the firft-made furrow, does not meafure more than three feet eight or nine inches.

2. AFTER THE FIRST YEAR'S LAY, the feed is generally fown on the flag.

3. AFTER PEAS, the farmer gives one two three or four plowings, and manages in every other refpect the fame as he does after the fecond year's lay.

4. AFTER BUCK HARVESTED, he is more confined in refpect of time, and feldom gives more than two, fometimes but one, plowing. If he plow twice, he fpreads his manure on the ftubble, fcales it in fleet, harrows, rolls, fows and gathers up the foil a mean depth into narrow

work. If he plow but once, he, in like manner, spreads his manure on the stubble; and, what seems very extraordinary to a stranger, sows his seed among his manure; plowing the whole in together, and gathering his soil up into narrow ridges; as if it had undergone the operations of a fallow.

There is, however, one very great evil attends this method of sowing wheat after buck; especially where rooks are numerous. The buck which is necessarily shed in harvesting the crop, and which is, of course, plowed under with the manure and seed-wheat, vegetates the succeeding spring, and becomes a weed to the wheat; and, what is of still worse consequence, should rooks get a haunt of it, they will not only pull the buck up by the roots, but the wheat plants with it; so as to leave large patches almost destitute of plants. But, by first scaling in the manure and self-sown buck very fleet, and harrowing the surface fine, the buck vegetates, and the evil consequence is thereby, in a great measure, prevented.

5. AFTER BUCK PLOWED UNDER.—This, as well as the preceding, is a favorite practice among good farmers; and the Norfolk plowmen perform the operation of plowing the crop

under,

under, in a mafterly ftyle. They fweep it
down by the means of a brufh or broom, made
of rough bufhes fixed to the front of the
" fickle-tow ;" or fore tackle of the plow, between the wheels ; fo as to bear down the buck
without lifting the wheels of the plow from the
ground. To prevent this, when the buck is
ftour, it is firft broken down by a roller, going
the fame way as the plow is intended to go.
This operation is performed when the plants
are in their fulleft bloom.

The furface is, fometimes, harrowed and
rolled after plowing : fometimes left rough :
the former is perhaps the moft eligible management.

In either cafe, the foil remains in that ftate
until after harveft, when it is harrowed and
taken up a full pitch, acrofs the warps.

At feedtime, it is harrowed,—rolled,—fowed,—and ufually gathered up into " narrow
work," in the manner above defcribed.

6. AFTER SUMMER FALLOW.—The practice
of fummer fallowing feldom occurs in this
Diftrict;—turneps or buck being generally introduced as a fubftitute for it. However, when
land has been worn down by cropping, and is
much run to " beggary" and weeds, a " right-

out fummerly" is efteemed by many judicious
hufbandmen as good management; and is, it
feems, fince the late failure of the turnep crops,
gaining ground every year.

The clofe of a fummer fallow is the fame as
that of a backward fummerly: the manure is
fealed in with the laft plowing but one, the feed
plowed in moderately deep, and the foil gathered into narrow ridges by the laft plowing.

7. AFTER TURNEPS.—In general, the foil is
plowed a mean depth, and the feed fown over
the firft plowing: if, however, the turneps be
get off early, the weeds are fometimes firft fealed
in, and the feed plowed under with a fecond
plowing; gathering the foil into narrow ridges.

GENERAL OBSERVATION.—Excellent as the
Norfolk practice of hufbandry may be, taken
all in all, it feems in this place neceffary to
obferve, that although there are fome fuperior
hufbandmen who put in their wheat crops in a
mafterly ftyle, a very confiderable part of the
land fown with wheat in Norfolk, is flovened
over in a moft unfarmerlike manner.

The fecond year's lays in general are broken
up too late, and receive too inconfiderable a
portion of tillage to bring them into a hufband-
like ftate.

Were

Were a Kentiſh, or any other good wheat, farmer, who had heard much of the ſuperiority of the Norfolk huſbandry, to ride through Eaſt Norfolk in the month of November, he would experience ſome difficulty in conceiving himſelf travelling in a country of which fame has ſo long ſpoken loudly. It is true, he would not unfrequently be ſtruck with a beautiful objeċt;—a kind of fluted frize-work, or any other ornament to the face of the country his fancy might picture to him; but he would not leſs frequently be diſguſted with the ſight of fields which he would little ſuſpeċt, on a curſory view, to be ſown with wheat. He would rather, at firſt ſight, take them for rough fallows, on which ſheep had been foddered with hay they could not eat; the whole ſurface being ſtrewed with tufts of roots and ſtems of withered graſſes, and with graſſy clods of every ſhape and dimenſion *.

* There are, nevertheleſs, men who argue in favor of this management; and, were it prudent to ſow wheat on very light " running ſands," it might be proper to preſerve part of the " wreck," as it is well termed, to prevent the ſand from being run together by heavy rains; but ſoils of this nature are, as has been already obſerved, generally improper for wheat.

P 3   In

In their culture of barley and of turneps, the Norfolk hufbandmen, no doubt, excel; but, taken collectively as a body of profeſſional men, they cannot, defervedly, be ranked among wheat farmers.

Neverthelefs, there are, as I flatter myſelf fully appears by the foregoing detail, ſome hufbandmen in Norfolk who merit no part of this cenſure; their management being, perhaps, the beſt that art can deviſe for the ſoil they act upon: while, therefore, I condemn them as a body (for reaſons which I flatter myſelf are obvious), I mean to except, with all due reſpect, a number of individuals.

V. The manure process,—Land which has been recently marled or clayed, requires no further addition ;—nor has land which has received fifteen or twenty loads of dung and mould for turneps,—the firſt year's lay having been teathed in autumn, and the ſecond fed off,—any need of another dreſſing for wheat.

Where the ſoil is good, and the wheat apt to run too much to ſtraw, ſome few judicious farmers ſet their manure upon the young clover, thereby checking the effect of rank-neſs to the wheat.

But

But the moft general practice is to spread
the manure upon the broken ground, in the
manner defcribed in the laft fection; or, if the
feed be fown upon the flag, to fpread it on the
turf and plow it under; or to fpread it on the
plowed furface, and harrow it in with the feed,
as a topdreffing.

The laft I have feen done in the following
judicious manner. Three or four bouts are
firft plowed in the middle of each warp, forming a narrow bed of plowed ground wide
enough to fet the manure upon, but not too
wide to be received between the wheels of the
cart; which, in fetting on the muck, run in
the plow-furrows on each fide the bed. The
manure is then fet in hillocks upon thefe plowed flips; the warps are finifhed plowing; the
manure fpread over them ;—the feed fown ;—
and the whole harrowed in together.

By this management the manure goes on
with eafe to the team, and without the newly-
plowed ground being cut to pieces by the
wheels of the cart, or torn about by the feet of
the horfes; for the cart being always, as it were,
on the .nail, the horfes have no obftacles to
ftruggle againft. In a wet feafon this practice
is fingularly eligible.

The quantity of manure set on for wheat is generally less than that set on for turneps. Of *dung*, eight to t n cart-loads (as much as three horses can conveniently draw) an acre is reckoned a tolerable dressing. Of *lime*, three to four chaldrons an acre. Of *rapecake*, a ton to three acres. Of *soot*, about forty bushels an acre.

For observations on the *species* of manure for wheat, see the article MANURE PROCESS.

VI. SEED PROCESS.—In describing this department of the culture of wheat, it will be necessary to perspicuity, to consider, separately,

1. The time of sowing;
2. The preparation of the seed;
3. The method of sowing;
4. The quantity of seed;
5. The method of covering;
6. The adjustment of the soil.

I. THE TIME OF SOWING.—An orthodox farmer never thinks of beginning "wheat-seel" until after St. Faith's fair; which is held on the 17th of October. So prevalent, indeed, is this custom, that, perhaps, nine of ten of the farmers in East Norfolk begin to sow wheat

between

between the 17th and 24th of October;—and continue till the beginning of December;—sometimes even until Christmas. If they finish in November, they consider themselves in very good time. Wheat sown in the ordinary broadcast manner is, however, here spoken of; for dibbling or setting of wheat, Michaelmas is esteemed the best time.

The reason which the Norfolk husbandmen give for sowing their wheat so late, compared with the practice of other lightland counties, is, that their early sown wheats are liable to be winterproud, and run too much to straw; whereas their late-sown crops afford less straw, but a greater " cast;" more especially on land which has been recently marled.

This last idea, perhaps, accounts for the origin of their present time of sowing. The present practice of husbandry, in Norfolk, was established a century, perhaps two or three centuries, ago; and has been handed down from father to son with but very little improvement or alteration.. The present time of sowing was, of course, fixed when the land was full of marl, and was no doubt judiciously founded on experience. Marl, however, has now, in some

measure,

meafure, loft its efficacy; and it feems probable, that not only the time of fowing wheat,
but the very fyftem of Norfolk hufbandry will
require, ere long, to undergo a confiderable
change. Suffice it, however, in this place to
fay, that there are fome fenfible, judicious
men, who already fee the folly of waiting for
St. Faith's fair, before they begin to fow their
wheat.

2. PREPARING THE SEED.—The ordinary
method of preparation is to fteep the feed in
brine, and candy it with lime, in a way fimilar
to that practifed in other counties; and, probably, with the fame effect.

There are, however, men in this county
who fpeak with firmnefs and confidence of that
they can prevent, by a preparation of the feed,
the fmut or "brand" of wheat. They, likewife, feem clearly of opinion, that all wheat
would naturally become fmutty, if not checked by a proper management of the feed; but
that were it become, through neglect, as black
as fmut itfelf, they would engage in three years
time to effect a radical cure. The firft year, it
is allowed, there will many grains efcape; the
fecond, fome; but the third year, there will not.

remain

remain in the whole crop one "brandy" ker-
nel.

This is fpeaking clofely to the point, and
deferves a hearing. The procefs, though fimple, is truly chemical; and the idea, I believe,
totally new to written agriculture.

Their method is this: Inftead of diffolving
the falt in a large proportion of water, in order
to form a brine to fteep the wheat in; it is
diffolved in a very fmall quantity of water;—
barely enough to bring on the folution. With
this *liquid falt* the lime is flaked; and with this
faline preparation, in its *hotteft* ftate, the wheat
is candled; having previoufly been moiftened,
for the purpofe, with pure water.

I fhall not, here, comment on this procefs;
but only obferve, that the wheat crops of the
perfons who pride themfelves on this practice,
are, in general, freer from fmut, than thofe of
their neighbours.

J. THE MODE OF SOWING.—Broadcaft is the
prevailing practice. Dibbling, or fetting, is
in much ufe on the Suffolk fide of the county.
—Dibbling and fluting rollers are alfo ufed by
fome few individuals. But what is remarkable, drilling is, in a great meafure, unknown in
Norfolk;

the feedfman fees to an inch how far he has
fown, and where each handful ought to fall; he,
of courfe, leaves no flips unfown, nor gives
others double feed.

If the foil be intended to be gathered into
fix-furrow ridges, the feedfman fows, on the
warps, about two thirds of his feed;—if into
four-furrow work, fomewhat lefs than two
thirds *.

The plowman then begins to fet out his
ridges, the fame way that the warps are drawn;
but without any regard either · as to their
ftraightnefs, or their width; they being intended merely to direct the feedfman, not the
plowman. In fix-furrow work, the middle-
bout plowman follows next, and after him the
feedfman, ftraining the remainder of his feed
in the trenches made by the middle-bout plow;
which is called " fowing the furrows." The
head plowman follows laft,—covers up the
feed, and finifhes the work. In four-furrow
work, the two firft furrows are fown, and the
ridgets made up in a fimilar way.

* See Min. 67, on this operation.

The

The ufe of fowing the furrows is to give the
outfides of the ridgets their due proportion of
feed ; thereby preventing the interfurrows from
being left too wide and naked of plants.—
Some farmers fow only one of the outfide
furrows; namely, that toward the worked
ground, and this is undoubtedly the more
requifite bufinefs; for the feed on this fide
having been all gathered up by the preceding
furrow, the crumb or fhovelling of the inter-
furrow is left naked; and there would, of
courfe, be no feed buried under it, if it were
not thus fown by hand, in the preceding plow-
furrow.

. In fix-furrow work, three plows employ a
feedfman, and finifh about three acres a day.
In four-furrow work, two plows find employment for a feedfman,—there being, in this
cafe, more furrows to be fown,—and finifh
about two acres.

The dibbling, "dabbing," or fetting of wheat,
is confined principally to the country about
Wyndham, Attlebury, Buckenham, Harling,
&c. In the other Diftricts of Norfolk it is
but little known, and no where *practifed*;
though fometimes tried by way of experiment.

                                               The

The propriety of the practice depends upon circumstances; such as the price of labour, the price of the seed, and the quality of the soil. There seems, however, one thing always essentially needful; that is, a good soil. And this may, in some measure, account for the slow progress which it has made in the more northern parts of East Norfolk; but why it should not gain ground in the Blowfield, South-Walsham, and Flegg Hundreds, is a matter of surprize. Perhaps, nothing but the sanction of custom and fashion is wanted to render it, in this well soiled quarter of the county, the universal practice.

For a full account of this process, see the MIN. 23. 26. 28.

The Dibbling Roller is made somewhat similar to the common spiky roller; with, however, these distinctions: it is in itself shorter, and the spikes, instead of standing perpendicular to the circumference, are bent obliquely thereto, that they may leave smooth and clean indentures, without pulling up or breaking the flags. Between each row of spikes is a scraper to disengage the roller from the mould, which is apt to stick between the spikes, and which

in

in moist weather renders it wholly useless.—
The seed is sown broadcast over the indentures, and swept in with a bush-harrow.

I have seen wheat come up very well after
the spiky roller; but an implement which a
shower of rain renders useless, seems ill-adapted
to the business of sowing wheat in November *.

4. QUANTITY OF SEED.—Three bushels an
acre, broadcast, is the favorite quantity of
seed, without much regard being had to the
time of sowing.

This accounts in some measure for the want
of success in the early sown wheats. Three
bushels of seed sown in September is equal to
four or five bushels sown the latter end of
November. It is no wonder, then, that the
straw should prove slender, and the grain light:
for the plants being too numerous, and the soil
weak and shallow, though perhaps in sufficient heart to push the plants through the winter and spring, the vigour of the soil is spent
before harvest, and the ears of course abridged
of half their load. Whereas, had there been
a due proportion of plants, the exhaustion
during winter and spring would have been less,
and the strength of the soil reserved for the

* The fluting roller I did not meet with.

more

more material purpofe of perfecting the plants
at harveft.

5. COVERING THE SEED.—The feed fown
over the rough furrows of the firft or fecond
plowing is covered in the ufual manner with
tined harrows: generally with two fmall harrows and two horfes led by a boy, and fometimes guided with a plow line ; the man or
boy following the harrows to lift them up, and
difengage them from the rubbifh; which too
frequently Incumbers them.

That fown after the hand dibbles or the
dibbling roller is fwept in with a bufh-harrow;
made of a gate; hurdle, &c. wattled with
thorns or other bufhes.

6. ADJUSTING THE SOIL.—The fubfoil of
Norfolk being in general of an abforbent
nature; crofs water-furrows are in many inftances unneceffary : however, where the fubfoil is a brickearth; which is not unfrequently
the cafe; crofs-furrowing becomes abfolutely
neceffary to good management, though not
always put in practice.

Some neat hufbandmen roll their " wheat-
figgs" immediately after fowing. A common
roller takes two ridges at once, the horfes draw-

ing in the furrow between them.   This gives
an immediate neatnefs ; renders the crop beautiful at firſt coming up ; anticipates the labour
of rolling in the fpring ; and thereby precludes
the danger of unlocking the weed feeds at
that vegetative feafon of the year.

VII. THE VEGETATING PROCESS.—*Handweeding* is the principal labour beſtowed upon
the wheat-crop between feed-time and harveſt.
If the interfurrows be wide and thin of plants,
or if the crop be otherwife broken, *the hœ* is
fometimes, but very rarely, ufed.

Paſturing wheat in the fpring, though it cannot be called a common practice, is, nevertheleſs, frequently done ; efpecially when
fpring food is peculiarly fcarce, as it was in the
fpring of 1782 ; when almoſt all the wheats
in the country were fed off : not by fheep, as
is ufually the cafe, but by every other fpecies
of live ſtock.   See MIN. 106.

If wheat abound with " red weed"—pop-
pies—*fwine* are frequently turned upon it to
eat out this troublefome weed ; which they
will do, with little or no damage to the
wheat.

For

For the method of · fcaring *rooks*; and obfervations on *game* ; fee the general fubject VEGETATING PROCESS.

VIII. THE HARVEST PROCESS.— I. THE TIME OF WHEAT HARVEST, in Norfolk, is fomewhat late. The feafons are later, here, than they are in the more fouthern provinces, and the Norfolk farmers, in general, fuffer their wheat to ftand until very ripe. In fome of their fmall " woodbound pightles," they are, indeed, under a degree of neceffity of letting it ftand until it can be cut and carried imme-diately; for fhould it, in this fituation, 're-ceive much wet in the fhock, they would find it difficult to get it dry again, before it re-ceived confiderable damage.

2. THE METHOD OF HARVESTING WHEAT, as has been obferved, is feldom cut by the acre ; every farmer providing harveftmen fufficient to get in his crops.

It is, almoft univerfally, " fhorn" with fickles; either with or without teeth, as beft fuits the hand or the fancy of the " fhearer." Of narrow work each man takes his rigg; a · method which makes the work go on regu-

Q 2   larly

larly and with great conveniency to the workmen. Sometimes each man binds his own corn;
but more frequently, two-and-two lay together;
the firſt making the band, the latter binding
the ſheaf. If they work ſingly, they drive the
corn before them with their feet, until having
collected a ſheaf, they ſtop and bind it up.
This method is more expeditious than that
of delivering the handfuls in detached reaps
or ſhoves, which, in this narrow work, would
be tedious to gather up; but, in appearance
at leaſt, it is waſteful, and at the ſame time
conveys, to a ſtranger, an idea of ſlovenli-
neſs. The bands are, in general, knotted;
the ſheaves made of indeterminate ſizes; tied
loofely, with the band about the middle; ſet
up in ſhocks, as cloſe as they can ſtand, and
with generally a ſheaf placed at each end, as
if ſtudiouſly intending to exclude the air entirely from getting into the ſhock. No caps
or head ſheaves are ever made uſe of. If the
crop be tall, the ſtubble is left eighteen inches
or two feet high. ·

Unworkmanlike as all this would ſeem to a
man of Kent, the Norfolk reapers have one
qualification which, in ſome meaſure, atones

for

for their fins of undoubted flovenlinefs: a common hired harveftman, who is not working for himfelf, but for his mafter, will clear with his own fickle, one day with another, from two to three roods of wheat; in proportion to the ftoutnefs of the crop.

If the fheaves receive much rain in the fhock, they are, the firft fine day, fet out fingly, in order to have the benefit of the fun and air; which, in the clofe ftate in which they are ufually huddled together, it is impoffible for them to receive. This is by no means fo tedious an operation as theory may fuggeft; but is, when the fheaves are very wet, an eligible expedient.

3. An excellent regulation is common, in this Diftrict, refpecting GLEANERS: every parifh, or parifhes in general, referving their fcattered corn for their own parifhioners. This is not only equitable; but refcues the farmers from thofe clouds of gleaners, which, in fome countries, ftroll about from parifh to parifh. But, even with this regulation, the number of gleaners which are fometimes feen collected together, is fhameful; generally including a number of ftrong healthy young women, who

Q 3   would

would be much more laudably employed, as they are in other Diftricts, in affifting to reap the crop. Some farmers allow the gleaners to follow the fhearers; but, in general, they are not permitted to enter the clofe until the fhocks are out of it.

4. LAYING UP THE WHEAT CROP. Formerly the wheat crop was put entirely into the fpacious barns, with which this Diftrict abounds; a wheat rick being a phenomenon : of late years, however, pillar frames have been conftructed ; and wheat ricks are now no longer an uncommon fight.

5. WHEAT STUBBLES. — Notwithftanding the length which ftubble is generally left, it is feldom mown for ftable litter: the general practice being to throw turneps upon it in autumn, and, when the bullocks have trampled it down, to pull it into " rucks"with a pair of harrows, and carry it home as litter for the yards,

IX. THE BARN MANAGEMENT.—After what has been faid already, on this fubject,· under the general head FARMYARD MANAGEMENT, little remains to be added here.

Wheat

Wheat ftraw, being of lefs value, in Norfolk, than in moft other places; owing to the great quantity of reed ufed in thatching; lefs care is obferved in thrafhing wheat, here, than in places where it is either fold for litter, as about London, or where it is in general ufe for thatch, as in moft parts of the kingdom: even when it is intended for thatch, it is thrafhed rough, and fhook off, heads-and-tails: it being the univerfal practice of thatchers, here, to blend their ftraw, and *draw* their thatch.

X. MARKET.—This, alfo, has been noticed in the general articles: fuffice it, therefore, here to add, that Norfolk abounds with corn, mills;—the fmall ftreams which are very abundant in this country, are convenient fupplies for watermills: befides which, numbers of windmills are difperfed over the face of the country; fome of them very capital and coftly. One lately erected in this Diftrict is faid to have coft twelve hundred pounds.

For obfervations on the effect of *berbery* on wheat, fee MIN. 13.

For an inftance of *mowing* wheat, fee MIN. 14.

For an experiment with different *manures* for wheat, fee MIN. 18.

For an experiment on the mode of *fowing*, fee MIN. 19.

For the origin and method of *fetting* wheat, fee MIN. 23.

For further obfervations on *fetting*, fee MIN. 26 and 28.

For the method of *plowing* for wheat againft *pheafants*, fee MIN. 41.

For an inftance of *fowing* wheat *between furrow*, fee MIN. 43.

For an exception to the common method of *fowing* wheat in four-furrow work, fee MIN. 67.

For obfervations on the practice of *pafturing* wheat, fee MIN. 106.

For an experiment made by planting *berbery* among wheat, fee MIN. 133.

28. BARLEY,

28,

B A R L E Y.

'THIS SUBJECT, likewife, requires to be divided into the following articles:

I. SPECIES.—The common long-eared bar-ley *(bordeum vulgare)* is the prevailing and al-moft only fpecies of barley fown in this Dif-trict.

II. SOIL.—The Norfolk foil is peculiarly well adapted to this crop: even the lighteft of it, if it be in fufficient heart, will bear tole-rable barley ; and the ftrongeft is not too heavy for this grain ; which is no where produced in greater perfection than in Norfolk ; whofe
barley

barley is coveted for feed throughout the kingdom.

III. Succession.—In the grand routine,
barley fucceeds *wheat* and *turneps*; and in
fome very light land farms, it is fown inftead
of wheat, after the *fecond year's lay*.

IV. Soil process.—1. After wheat ;—
the ftubble having been trampled down with
bullocks at turneps, and wheat-feel being
finifhed, the farmer begins to " fcale in his
wheat ftubbles" for a winter fallow for barley.
If the land lie in narrow work, the ridgets
are fplit; if in warps, the ground is likewife
plowed clean, but very fleet.   The beginning
of March, the land is harrowed; and, prefently
after, the farmer "takes up his wheat ftubbles," by a full-pitch crofs plowing; or, if the
feafon be wet and the foil heavy, he reverfes
the ridges.   In April he harrows, and begins
" ftirring for barley," with another full-pitch
plowing, lengthway; generally gathering the
foil, by this plowing, either into five-pace, or
into ten-pace warps; in which it lies until
feedtime ;—when it is harrowed; rolled;
                                        fown;

fown; plowed fleet; reverfing the warps, and
" flading down" the furrows,—fo as to render
the entire furface as even and level as may
be. ·

2. AFTER TURNEPS,—the foil is generally
broken up as faft as the turneps are got off;
if early in winter, by rice-balking; if late, by
a plain plowing. The general practice, if
time will permit, is to plow three times; the
firft fleet; the fecond full-pitch; the laft a mean
depth; with which laft the feed is plowed in.

But when it is late before the turneps are
got off, different ways of management are followed, according to the ftate of the foil, and
the feafon, and the judgment of the farmer.—
Sometimes the ground is plowed only once,
and the feed fown above; but more frequently
it is broken by three plowings, as above; notwithftanding, perhaps, the farmer has not more
than a week to perform them in.

This at firft fight appears injudicious management: the plowings being fo quick upon
each other, neither the root weeds have time
to wither, nor the weed feeds to vegetate; yet
a principal part of the moifture of the foil (a
thing peculiarly valuable in Norfolk at that
tune

time of the year) is neceffarily exhaufted. But
this being a frequent practice of fome of the
beft farmers in the Diftrict, we may reft affured that two plowings and harrowings are not
wantonly thrown away. The Norfolk farmers
in general are mafters in the art of cultivating
barley. They feem fully aware of the tender-
nefs of this plant in its infant ftate, and of its
rootlings being unable to make the proper
progrefs in a compact or a cold foil: they
therefore ftrive by every means in their power
to render the foil open and pulverous. To
this intent it is fometimes two-furrowed, and
fometimes a fourth earth is given ; efpecially
in a cold wet feafon.

The backward fpring of 1782 tried their
fkill: fome lands were two-furrowed twice-
over, laying the foil up in ridgets, dry and
hollow ; fo that two or three fine days fitted it
for the reception of the feed ; breaking under
the feed-plowing as fine as afhes.

Nor is this caution confined to " turnep barley," but is extended more or lefs to " ftubble
barley ;" which, however, does not require fo
great a degree of care ; the foil in this cafe
being kept open, in fome meafure, by the un-
digefted

digested stubble, and the roots of grasses and other weeds; which a turnep fallow is, or ought to be free from.

This, perhaps, accounts fully for the superiority of stubble barlies, over those produced by a well tilled, well manured turnep fallow :. a mysterious fact, which cannot, perhaps, be explained on other principle.

3. AFTER LAY,—the turf is generally broken by a winter fallow, and the foil treated in other respect, as after wheat. (For an exception see MIN. 57.)

V. MANURE PROCESS.—Barley is seldom manured for; except when sown after lay; when it is treated as wheat. After turneps, no manure can be requisite; nor after wheat, if this has been manured for : if not, the turnep crop following immediately, the barley is left to take its chance ; unless the opportunity be embraced for winter marling.

VI. SEED PROCESS.—1. TIME OF SOWING. —Notwithstanding the dryness of the Norfolk foil, barley may be said to be sown late, in this District. There is little sown before the middle of April, and the seedtime seldom closes
until

until towards the middle of May. The time
of fowing, however, depends in fome meafure
on the feafon; which, with refpect to fowing
barley, is more attended to In Norfolk than
perhaps in all the world befide. Until Lin-
næus hit upon the idea of fowing by the foliation of trees, the republic of agriculture never
heard of any other guide to the time of fowing
than the almanack; which is ftill followed im-
plicitly in every Diftrict in this kingdom except Norfolk: where a maxim, probably as old
as the prefent fyftem of hufbandry, fhews that
her hufbandmen are not inattentive to the foliation of trees with refpect to the proper feafon of fowing; their maxim importing, that
the fowing of barley ought to clofe with the
foliation of the oak :—

    " When the oak puts on his goffling grey,
    " 'Tis time to fow barley night and day;"

that is, when the oak puts on that fallow appearance which it does at the time the buds
are breaking, a few days previous to the expanfion of the leaves, no time fhould be loft in
getting the feed of barley into the ground;
                        that

that being the happy juncture which ought to be embraced.

In the backward fpring of 1782, barley was fown in June, with confidence, and with fuccefs: I have, by me, a fample of exceedingly good barley, produced from feed fown, by an experienced hufbandman, the fourth and fifth of June. See note to MIN. 125, for remarks on this incident.

2. PREPARING THE SEED.—I never met with an inftance either of fortifying it againft difeafe, or of fteeping it to forward its vegetation in a dry feafon, or a backward feedtime. This is ftrong evidence, though not a proof, that fteeping barley, with intent to promote its vegetation, has no beneficial effect.

3. THE METHOD OF SOWING.—All fown broadcaft; and almoft all *underfurrow!* that is, the furface having been fmoothed by the harrow and roller, the feed is fown and plowed under with a fhallow furrow: a circumftance this, which, until I obferved it in Norfolk, had never occurred to me, either in practice or theory; though admirably adapted to a light dry foil; and, indeed, to any foil which is light enough to produce good barley; provided it be

be rendered fufficiently fine, and the feed be not buried too deep.

Whether through general cuftom, or from particular experience, the Norfolk farmers are very partial to this method of putting in their barley: however, if the feafon be wet, and the foil cold and heavy, good farmers not unfrequently fow barley above. And, in all probability, the diftinction is well founded. In a dry fpring and fummer, fowing under muft, to all human reafoning, be eligible; and in a cold fpring, or when the foil is rough with clods, fowing above may be equally good management. Neverthelefs, I have known a judicious farmer give, under thofe circumftances, an earth extraordinary, rather than not have an opportunity of plowing in his feed.

In a forward fpring, and when the laft piece of turneps happens to be eaten off late, the ground is fometimes, at a pinch, obliged to be plowed only once, and to be fown above; but, even in this cafe, there are men who are not at a lofs for an expedient. Inftead of turning over the whole thicknefs of the foil at once, they " two-furrow" it, and fow *between* in the manner defcribed in Min. 43.

This

This method, if the under plit be fufficiently moift and mellow to break kindly with the harrow, appears to be moft eligible management.

4. THE QUANTITY OF SEED.—Three bufhels of barley an acre may be taken as the neareft medium quantity of feed.

5; 6. COVERING,—ADJUSTING.—Whether or not grafs feeds be fown over the barley, the furface is harrowed, prefently after the laft plowing; and, when the barley is up, run over with a light roller.

VII. VEGETATING PROCESS.—Handweeded.

VIII. HARVEST PROCESS.—1. TIME OF CUTTING. Barley, like wheat, is generally fuffered to ftand until it be *very ripe.*

2. METHOD OF CUTTING.—It is univerfally *mown into fwath;*—with a fmall bow fixed at the heel of the fithe.—Cradles are not in ufe; and the North-country method of fetting it up in finglets, is unknown.

3. METHOD OF DRYING.—If barley receive wet in the fwath, it is treated in a fingular method in Norfolk. It is not turned, but

VOL. L.   R   " *lifted:*"

" *lifted* :"—that is, the heads or ears are raised
from the ground, either with a fork or the
teeth of a rake; thereby admitting the air
underneath the fwaths; which, though they
be fuffered to fall again immediately, do not
fall fo clofe to the ground as they lay before
they were lifted; the air having free admiffion
under them. This method of lifting is thought
to ftop the ears from vegetating nearly equal
to that of turning; which requires more labour; befides breaking and ruffing the
fwaths; which, by repeated turnings, lofe
their ftiffnefs, becoming weak and flabby,
and liable to fall into clofe contact with the
ground; in which ftate the corn prefently begins to fprout. When the fwaths are become
thoroughly dry, and ftiff on the upper fide,
they are then *turned*, that the other fide may
be got into the fame ftate; and, if the weather be fuitable, rendered fit for

4. COCKING.—This is never done until a
fair profpect of carrying offers itfelf; it being
efteemed in Norfolk, as it is in the fouthern
counties, negligent management to leave barley all night in cock. The method of cocking, or, as it is provincially, and more properly,

perly, called—" gathering,"—is, in Norfolk, performed in a particular manner. Some small part may be gathered by men, with " gathering forks,"—common *corn forks* ;—but the principal part of the barley crop is gathered by women, with " gathering rakes :"—namely, strong rakes, with long teeth—with which the swaths are rolled up into wads of about a pitch, or forkfull, each, the women, at the same time, raking the swathsteads. This rids work, saves men, and puts the barley into a convenient form for pitching ; a roll hanging better together upon the fork, than a cock made up in layers in the Kentish manner.

5. CARRYING.—Generally two pitchers and two loaders ; who load with the hands only : women rake after the carriage : men, at leisure times, rake the stubble with drag rakes : trot with empty carriages : tread mows, and sometimes ricks, with horses : frequently make a " well,"—that is, carry up a flue or chimney, in the middle of a barley rick ; and sometimes, when the season is catching, use the same judicious precaution in a " gulph," or mow, in a barn.

IX. BARN-

IX. BARN MANAGEMENT.—See the general head.

X. MARKET.—Befides what is fhipped off to the London and other markets, a confiderable quantity is malted in the country; both for a market and for home confumption : this, however, is fmall, compared with that of other countries of equal extent and populoufnefs : fmuggled fpirits leffen the quantity; —and the quality of malt liquor, in Norfolk, is lower than in many parts of the kingdom; the "harveft beer" excepted; which is ufually brewed in October, and kept round till the enfuing harveft.

For an inftance of fheepfold being of great ufe to barley, fee MIN. 11.

For an experiment with lime for barley, fee MIN. 29.

For a fingular foil procefs for barley, fee MIN. 57.

29.

O A T S.

THE QUANTITY of oats grown in *this* Diſtrict is inconſiderable, when compared with that of barley.

The only SPECIES I have obſerved is a white oat, of a quick growth, and probably of Dutch extraction.

They are grown occaſionally on all SOILS ; but moſt frequently on cold heavy land, or on very light unproductive heathy ſoils.

Oats moſt frequently SUCCEED wheat or olland barley ; but there are no eſtabliſhed rules reſpecting any part of the culture of this time-ſerving crop,

The SOIL PROCESS is uſually the ſame as that for barley : the ground being, generally, broken by a winter fallow of three or four plowings ; oats, however, are ſometimes ſown on one plowing.

The SEED PROCESS, too, is frequently the ſame : except that oats are more commonly ſown abovefurrow than barley is. The *time*

of ſowing oats is generally made ſubſervient to
that of ſowing barley ; ſome being ſown before ; others after barley-ſeel : an uncommon
circumſtance. I have ſeen oats ſown in June ;
and it is remarked by men of obſervation,
that oats ſown late, grow ripe earlier than barley ſown at the ſame time. This ſhews that
the Norfolk oats are of a quick-ripening kind.
The *quantity of ſeed* from four to five buſhels
an acre.

I met with one remarkable inſtance re ſpect-
ing the culture of oats. The ſurface of a
piece of ground, which had been ſown ſeveral
days with oats, but which were not yet up,
was " run," by heavy rains, into a batter ; and
baked by ſucceeding dry days to a cruſt ; ſo
that the owner deſpaired of a crop : he therefore, as an expedient, plowed the ground ;
turning the oats, notwithſtanding they had
begun to vegetate, under a fleet furrow. The
ſucceſs was beyond expectation.

This operation, however, was not altogether
a game of hazard : there being, it ſeems, a
farmer, ſomewhere in the Diſtrict, who uſes it
in common practice ; plowing in his oats with
a very fleet furrow ; and, after they have
" chicked,"

"chicked," but before they appear above-ground, turning over the foil a full pitch: and he is faid to find his account in this fingular management.

Two things are, undoubtedly, obtained by this practice : weeds of every fort are either totally deftroyed, or fufficiently checked to give the corn an opportunity of gaining full poffeffion of the foil : which, by this opera-tion, if performed in proper feafon, acquires a degree of porofity, giving a degree of free-dom to the rootlings of the young plants, which, perhaps, no other procefs could give.

The opennefs and freedom communicated by this operation, feems to be fingularly well adapted to the infant plants of BARLEY ; which, it is highly probable, might frequently receive benefit from this extraordinary opera-tion.

The HARVEST PROCESS,—BARN MANAGE-MENT, &c. of oats, are fimilar to thofe of BARLEY.

30.

P E A S.

PEAS cannot be called a ftaple crop of this country: neverthelefs they are every year grown, in greater or fmaller quantities; according, perhaps, to the demand of the preceding year, and according to the comparative prices of peas and barley; which, in Norfolk, may be called rival crops; peas being ufually fown on wheat ftubbles, or on light-land lays, which, in the common courfe of culture, are objects of the barley crop.

The very low price of barley in the winter 1781-2 fickened the farmers of that crop; and, in the fpring of 1782, more peas were fown in Eaft Norfolk, than, perhaps, had ever been known in any preceding year. This circumftance afforded me a favourable opportunity of making remarks on the different modes of cultivation made ufe of in producing this crop; which, as will appear by the following fketches, has not, here, any fettled mode of culture appropriated

to

to it. Yet no crop, perhaps, affords greater proofs of the ingenuity of the Norfolk husbandmen, and of their talent for expedients, than that which is now before us.

B——m *dibbled** seven pecks of white peas an acre, on *olland*, once-plowed, in flags, " as wide as he could whelm them." Two rows of holes on each flag; the holes about three inches apart in the rows; namely, " four holes in the length of the foot," one pea in each hole. Gave 4s. 6d. an acre for " dabbing;" and hired " droppers" by the day (children belonging to the parish); which cost him about 4s. an acre more. The men offered to dibble and drop for 9s.—The soil free from stones. Finished 27 Feb.

II———d *sowed* four bushels an acre of white peas, broadcast; on *barley stubble*, after turneps—the clover missing. Soil light and shallow. Finished 1 March.

M——s *dibbled* two bushels of white peas an acre on *wheat stubble*. Gave 8s. an acre for dabbing and dropping. Finished the beginning of March.

* Dibbling: for particulars respecting this operation, see MIN. 23.

S————n

S———n *fowed* four bufhels, broadcaſt, on *olland*;—part once plowed; part rice-balked, and afterwards plowed a mean pitch; the whole fown abovefurrow, and rolled before fowing.

G———n *dibbled* two bufhels on *olland*; the price four fhillings a bufhel for dabbing and dropping: about three holes and a half in a foot: one pea in each hole. Flags narrow.

D———l *dibbles* nine pecks on *any thing* which is in heart. Gives any price to have them done well, and put in thick. His dibbled peas, laſt year, produced ten coomb an acre: dibbles about twenty acres this year: almoſt done; 21 March.

F———r has *fown* upwards of twenty acres this year on *wheat ſtubble*, inſtead of barley: fows four bufhels of white an acre. Plows three or four times, and plows in the feed underfurrow. Finifhed 2 April.

B———r *fowed* four bufhels of white an acre, broad-caſt, on a *wheat ſtubble* winter-fallowed: namely, fcaled in—two-furrowed acrofs—ſtirred—harrowed—fowed—and *plowed under*, about three inches deep; the outfide furrows fown, and fladed down, and the whole harrowed acrofs once in a place the beginning of April.

B—d.

B—d *sows* three bushels of grey peas, broad-cast, the beginning of April. He thinks three bushels of grey are equal to four of white.

B——d, on light thin-skinned *olland*, dibbled part with two bushels an acre; and *two-furrowed* the rest with three bushels, *sown* by hand *between the furrows*; each of them about one inch and a half thick l ' The Norfolk plow singularly adapted to this work; and, in loose broken ground, the procefs would be excellent; but, in whole ground, the back of the firft furrow being *smooth*, and the peas round and flippery, they do not reft where they fall, but roll more or lefs into the feams and hollows, notwithftanding the operation was, in this inftance, performed in a mafterly ftyle.

Thus it appears that various ways are practifed in putting in the pea crop; but, from thofe and other inftances, I may venture to draw two general inferences. Lays are feldom plowed more than once for peas; and the feed is, in general, DIBBLED IN, upon the flag of this one plowing. But STUBBLES are, in general, broken by a winter fallow of three or four plowings; the feed being sown BROAD-CAST; and PLOWED IN, about three inches deep, with the laft plowing.

                              31. VETCHES.

31.

V E T C H E S.

WHEN we confider the nature of the Norfolk foil, and the excellency of the Norfolk
hufbandry, we are, at the firft fight, furprifed
that vetches are not more in ufe, as fummer
food for farm horfes;—and nothing, perhaps,
but the eftablifhed prevalence of clover can
account for it.   Clover is not only mown for
foiling horfes in the ftable; but, as has been
already noticed, horfes are frequently "roped"
or teddered on clover; as well as turned upon
it loofe.

This practice was, probably, eftablifhed
when clover was new to the foil, and the crops
of courfe large and luxuriant; and it was then
no doubt the moft eligible management : neverthelefs, it may, now, when the foil is no
longer the favorite of clover, be worth the attention of farmers, of the prefent day, to try
whether more vetches, and pre porzionably lefs
clover, would not be the meft eligible management.

32. BUCK.

32.

B U C K.

BUCK is an object of the Norfolk culture,
in a twofold light. It is propagated as GRAIN;
and as MANURE: and it will be proper to view
it in thefe two lights. However, the main intention of its propagation, whether as a crop,
or as a melioration of the foil, being the fame ;
namely, the cleanfing of foul land ; it will be
convenient to keep the two objects in nearly
the fame point of view.

I. With refpect to SPECIES, there is only
one ; this grain having not yet, I believe, run
.into any *varieties* fufficiently ftriking to have
diftinguifhing names appropriated to them.

II. It is fown almoft indifcriminately on
all fpecies of SOILS; except that light poor
land has the preference: indeed, it is to this fpecies of foil that buck feems moft efpecially
adapted.

III. It

III. It likewife succeeds every fpecies of crop; the ftate of the foil, as to foulnefs and poverty, being generally more attended to than either the nature of the foil or the crop it bore laft.

IV. The soil process depends upon the ftate of the foil, and the intention, jointly: if the foil be tolerably clean, and the buck be intended to be plowed under as a manure, it is fown on one plowing: but, in general, the ground is broken, as for barley or peas, to forward the fallow, and fecure a crop.

V. The seed process is the fame for both intentions; excepting that, for a crop, the feed is fown firft; namely, immediately after barley-feel: and that intended to be plowed under, is fown as foon afterwards as the ground is in a ftate fit to receive the feed. It is univerfally fown abovefurrow. The quantity of feed fix pecks to two bufhels an acre.

VI. No vegetating process takes place: the growth of buck is fo rapid as to outftrip and fmother almoft every fpecies of weeds; an excellency peculiar to this crop.

VII. The

VII. The method of PLOWING BUCK UNDER, and the after management of buck fallows, have been defcribed under the article WHEAT.

VIII. For the HARVEST PROCESS of buck, we refer to the head BARLEY; the harveft management of both crops being fimilar.

IX. The FARM-YARD MANAGEMENT of harvefted buck is alfo fimilar to that of barley; except that the ftraw being fit for litter, only, and the grain being wanted for the fatting of pigs, in autumn, and the beginning of winter, it is frequently thrafhed out prefently after harveft, before the liveftock are taken into the yards.

X. MARKETS. Notwithftanding it is highly probable that there is more buck grown annually in Norfolk, than in the other thirty-nine counties of the kingdom, it is all confumed in the neighbourhood of its growth. It is the univerfal food of fwine and poultry; both of which it fats quickly and well. It is fometimes crufhed for pigs, and fometimes given to them whole: in this cafe, however, fome

judicious

judicious hufbandmen mix a few oats or peas
with it, in order that the fwine may grind it
down the more effectually, and thereby prevent its paffing through them whole.

33.

T U R N E P S.

THE TURNEP CROP is the grand bafis
of the prefent fyftem of Norfolk hufbandry.
I fhall, therefore, endeavour to defcribe its
culture as amply as comprehenfivenefs will
permit. In doing this it will be neceffary to
confider,

1. The fpecies,   5. Manure procefs,
2. The foil,   6. Seed procefs,
3. The fucceffion,   7. Vegetating procefs,
4. The foil procefs, 8. Application.

I. SPECIES.—There are four different fpecies, or, perhaps, *varieties* of one fpecies, fown
in Norfolk.

1. THE

1. "THE COMMON WHITE STOCK,"—white-loaf—white-round—white-rind—or, as it is called in many places, THE NORFOLK TURNEP.

2. "THE PURPLE STOCK." This, in its shape and the manner of its growth, is similar to the common turnep ; but its rind is of a dark red or purple colour, its size, in general, smaller, and its texture closer and firmer than that of the common white stock ; and it is allowed to stand the winter better, and to preserve its firmness and succulence later in the spring than the common turnep. But it seems to be a fact well established, that the purple turnep is not so well affected by cattle as the other species : this circumstance, added to the smallness of its size, confines its culture within narrow limits.

3. "THE GREEN STOCK." This resembles, still more, the common white turnep ; from which it differs principally in the colour of its rind. It is in the hands of very few : these few, however, *say*, that it is preferable to the common stock.

4. "THE PUDDING STOCK *." This, in its shape, is so perfectly different from the

* The *tankard turnep* of the midland counties.

common fort, that it might well be ranked as
a diftinct *species*. Inftead of fpreading itfelf
flat upon the ground, or burying itfelf partially in the furface mould, it rifes in a cylin-
drical form, eight, ten, or twelve inches high;
ftanding in a manner wholly aboveground;
generally taking a rough irregular outline, and
a fomewhat reclining pofture. In colour, contexture, and quality, it refembles very much
the common turnep; of which it is by much
the moft formidable rival. Indeed, for early
fowing, to be eaten off in autumn, this long-
rooted fpecies feems to gain a preference even
to the common white-rounds: the roots are
of quick growth,—acquire a great fize,—and,
ftanding wholly aboveground, are readily
drawn; or, if eaten off by fheep, are confumed with little wafte; the refufe fhells being
fmaller than thofe of broad flat turneps half
buried in the ground.

But this very circumftance renders them
wholly unfit to be fown as a fpring food; for,
ftanding, as they do, expofed on the furface,
they become liable to the attack of every
froft; and, from annual experience, it is
known that they fuffer fooner, and more, from
the

the feverities of winter, than THE COMMON WHITE-ROUND STOCK ; which, taken all in all, is, I believe, the beft fpecies of turnep known, at prefent, in thefe kingdoms.

II. SOIL. Turneps are fown on every fpecies of foil, in ufe as arable land.   It is obfervable, however, that the ftronger, heavier foils, of the fouthern parts of this Diftrict, will not bring turneps freely without marl ; which, perhaps, by rendering the foil more friable, and confequently *lighter*, fits it for the tender fibrils of the turnep plant in its infantftate; or, perhaps, the marl itfelf is acceptable to this *luxurious* plant.

Be this as it may, marl is found highly beneficial to the crop ; and the fact proves, that a foil by nature ungenial to turneps, may in fome cafes be rendered agreeable to them, by art.   See MIN. 136.

III. SUCCESSION. In the regular courfe of management, turneps fucceed barley after wheat ; and in *this* part of the Diftrict, where the hexennial round is obferved with confiderable regularity, they feldom fucceed any other

S 2   crop;

crop; excepting fome few fown on wheat or pea ftubble after harveft; but this is not a general practice.

IV. SOIL PROCESS.—1. The farmer having finifhed fcaling in his wheat ftubbles for barley, he begins about Chriftmas to BREAK UP HIS BARLEY STUBBLES, for turneps.

In this inftance, he quits his general rule of beginning to break up a fallow with a fleet plowing; for, in breaking up a turnep fallow, he goes the full depth of the foil—" turning it " up a full pitch to take the winter."—His motive in this, as in moft other cafes, is a good one. In this inftance, indeed, his practice obvioufly proceeds from a degree of neceffity; his general plan of management not allowing him time to plow his turnep fallows more than once, during the winter feafon. For, no fooner has he given them this one plowing, than his wheat ftubbles require to be taken up for barley; which, with his other fpring crops, engage every hour of his time, until the clofe of fpring feedtime.

2. This finifhed, he begins TO TAKE UP HIS TURNEP FALLOWS. In doing this, too, he de-

viates

viates from general practice; for the second plowing of a turnep fallow is not acrofs but lengthway. But here, likewife, he acts from a degree of neceffity; for the firft plowing having been given the full depth of the foil, there is no whole ground left for the plow to lay hold of in crofs plowing; and the flags, of courfe foul, having lain fome months unmoved, are become too tough to be cut readily with the coulter; but would, of courfe, drive into rucks before the plow.

3. This loofe woolly ftate of the turnep fallows is, however, fometimes leffened by harrowing them in the beginning of April; and, while the lays are fhut up, THROWING TUR-NEPS upon them for bullocks; the treading of which gives the foil a degree of firmnefs, and renders the fecond plowing more tolerable.

4. The teams, from the middle of May to the beginning of July, are almoft wholly employed in plowing, harrowing, and manuring the turnep grounds: for the fecond plowing finifhed, and the furface fmoothed with the harrow, a THIRD PLOWING is given.

5. This plowing being well reduced with the harrow, and the root weeds collected, and

S 3	burned

burned or carried off, the DUNG is set on, and,
if time will permit, scaled in fleet by a FOURTH
PLOWING.

6. After which, the soil and manure are intimately blended with the harrow; and, in
due season, the SEED PLOWING takes place.

The fourth plowing, is, however, frequently
omitted; either through want of time or
other reason; the manure being in this case
turned in immediately with the seed plowing,
which, in either case, is of a mean depth.   The
former is, no doubt, to appearance, the most
husbandlike practice, and, in a light soil and
moist season, may be the most eligible management;—but, in a dry time, and on a stout
close-textured soil, the latter, provided the
manure be finely broken, and evenly spread,
may be more eligible.   See MIN. 71. on this
subject.

V. MANURE PROCESS.—1. The SPECIES of
manure which is principally depended upon
for turneps is " *muck* ;"—that is, dung, with
a greater or smaller admixture of mould,
marl, &c.—*Maltcombs* are in good repute;
and *oilcake* is sometimes used by some few individuals;

dividuals; but it may be said, that nine acres of ten of the turneps grown in East Norfolk are manured for with " muck." The quantity of malt-coombs made in the county is inconsiderable, when compared with the number of acres of turneps annually sown in it;—and rape-cake is principally confined to the north coast: nor are either of these manures equal to the task of keeping up the soil thro' the barley and the two grass crops; much less of assisting to support it under the succeeding crop of wheat, in the manner which may reasonably be expected from a proper dressing of dung; the whole quantity of which, made upon a given farm, ought, in my opinion, to be applied solely to the turnep crop: and, if the soil require support under the wheat, let it be assisted with lime, maltdust, soot, oilcake, or other light manures; which may not be only adequate to securing a crop of wheat, but may be more or less serviceable to the succeeding crop of barley. This has already been mentioned; but I think it merits a repetition in this place.

2. The QUANTITY of dung set on for a crop of turneps, generally depends on the

S 4   quantity

quantity on hand, and the quantity of turnep
ground to be manured: there is little danger
of fetting on too large a quantity: ten to fifteen cart-loads of good *muck* are confidered as
a fair dreffing. Of *oilcake*, about a ton to
three acres: of *maltcoombs*, fifty or fixty;—
and of *foot*, forty or fifty bufhels an acre.

For the method of carrying out, compoft-
ing, and fetting on muck, fee the article
MANURE PROCESS.

VI. THE SEED PROCESS.—I. THE TIME OF
SOWING depends upon the application.—When
turneps are intended for early confumption, they
are fown as foon as the foil can be got into proper order for them: but if they be intended to
ftand the winter, the beginning of July is
thought to be early enough. The moft general rule is, to begin to fow about a week
before Midfummer, and continue fowing, from
time to time, until about a fortnight after
Midfummer;—fay, from the feventeenth or
eighteenth of June, to the feventh or eighth of
July.

It

It is a fact well afcertained, that late-fown
turneps ftand the winter better than fuch as are
fown early; which are fubject to the blight;
liable to be rotted by much wet, as well as by
froft; and become tough and woolly in the
fpring, when the later-fown ones are in full perfection.

If a Norfolk farmer could infure his firft
fowing, he would fow later than he now does;
but liable as the turnep crop is to numerous
accidents and mifcarriages, it is prudent to
have a week or two in referve for a fecond
fowing, in cafe the firft fowing fhould fail.

2. Old feed is fometimes PREPARED by
fteeping it in water, in order to forward its vegetation; but this is by no means a general
practice. Experiments have been tried on
coating the feed with fulphur, foot, &c, as a
fecurity againft the " fly ;" but the refults have
not been fuch as to eftablifh any practice of
this nature; the feed, whether old or new, being ufually fown dry, and unprepared.

3. THE METHOD OF SOWING is univerfally
broadcaft. The feed plowing having been
gone over, once in a place, with the harrow,
the feed is fown with a wide high caft, the
feedfman

feedfman going twice over the ground; agreeably to the prevailing, though not the general, method of fowing.

4. THE QUANTITY OF SEED, two pints an
acre.

5. The feed is COVERED by two tines of a
pair of light harrows, ufually drawn "backward;" that is, wrong-end-foremoft, to prevent the tines, which are generally fet fomewhat pointed forward, from tearing up the
clods, and burying the feed too deep.   The
horfes are univerfally walked one way, and
trotted back again in the fame place.   This is
an excellent cuftom; the quick zigzag motion
of the harrows at once affifting to level the furface, and to diftribute the feeds more evenly.

VII. THE VEGETATING PROCESS.   Turneps
are univerfally hoed : and, unlefs they be fown
very late, are generally hoed twice.

1. The diftance of TIME between the fowing and the FIRST HOING is very uncertain;
depending on the foil and the feafon : the fize
of the plants is the only guide.

If turneps be fuffered to grow too large before they be hoed, the plants are difficult to be
                                            fet

fet out fingly, and are liable to be drawn up by weeds; thereby acquiring a flender upright tendency; whereas their natural growth, in their infant ftate, is procumbent, fpreading their firft leaves on the ground, and taking the form of a rofe.

If the hoe be put in too foon, the plants which are fet out are liable to be buried, and their tender rootlings difturbed, in the act of fetting out the neighbouring plants.

The critical ftate obferved by judicious hufbandmen, is, when the plants, as they lie fpread upon the ground, are about the fize of the palm of the hand: if, however, feed-weeds be numerous and luxuriant, they ought to be checked before the turnep plants arrive at that fize; left, by being drawn up tall and flender, they fhould acquire a weak fickly habit.

2. The method of hoing turneps is difficult to defcribe: nothing but practice can teach it:—and, like other manual arts, it ought to be learnt in youth.

A boy in Norfolk, by the time he is the height of a hoe, begins to make ufe of one: confequently every man who has been bred to

country

country bufinefs is a turnep hoer; yet not always, even with this advantage, an expert one.

The operation, to be performed quick and well, requires a quicknefs of eye, and a dexterity of hand, which every man is not favored with: while fome men catch the proper plants to be fingled, and fet them out, with a rapidity and neatnefs of execution, very pleafing to the obferver.

The hoe is generally drawn round the plant, with a long fweeping ftroke; and, when the plants are fmall, this is the only ftroke that can be ufed with propriety; but, when the plants are out of danger of being buried, a fhort ftraight ftroke is more expeditious, and, in the hands of fome few, makes tolerably good work.

Upon the whole, it matters not which way the operation be performed, provided the ground be ftirred, and the weeds eradicated; the plants fet out fingly, and at proper diftances.

3. The proper DISTANCE depends upon the foil, and the time of fowing; jointly, and feparately.

Turneps

Turneps fown, early, in a rich productive foil, require to be fet out wider than thofe fown late, on a foil of a contrary nature.

If the foil be at par, the time of fowing ought to regulate the diftance: if this be at par, the nature or ftate of the foil fhould be the regulator.

Thefe rules, however, felf-evident as they undoubtedly are, are not attended to by the generality of farmers; who, led away by long-eftablifhed cuftom, or by the interefted perfuafions of their labourers (farmers in all countries being more or lefs warped by the opinion of their workmen) fuffer their turneps to be hacked out fourteen or fifteen, or perhaps eighteen inches afunder, without any regard to the ftate of the foil, or the feafon of fowing.

This practice was eftablifhed while the Norfolk foil was full of marl, and new to turneps; and when, it is probable, eleven or twelve inches in diameter was no uncommon fize; with tops proportionally large and fpreading: and fourteen or fifteen inches might, then, be a proper diftance.

But, now, when the efficacy of marl is leffened, and the foil no longer the favorite of turneps,

turneps; which seldom reach more than seven
or eight inches in diameter, it is ruinous and
absurd to continue the practice.

But the present price of hoing was likewise
established when large turneps were grown,
and when wide hoing might, perhaps, be proper; and a workman cannot, at the present low
wages, *afford* to set out the plants at a
shorter distance; for though, in either case, he
stir the whole ground, yet the more plants he
has to single, the more tedious the operation
becomes.

If the plants be set out at eighteen inches—
each square yard contains four plants: but, at
twelve inches, the same space of ground contains nine plants: so that in this case the hoer
has more than twice the number of plants to
single and set out.

But does it not follow, that the farmer has
more than twice the number of turneps to fat
his bullocks upon? and is not this interesting
fact a sufficient inducement to farmers in general to break through a custom whose original
foundation no longer exists, and to silence the
persuasions of their men by an adequate advance of wages?

There

There are men, whofe good fenfe and dif-
cernment have fhewn this matter to them in its
true light, and who are fully aware that the
" proof" of their turnep crop depends more on
its " thightnefs" than on the fize of the plant.
And it is the practice of thefe men I wifh to
hold out in ftriking colours, in order that it
may become the general practice of the Diftrict ; as well as to endeavour to do away a pernicious idea which has gone abroad refpecting
this part of the culture of turneps, in Norfolk ;
where good farmers do not fuffer their turneps
to be fet out fifteen or eighteen inches apart ;
but rather from ten to fourteen, accordingly
as circumftances point out; and according to
the fituation of the plants with refpect to each
other.

Thus, if three plants ftand in a line, the two
outer ones fourteen inches afunder, the intermediate one is, of courfe, taken out: but
fhould two healthy plants ftand in a wide vacancy, thoufands of which vacancies generally
occur in every piece of turneps, they are both
of them fuffered to remain, though they ftand
not more than fix or eight inches from each
other; for when the tops have room to fpread

and

and wax large, the roots will increafe in proportion; and it is well known to thofe who
make obfervations on the growth of turneps,
that, when the roots of two plants, thus
fituated, fwell out till they touch each other,
they become flat on the fide in contact, but
continue to fpread on every other fide, as if
not incommoded by their contiguity; which,
indeed, has one good effect: for, in endeavouring to preferve their rotundity, they force
each other into a heeling pofture, thereby giving their tops more freedom of expanfion;
and it feems to be an undoubted fact, that the
vigour of a given plant will ever keep pace
with the fize and number of its leaves.

This leads us to a general rule for afcertain-
ing the proper diftance of turnep plants;
which ought to be fuch as will give them room
to keep themfelves in a ftate of vigour and full
growth; without leaving any fpace of ground
unoccupied by, or thinly filled with, leaves.

And this leads us round to the firft pofition,
—that the diftance ought to be in proportion
to the ftate of the foil and the time of fowing.

For, fuppofing a root of fix inches diameter
to require a fpace of twelve inches fquare,

to

to diffuſe its top in, the top of a root of ten
inches would be crouded in the ſame ſpace;
while one of a ſmaller ſize would leave the
vacancy unfilled. And as turneps in this Diftrict, now, run from four to eight inches in
diameter, twelve inches may be taken as a
proper *medium diſtance.*

. To talk of *preciſe diſtances*, of turneps ſown
broadcaſt, would be ridiculous, and beſpeak
a want of knowledge of the ſubject: if a piece
of turneps be examined after hoing, though
done by a workman, the variety of diſtances
is endleſs; ſcarcely any two interſpaces being
the ſame.

4. With reſpect to the SECOND HOING, little can be ſaid; the firſt being a guide to this:
the main purport of it is to looſen the mould,
and draw it in ſome meaſure to the roots of the
plants; to reduce the weeds effectually; and
to ſingle ſuch plants as have been left double
by the firſt hoing; as well as to remove ſuch
as have been miſſed; or, having been buried
in the looſe mould in moiſt weather, have
ſtruck root again in improper places.

It would be well, if at the time of the ſecond
hoing ſome of the ſupernumerary plants could

VOL. I. T be.

be tranfplanted into the vacant patches, in the manner that rape plants are ufually done. This, however, cannot be practifed with profit : turnep plants may be got to live, but not to thrive after tranfplantation. Does it not, therefore; behove the turnep grower to fee, that, in the firft hoing, no artificial vacancies be added to thofe, which too frequently abound, accidentally, or for want of a proper quantity of feed, in almoft every turnep ground ?

On the contrary, a fupernumerary plant may be removed on a certainty, and without additional labour or expence ; for the ftroke which loofens the foil, and eradicates the remaining weeds, difplaces a fupernumerary plant. Is it not, therefore, unpardonable management to fet out the plants too thin the firft hoing?

The workmen, fome farmers, and theorifts in general, hold out a plaufible idea, which has fome fmall degree of truth in it : namely, that if the plants are not fet out regularly the firft hoing, they cannot afterwards be regulated.

This, in rows of drilled turneps, would have fome weight; *provided* every plant which was left could be infured to *live*, and become a *thriving plant.* But, in a field of turneps fown

at random, there is no such thing as regularity
of diftance ; and, here, the notion has little or
no foundation.

Nor is regularity here neceffary : for, fuppofing nine plants to grow in a yard fquare, it
appears to me a matter of fmall confequence,
whether they ftand exactly a foot apart ; or
whether fome of them be fifteen and others
only nine inches afunder ; provided they be fo
diftributed, that their tops fill up a fquare yard
of fpace above them: for, in the fame manner
as the tops of plants feek out for air and head-
room above, in a fimilar manner do their roots
feek out for food and moifture below.

I grant, that if I had my choice, I would prefer an exact regularity of diftance ; but I would
much rather forego the mental gratification,
than give up three or four turneps in a yard
fquare of ground.

Upon the whole, it ftrikes me, that the object of the firft hoing, inftead of being that of
fetting out the plants at exact and wide diftances, fhould be merely that of checking the
weeds, and thinning the plants, to prevent their
crowding each other ; and that the regulation
of diftances fhould be left in a great meafure to

T 2   the

the laft hoing: in the firft, *(by reafon of the many accidents young turnep plants are liable to)* it is a work of hazard and uncertainty; in the fecond, not only proper diftances, but proper plants, may be chofen, with a degree of certainty and fafety.

With refpect to timing the fecond hoing, it ought to be given before the leaves become too large, to prevent the plants from being properly fingled and fet out, or the weeds from being effectually cleared away; but the longer they ftand before the laft hoing, the more effectually will the weeds be overcome.

5. The length of the HOE fhould be in proportion to the *medium diftance* between the plants, and *this* to their *expected fize*.

The Norfolk hoes are, at prefent, out of all proportion to the prefent fize of plants; and, confequently, out of proportion to the proper medium diftance. I have meafured them nine inches and a half; there are many, I believe, of ten inches long: too long, in my opinion, for any turneps I have feen in Norfolk, by at leaft two inches.

It is the hoer's intereft to work with a long hoe; for in a foil free from obftructions, the
larger

larger the hoe the quicker he gets over the
ground, and the fewer plants he has to fet out;
but unfortunately for the inattentive farmer,
his intereft is, in this cafe, in direct oppofition
to that of his workmen.

There are, however, as has already been
obferved, fome good farmers who pay proper
attention to their turnep hoers, and who are
well aware that a little attention, and a fhilling
an acre extraordinary, beftowed upon the hoings, is no object when compared with the
difference between a "thight" and a thin crop of
turneps;—between a crop worth forty fhillings,
and one worth four pounds an acre. The expence of rent, tillage, manure, and feed is, in
either cafe, the fame.

6. The prefent PRICE is fix fhillings an acre
for the two hoings, which are almoft always
let jointly: if they be feparated, the firft is from
three fhillings and fixpence to four fhillings;
the laft from two fhillings to two fhillings and
fixpence.

Thefe are low prices when compared with
thofe of other countries, where eight fhillings,
ten fhillings, or twelve fhillings, an acre, are
given for the two hoings. But there are two

reafons

reafons for this difparity. In Norfolk every countryman is a turnep hoer, and is generally expert, compared with thofe of other places; where hoing turneps is a myftery, known only to gardeners, and a few individuals who, though inexpert, have it in their power to make their own prices. The other is the friability of the Norfolk foil, and its freenefs from obftructions; while foils, in general, are either in themfelves ftubborn, or contain ftones or other obftructions of the hoe.

8. The APPLICATION. Turneps are either cultivated

> For feed,
> For fale, or
> For confumption.

1. SEED.—Many farmers raife their own feed: though this is not a general practice; yet moft good farmers, who are curious in their ftock, either raife it themfelves, or have it raifed from their own ftock by a labourer or other neighbour.

The Norfolk farmers are mafters in the art of raifing turnep feed, in which, as in many other fubjects in hufbandry, their ideas are remarkably clear and accurate. It is generally underftood, understood, in other parts of the kingdom, that no turnep seed is fit to be sown, which has not been raised from transplanted roots. But not so in Norfolk, where seed is frequently raised from untransplanted turneps.

It is a fact well understood by every husband-man, here, that if the seed be gathered repeatedly from untransplanted roots, the plants from this seed will become "coarse-necked" and "foul-rooted;"—and the flesh of the root itself will become rigid and unpalatable. On the contrary, if it be gathered, year after year, from transplanted roots, the necks will become too fine, and the fibres too few; the entire plant acquiring a weak delicate habit, and the produce, though sweet, will be small. For the neck, or on-set of the leaves being reduced to the size of the finger (for instance), the number and size of the leaves will be reduced in proportion; and in a similar proportion will the number and size of the fibrils be reduced.

From a parity of reasoning it may perhaps be inferred, that when the neck acquires a thickness equal to that of the wrist, the size of the root will be in proportion.

T 4

With

With refpect to the *fibres* or rootlings, this is a juft inference ; but with refpect to the *bulb*, it is in great meafure erroneous. For a few generations the fize of the bulb will keep pace with the increafe of leaves and fibres; but after having once reached the limits, which nature has fet to its magnitude, it begins to revert to its original ftate of wildnefs, from which to its prefent ftate it has, beyond difpute, been raifed by tranfplantation.

The farmer has therefore two extremes, both of which he ought to endeavour to avoid. The one is difcoverable by the thicknefs and coarfe- nefs of the neck, the fcaley roughnefs of the top of the bulb, the thicknefs of the rind in general, the foulnefs of its bottom, and the forkednefs of its main or tap root : the other, by the flendernefs of the neck, the finenefs of the leaves, and the delicaey of the root. The former are unpalatable to cattle, and are there- by creative of wafte ; the latter are unproduc- tive ; are difficult to be drawn ; and do not throw out fuch ample tops in the fpring, as do thofe which are, by conftitution or habit, in a middle ftate between thofe two extremes.

There

There is not, however, any general rule respecting how many years turneps ought to be transplanted succeffively, and how often they ought to be fuffered to run up from the feed bed: the foil and fituation have, and other circumftances may have, influence on the habit or conftitution of vegetables, as of animals; and the farmer muft attend alone to the ftate of the turneps themfelves. Whenever he judges that by repeated tranfplantation they have paffed the acme of perfection, have paffed that height to which nature has faid, "So far fhalt thou go, and no farther," then it is his duty and intereft to let them run up to feed without tranfplantation.

In Norfolk it has been found from long experience, that tranfplanting two, three, or four years, and letting the plants run up the third, fourth, or fifth, will keep the ftock in the defired ftate.

The time of tranfplanting is from old Chriftmas to old Candlemas.

In *the choice of plants,* the farmer is not guided by fize; but " picks the cleaneft plants," without regard to the fize : or, more accurately fpeaking, he makes choice of fuch

as

as are near, but not at, or above, the state of
perfection. In almost every piece of turnep
there are plants in various states : much judgment, therefore, is requisite in the choice of
plants.

The choice of soil and situation for this purpose
is pretty uniform ; a piece of good ground,
near a habitation, being generally pitched
upon.

But *the method of planting* is various ; the
plants are generally set in rows : but the distance between the rows, and between plant and
plant in the rows, is uncertain. I have mea-
sured the rows sixteen or eighteen inches apart,
and the plants eight or ten inches asunder. I
have also observed them planted in two-foot
rows, and twelve inches in the rows. But
the practice of a man who indisputably stands
near the head of his profession, is to plant them
in rows about two feet asunder, without any
intermediate space in the rows ; in which the
plants stand in contiguity.

The vegetating process consists in keeping the
intervals clean-hoed ; and when the seed verges
towards ripeness, in preserving as much of it as
possible from birds. If the plot be large, a
boy

boy is generally employed to scare them. —
When the plot has been small and near the
house, I have known a simple expedient used
for this intent with success. On a slender post,
rising in the midst of the patch of seed, was
fixed a bell; from which a line passed into the
kitchen; in the most frequented part of which
hung the pull. Whoever passed the pull, rung
the bell; so that in a farm-house kitchen,
where a mistress and two or three maids were
some of them almost always on the foot, an
incessant peal was kept up; and the birds,
having no respite from alarms, forsook their
prey.

2. SALE. It is not a practice among the
generality of farmers to raise turneps for sale;
nevertheless there are every year more or fewer sold. Little farmers, who want conveniency or skill, and larger ones who want money
to lay in a proper stock, or who from the
prices of stock and turneps, comparatively,
judge it more eligible to sell than to " graze,"
— sell their turneps to those who have judgment, money, and spirit to buy stock.

Sale turneps are usually consumed on the
premisses they grow upon. Sometimes the
buyer

buyer and fometimes the feller draws the crops, and tends the cattle; for which fometimes the one and fometimes the other finds ftraw.

The medium price of a middling crop of turneps is about 50s. an acre; but the price is fubject to great and fudden fluctuations, as will appear in Min. 68.

3. Consumption. This is the grand purpofe for which the turnep crop is principally cultivated.

Turneps are almoft univerfally " pulled;" that is, drawn up by the roots. The practice of hurdling them off with fheep, as they ftand, the almoft only practice of other countries, is not in ufe in Eaft Norfolk. I do not recollect to have obferved one inftance of this practice, unlefs when the turneps were very fmall, or very thin.

But the Norfolk practice is not more fingular with refpect to the mode of application, than with refpect to the fpecies of ftock to which turneps are applied. In moft places sheep are the chief confumers; but, here, cattle are almoft the only object of the turnep culture. I fpeak more particularly of the practice of *this* Diftrict: in which, as I have

before

before intimated, the genuine fyftem of Norfolk hufbandry is practifed.

There are three ways of *harvefting* the turnep crop:

    A. Drawing and carting-off the whole crop.

    B. Drawing and diftributing the whole over
       the turnep-ground.

  · C. Carting off half, and diftributing half.

    The two laft, however, are in ufe only where
fheep are the fole or joint confumers. The
firft, therefore, may be called the general
practice: and it is probable that nine tenths of
the turneps grown in Eaft Norfolk are harvefted in that way.

    A. CARTING-OFF THE WHOLE.   This pro-
cefs merits a minute defcription.

  · *a. The time of drawing* commences about
Michaelmas, and continues until the plants be
in blow.

    b. The procefs of drawing.   This, in fevere
weather, is an employment which nothing but
cuftom could reconcile, to thofe whofe lot it is
to go through it: namely, ftout lads and
youths; whofe hands are frequently fwelled
until the joints are only to be difcerned by the
dimples they form; neverthelefs, I·have not
                     heard

heard an inftance of ill confequence from this circumftance.

Their method of pulling, when the tops will bear it, is very expeditious: they pull with both hands at once; and, having filled each hand, (one on one fide of them, the other on the other) they bring the two handfuls together with a fmart blow, to difengage the foil from the roots; and, with the fame motion, throw them jointly into the cart.

If the tops be cut off by the froft, or if this be in the ground, they are pulled with " crooms"—two-tined hooks.

If a deep fnow bury the roots, it is removed with the fnow-fledge (fee IMPLEMENTS).

It is cuftomary to begin pulling under the hedges, clearing the headlands and fidelands firft; and then, if the whole crop be carried off, to begin on one fide, and clear the ground progreflively for the plow.

If the area be broken into,—a lane is made for the horfe and cart, by drawing the turneps; and, while their tops remain fucculent and valuable, fetting them in double handfuls on each fide the road; by which means the tops are preferved as free from dirt and taint,

taint, as if the handfuls were thrown immediately into the cart.

It is cuftomary, in drawing turneps, to clear
them away entirely, great and fmall: I met
with one inftance, however, and that in the
practice of a good hufbandman, of the fmall
ones being left upon the ground : not more to
encreafe in fize, than to throw out tops in the
fpring; it being obfervable, that a fmall turnep
fends up a top nearly equal to that of one whofe
bulb is larger.   There is one inconveniency
arifing from this practice : the plow is prevented from entering upon the foil until late
in the fpring; and this, upon fome foils, is an
unfurmountable objection.   Upon land, however, which will bring good barley with one
plowing after turneps, it may be very eligible
management.

· *c. The method of giving them to cattle.*   This
is threefold.

Firft, They are thrown on ftubbles, grafs-
lands, and fallows, to cattle abroad in the fields.

Second, They are given in bins, in the
ftrawyard, in which the cattle go loofe.

Third, They are given to cattle tied up in
houfes or under fheds.

The

The *first* is the prevailing practice: perhaps, three fourths, or perhaps, a greater proportion, of the bullocks fatted on turneps, in this District, are fatted abroad in the fields.

The general practice is to begin with the wheat stubbles; on which turneps are usually thrown, until they be broken up for fallow for barley. The next throwing ground is frequently the barley stubbles, which receive the bullocks as the wheat stubbles are scaled in, and retain them until they, in their turn, are broken up for turnep fallow. From about Christmas until the beginning of April, the clover lays, only, are thrown upon: and after these are shut up, (in order to acquire a bite of ray grass for the unfinished bullocks,) the turnep fallows, sometimes, become the scene of throwing.

These rules, however, are not always strictly observed: some farmers objecting to throw turneps on land intended for turneps the ensuing year, under an idea that it is productive of the Anbury. In this case, the clover lays succeed the wheat stubbles, some part of them being kept open until the turnep crop be finished in the spring. Young clovers are
some-

sometimes thrown upon; but this is seldom done, unless there does not happen to be a clover stubble in the neighbourhood of the turnep piece; and even then, it is considered as bad management; unless the season be very dry, and the surface sound.

In a wet season, the Norfolk farmers, even on their dry soil, are sometimes put to inconveniences for clean ground to throw upon; and, notwithstanding the value of teathe, when the land will bear the bullocks, I have known a farmer ask leave of his neighbour to let him throw turneps upon an adjoining piece of sound olland; rather choosing to lose his teathe than check his bullocks.

Hence, in laying out a Norfolk farm, it is proper to endeavour to intermix the crops in such a manner that a piece of turneps shall have, at least, two pieces of lay in its neighbourhood.

The method of throwing turneps is similar to that of setting on manure; the carts beginning on one side of a close, and working regularly to the other, giving every part an equal share; and never throwing twice in the same place, until the whole has been gone over.

At the beginning of the throwing feafon, while grafs is ftill in plenty for lean ftock, it is ufual to keep the fatting cattle conftantly in the fame piece of wheat ftubble, giving them a frefh fupply of turneps every day, or every two days at fartheft.

But the clover ftubbles being cleared from grafs, and the ftore beafts beginning to want affiftance from turneps, the fatting cattle have their "followers,"—that is rearing cattle:— lean bullocks, cows, or ftore fheep follow them to pick up their leavings.

In this cafe it is convenient to have three "fhifts," namely, three pieces of throwing-ground, going on at the fame time :—one for the head beafts, one for the followers, and a third empty to throw in.   Two pieces, or two divifions of the fame piece, are indifpenfibly necefiary.

Sometimes a row of hurdles is run acrofs a throwing piece to divide the "bullocks" from the "followers;" and I have known a boy em-ployed for the fame purpofe.

Good farmers are very attentive to having the turneps thrown evenly and thinly ; it being a maxim, that while a bullock is breaking one

turnep, he fhould not have it in his power to
tread or dung upon another. This, however,
is feldom effectually guarded againft. If turneps be fcattered a yard afunder, they are not
ill thrown: it is too common to fee them
thrown in " rucks" and " ringes" by half
dozens together.

They are thrown by hand, by a boy ftanding in the cart, which keeps going on as he
throws them out,—with their tops and tails on,
as they were drawn out of the piece.

Bullocks at turneps abroad, are fometimes,
when the diftance is not too great, driven into
the ftrawyard at night;—and fometimes have
a little ftraw given them under the hedge of
the throwing piece, where they fleep, entirely
abroad. See MIN. 69.

The quantity of ftraw carried to them Is
very fmall, being meant merely to " clean
their mouths" from the dirt of the turneps;
which, alone, are depended upon for bringing
the cattle forward.

It is indeed an interefting fact, that not one
In ten of the high finifhed bullocks, which are
annually fent to Smithfield market out of Norfolk, tafte a handful of hay; or have any other
food,

food, whatever, than turneps and barley ftraw ;
excepting fuch as are finifhed with ray grafs in
the fpring ; and excepting fome few fatted by
fuperior graziers, who make a point of giving
their bullocks at turneps a little hay, towards
fpring, when the turneps are going off, before
the ray grafs lays be ready to receive them.
An excellent practice, this, which ought, if
poffible, to be univerfally copied : for without
this precaution, bullocks are liable to receive a
check between turneps and grafs.

The *fecond* method of fatting cattle with
turneps is, to keep them in a loofe ftrawyard ;
giving them turneps in clofe bins ; namely, a
kind of fmall cowcrib with boards, or bars
nearly clofe, at the bottom.

Thefe bins are diftributed about the yard,
and the turneps ufually put into them whole ;
but, in this cafe, they are always " tailed"—
that is, have their tap-root lopped off—in the
field ; and, unlefs the tops be frefh and palatable,
they are ufually " topped-and-tailed," giving
to the fatting bullocks the bulb only ; the
tops, if eatable, being given to ftore cattle.

Bullocks in the yard have fometimes their
ftraw given them in cribs ; and fometimes have

it

it fcattered in little heaps about the yard, two
or three times a day: the quantity of it eaten
is in either cafe fmall; and, with the latter
management, the yard becomes evenly littered
without further trouble.

This method of fatting bullocks on turneps
is fomewhat more troublefome than that of
throwing to them abroad; which, if the foil
be dry enough to bear ftock, and light enough
to require "jamming,"—is, perhaps, upon the
whole, the moft eligible management: but in
a deep-land fituation, and in a wet, or a fevere
feafon—the yard, if it be kept dry and well
littered, is the more comfortable place; efpecially if it be provided with open fheds for the
cattle to take fhelter under in inclement feafons.

The teathe of bullocks abroad is no doubt
highly ferviceable to land; efpecially to a light
foil; while bullocks at turneps in a yard well
littered make a great quantity of good manure.

The *third* method is to keep the cattle tied
up in hovels, or under open fheds, with
troughs or mangers to receive the turneps;
which, in this cafe, are frequently "chopped;"

that is, cut into *slices*; or more generally, though perhaps less eligibly, into *quarters*, with a small hedging bill, or other chopper, upon a narrow board or stool, with a basket underneath to catch the pieces as they are chopt off. The turnep in this operation is held by the top; which, when wholly disengaged from the root, except the coarse part immediately about the crown, is thrown aside for the store cattle. The tap root and bottom rind are sliced off with the first stroke, and suffered to drop on one side the skep; so that the fatting cattle, in this case, have only the prime part of the bulb.

This accounts for the quick progress which "shed bullocks" sometimes make; especially in cold weather. But on account of the extraordinary attendance they, in this case, require,—not only in cutting the turneps, but in littering and cleaning out their stalls,—besides the checks which they are liable to receive in close muggy weather—the practice is seldom followed by large farmers in *this* District; unless to push forward some particular individuals.

Among little farmers, who have leisure and inclination to tend their own sheds, the practice

tice is not uncommon; and much depending
on care and management in this bufinefs, they
may, probably, find their account in it. Under this treatment, the cattle have a little barley ftraw given them, from time to time, to
clean their mouths, and dry up the fuperfluous
juices of the turnep.

Sometimes fhed bullocks are " blown up"
with pollard and barley meal; but this is confidered as an unfair practice by the butchers in
Smithfield, who prefer turneps and hay in
winter, and ray grafs in the fpring, to every
other kind of fatting.

In the fouthern Hundreds of this Diftrict,
the foils of which are, in general, too tender
to bear cattle with propriety in a wet feafon,
the yard and the fhed are more common receptacles of bullocks than they are in *this*
neighbourhood.

In Blowfield Hundred, a commodious but
expenfive fhed prevails: it has one main advantage over the little hovels in which bullocks are fometimes cooped up: the lofty,
fpacious area in which the bullocks breathe,
affords them a plentiful fupply of frefh air,
and keeps their bodies in a due degree of tem-
perature.

U 4   Fer

For a defcription of one of thefe fheds, fee
MIN. 118.

B. DRAWING AND DISTRIBUTING THE
WHOLE CROP OVER THE TURNEP GROUND.
This being only in ufe where a large flock of
fheep is kept and few bullocks are fatted, it is
feldom practifed in Eaft Norfolk. It differs
from the ordinary method of hurdling off turneps, in that the fheep, inftead of being put
upon the plants as they ftand, are kept back
upon the cleared ground, upon which the turneps are thrown. But as, in this cafe, the turneps muft either be thrown in part over the
ground already foiled by the fheep; or be
confined to a fpace fimilar to that off which
they are drawn ;—by which means the principal intention of drawing is fruftrated ;—a third
method of harvefting has been invented ꞉
namely,

C. CARTING OFF HALF AND DISTRIBUTING
HALF. This ingenious method is, I believe, of modern invention; and is now
chiefly practifed by a few capital farmers, who
fat large quantities both of cattle and fheep.

In

In this cafe, the headlands and fidelands being cleared, the area is drawn and carried off, warp for warp; leaving the piece in stripes, about ten paces wide.

The firft drawing is expended on the bullocks in one or other of the ways already defcribed; while the remaining ftripes are drawn and fcattered over the entire ground for fheep.

By this means the principal intention of drawing is obtained; namely, that of diftributing the turneps evenly and thinly; fo that while one is eaten, another may not be foiled: a principle which, it may be taken for granted, is well founded; as it is ftrictly and invariably attended to by good farmers in general.

This advantage, however, does not appear to me to be the only one obtained by drawing turneps for fheep in the fold.

When a flock of fheep are turned upon a fhift of ftanding turneps, the firft thing they do is to run over the whole; and, then, to eat fuch of the tops as they have not trampled down in running over them. While they are doing this, they ftand upon the roots: which, being firm in the ground, and flat on

the

the top, are no way inconvenient to ftand upon. But what is worfe, if the foot happen to fall near the edge of the turnep, the fharpnefs of the hoof, and the fixed fituation of the root, renders it liable to be barked, as well as fouled, and rendered unfavory to this faftidious animal.

On the contrary, if fheep be put upon drawn turneps, their tops may be in fome meafure injured, but their roots cannot; for being round, and lying loofe upon the furface of the ground, they afford no foothold to ftand upon. And, if the hoof be put upon the edge, the turnep roiling with the flighteft touch, the foot flips, and the rind is faved. Thus the roots in this cafe, inftead of being footftools become ftumblingblocks to the fheep; who, carefully avoiding the turneps, ftand, in this cafe, entirely upon the ground; which, under thefe circumftances, is left almoft wholly free for their feet; the turneps touching it with a fmall portion of their circumferences only; whereas, in their natural ftate of growing, they occupy a confiderable portion of the furface.

For

For obfervations on *fteeping the feed*, and *re-fowing*, fee MIN. 3.

For obfervations on the *turnep caterpillar*, fee MIN. 12.

For obfervations on the *grub* and *Anbury*, fee MIN. 20.

For an inftance of the "*fly*" being checked by the fheepfold, fee MIN. 21.

For preventatives of the *Anbury*, fee MIN. 22.

For experiment with *lime* for turneps, fee MIN. 29.

For the *quantity* of turneps eaten by bullocks in the yard, and calculation on their *produce value*, fee MIN. 56.

For an incident refpecting the "*proof*" of turneps; and reafons accounting for it by a particular *foil procefs*, and *clofe being*, fee MIN. 57.

For a fimple way of *preferving turneps* in winter, and refiections upon it, fee MIN. 61.

For inftances of the *price* of turneps, fee MIN. 68.

For comparative obfervations on *fhed* and *out-door* bullocks, and on the practice of *indi-viduals*

viduals in fatting *bullocks* on turneps, fee
Min. 69.

· For a particular *feed procefs*, fee Min. 71.

For the practice of fundry *individuals* in the
confumption of turneps on *ftore cattle*, fee
Min. 74.

· For an opinion refpecting the great ufe of
turneps to *cows* in the fpring, fee Min. 83.

For a defcription of the manner in which
bullocks *break* their turneps, fee Min. 84.

· For obfervations on the expenditure of turneps in *Fleg*, fee Min. 106.

·For further obfervations on the turnep *Ca-*
terpillar, and of the *Tentbredo* which produces
them, fee Min. 122, 124, 129, and 131.

For further obfervations on the *application*
of turneps, fee the article Bullocks, and the
Min. from thence referred to.

34.

CULTIVATED GRASSES.

UNDER THIS HEAD it will be proper
to confider,

     1. The fpecies,
     2. The foil,
     3. Succeffion,
     4. Seed procefs,
     5. Vegetating procefs,
     6. Firft-year's lay,
     7. Second-year's lay.

I. SPECIES.   The cultivated graffes of this
Diftrict are,

   Darnel,—*lolium perenne*,—ray grafs;
   Clover,—*trifolium pratenfe*—red clover;
   Suckling,—*trifolium repens*—white clover;
   Black nonfuch *,—*trifolium agrarium*,—tre-
      foil hop clover,—or yellow clover;
   Suffolk grafs,—*pea annua*,—dwarf meadow-
      grafs.

  * By "black nonfuch" is meant trefoil in the hufk;
in contradiftinction to darnel, which is frequently called
                            "white

the quantity of ray grafs being fmall ; the
feedfman taking care to ftir them up, from
time to time, to prevent the fmalleft and
heavieft from fettling at the bottom of the bowl
or hopper.

4. QUANTITY OF SEED.—This varies with
the quality of the feed, and the opinion of
the farmer: half a peck of ray grafs l and *to
the amount of* twelve or fourteen pounds of
clover, an acre, may be taken as the medium
quantity: if two or three pounds of fuckling,
or three or four pounds of " hulled nonfuch,"
or a proportional quantity of " black nonfuch,". be fown, the quantity of red clover is
proportionably lefs.

5. The feeds are generally COVERED with a
pair 'of fmall harrows, drawn backward to
prevent the teeth from tearing up the clods,
difturbing the barley, or burying the grafs
feeds too deep.

V. VEGETATING PROCESS. The " young
feeds" are ftudioufly kept from *fheep* the first
autumn and winter. They are, however, *eaten*
freely with young ftock and other ftore *cattle* ;
and for conveniency have fometimes turneps
thrown

thrown upon them : but this, as has been obferved, is not a general practice ; nor is it
efteemed a judicious one ; unlefs the foil be
very firm and the feafon dry. They are fometimes *top-dreffed* in winter, with dung or compoft; but this is a practice confined to a few
individuals. In the fpring of the firft year,
they are univerfally *ftonepicked*; but, extraordinary to relate, they are rarely, if ever, *rolled*
either the firft or the fecond fpring.

VI. FIRST-YEAR'S LAY.—1. This is generally SHUT UP in the month of April, and
either fuffered to ftand for hay, or is paftured,
or roped upon, by the working horfes. See
HORSES.

2. CLOVER HAY is mown with the fame
fithe, and is lifted or turned in the fame manner, as BARLEY. The great fingularity refpecting the treatment of clover hay, in Norfolk, confifts in its being univerfally made
into large cocks, as foon as it is weathered
enough to prevent its damaging in thefe
cocks; in which it frequently ftands a week,
or, perhaps, a fortnight.

X 2   By

By cocking it in this manner, before it becomes too crisp, the leaf and the heads are
saved; but heavy rains sometimes do it great
injury in this state. From slighter rains and
transient showers it is, however, much safer
in these large cocks (four, five, or six of
which will generally make a load), than in
swaths; whose surfaces being large in proportion to their bulk, and their situation being
low, are liable to receive damage from every
shower; while the surfaces of large cocks are
comparatively small, and, their situation being
elevated, the wet is licked up by the first
breeze of wind.

Clover is seldom mown more than once;
except for seed; the second crop being usually
eaten-off with store cattle; for which the
clover stubbles are necessary receptacles, after
the ray-grass lays are broken up for wheat.

3. RAISING CLOVER SEED is not a practice
of this District. The principal part of that
.which is sown in it is raised in Suffolk, and
the Suffolk side of Norfolk; the quantity saved
in this part of the county being small, compared with the quantity sown. See MIN. 101.

VII. THE

VII. The second-year's lay. This is invariably paſtured (unleſs ſome ſmall ſhare be ſuffered to ſtand for darnel ſeed), the ſpring ſhoot being uſually expended in "topping up" turneped bullocks: for which purpoſe no other vegetable, perhaps, is ſuperior to ray graſs.

Store cattle follow the bullocks (which generally are all ſent to Smithfield by the middle of June), and keep poſſeſſion of the ſecond-year's lays, until they be broken up for wheat, in July, Auguſt, September, or October; agreeably to the SOIL PROCESS made uſe of for WHEAT; which ſee.

For an inſtance of ſowing clover in autumn, ſee MIN. 24.

For an account of Norwich clover-ſeed market, ſee MIN. 101.

For a ſingular effect aſcribed to clover, in Fleg, ſee MIN. 106,

35.

NATURAL GRASSES.

IN DESCRIBING the management of the different kinds of GRASSLANDS, it will be necessary to treat separately of each species, namely,

    1. Grazing grounds,
    2. Meadows,
    3. Marshes,
    4. Fens.

I. GRAZING GROUNDS.—If we except the parks and paddocks of men of fortune ; who, through economy or fashion, have, in general, disparked their deer, and converted their parks and paddocks into sheep-walks and grazing grounds ; we find very little upland grass in *this* District : I recollect only one piece, of any extent, in the occupation of farmers.

There are two causes of this scarcity of natural grassland : the soils of this neighbourhood, and

and of the entire county, taken in a general
point of view, are of a quality ungenial to the
native grasses. If a piece of arable land be
laid down to grass, in the course of a very few
years it becomes mossy and unproductive, and
calls aloud for the plow and harrow.

The other is, the high price which corn bore
a few years ago. This urged the farmer to increase his arable land to the stretch : not only
UPLAND grass, but even bogs appear to have
been subjected to the arable process; though, in
their present state, too moist and chilly to bear
even the finer grasses ; much more to support
and mature profitable crops of corn.

This is far from being intended as a general
censure of the anxiety of the Norfolk husbandmen to increase the quantity of arable land;
for I am of opinion, that there is scarcely an
acre of land in the county which is not worth
more under the Norfolk system of aration than
it would be in any other state; *except* the MEA-
DOWS, the MARSHES, and the FENS; which I
am equally clear in opinion ought to be improved as grassland, or as sources of turf,
reed, oziers, sedge, or other aquatic and palu-
strean productions ; and ought not, under any

X 4   pretence

pretence whatever, to be attempted to be reduced to arable land.

II. MEADOWS. The species of grassland
which passes under this denomination in Norfolk, is confined to those bottoms, or vallies,
which accompany, almost uniformly, the rivulets which abound in East Norfolk.

These vallies vary in width and depth. In
some places the bed of the rivulet is sunk
deep and narrow, in an almost level surface;
so that the arable land comes down to its brink;
in others, the valley is wide, and the bottom
flat; and, in this case, the sides of the valley
are sometimes low with an easy swell, sometimes bold and lofty: this however is seldom
the case; the Norfolk meadows in general
lying in gentle dips a few feet below the level
of the upland, and from half a furlong to two
or three furlongs wide.

These dips, gentle as they may be, subject
them, in general, to a pernicious redundancy of
subterranean moisture.

The Norfolk soil, in general, is, as has
been repeatedly observed, of a nature unusually
absorbent; drinking up rain water as fast
as

as it reaches the earth: a flood is feldom heard of in Norfolk. The waters thus abforbed are liable to be obftructed by beds of marl and clay: if an obftruction take place on the verge of a valley, the waters obftructed ouze out, or attempt a paffage, on its fides; or rife, or attempt to rife, out of its bafe. Thus, land-fprings, quickfands, hanging tumours, and bogs, occur in almoft every meadow: and where none of thefe actually take place, a coldnefs ufually prevails in every part of the area (except in very dry feafons); owing to the lownefs of the fituation, compared with the neighbouring upland; whofe abforbed waters, though they fink beneath the corn-mould, and though they may meet with no particular obftruction, yet, in a wet feafon, are, in all human probability, collected, more or lefs, at the depth of a few feet below the fur-face.

Be this as it may, the chilnefs which pre-vails in the lower parts of the meadows, de-ftroys or checks the better graffes, and pro-duces or encourages alders, fedges, rufhes, and the whole tribe of paluftrean weeds: while

the

the upper margins are productive of furze, fern, and anthills.

Such, from fituation, is the *natural ftate* of the Norfolk meadows; and forry I am to add, that, with a few exceptions, *fuch is their prefent ftate*.

Admirer as I am of the arable management of this country, and cautious as I wifh to be of cenfuring, without caufe, any department of its rural economy; I cannot refrain from condemning, in full terms, its grafsland management.

Having, however, minuted my fentiments on this fubject, as they occurred from time to time, in the courfe of my obfervation or practice; I fhall, in this place, only give a fketch of the prefent management, fuch as it is, and draw what appears to me the general *outline* of improvement.

In winter, or towards fpring, when the landfprings are flowing and the bogs full of water, a few paltry grips are, fometimes, made acrofs fuch parts of a meadow as are no longer able to bear pafturing ftock: thefe grips being ufually run in a perpendicular direction, from the rivulet toward the upper margin.

But,

But, frequently, even this is omitted ; or, if once done, is so long neglected, that its effect is lost.

Besides this faint attempt at improving the substratum, the rushes and other tall weeds on the surface are *sometimes* swept down with the sithe ;—and sometimes left to enjoy their natural right.—Thus much as to *improvements.*

With respect to the *uses* to which these morasses are applied, they are principally confined to that of keeping young cattle from starving : cows are sometimes trusted in them ; but in general their surfaces are too rotten, and their herbage too rank for this species of stock : and common prudence, resulting from dear-bought experience, generally prevents the farmer from trusting either his sheep or his horses in his " meadows;"—lest the former should be subjected to the rot, and the latter be smothered in the peatbogs.

When the young cattle have picked out the little grass they can find,—the sedges and other aquatic weeds of the bogs are sometimes mown, and carried off by hand, for litter ; and sometimes suffered to die and rot .on their native bogs, whose depth is thereby annually increased.

creafed. Upon the founder better parts, the
ru!hes and rough grafs are, fometimes, made
into a kind of coarfe hay, for winter fodder for
ftore cattle.

The common rental price of meadow land
is, from five fhillings to ten fhillings an acre ;
and, in their prefent ftate, it is their full rental
value ; taking one year with another: in a
very dry feafon they are frequently, on a par,
worth ten fhillings an acre to a farmer; pafturage of any kind being, in that cafe, fingularly valuable in Norfolk ; but, in a common
year, they are not, in their prefent ftate, I apprehend, worth, on a par, more than feven
fhillings an acre.

If we confider the natural fituation, and the
prefent ftate of the Norfolk meadows, the following IMPROVEMENTS fpontaneoufly offer
themfelves.

1. DRAINING the furface and fubftratum
from fuperfluous moifture.

2. CLEARING and LEVELLING the furface-
mould; and increafing its contexture and FIRM-
NESS.

3. Improving the QUALITY OF THE PRO-
DUCE, by GRASS SEEDS; or, by PLANTING.

4. In-

4. Increasing the QUANTITY, as well as the quality of the herbage, by MANURING and WATERING.

The laſt, namely WATERING, is a practice entirely unknown to the generality of Norfolk huſbandmen. Indeed, until the ſurface of their meadows be adjuſted, and the ſubterranean waters removed, a knowledge of the practice would be uſeleſs to them.

Without this advantage, great as it would be in addition, I will venture to aſſert, from an extraordinary attention to this ſubject, that the preſent rental value of the meadows of Eaſt Norfolk might be doubled; and this at the expence of one third of the improved value. I will venture to go farther, and give it as my clear opinion, that the meadow lands of Eaſt Norfolk, with a ſimilar proportion of expence, might, on a par, be improved ten ſhillings an acre.

We have, in a former ſection, eſtimated the number of arable acres in Norfolk to be ſix hundred thouſand. Suppoſing the proportion of arable to meadow land to be as twenty to one (ten to one would, perhaps, be a nearer proportion) the number of acres of meadow will be thirty thouſand, which, at ten ſhillings

an

an acre, is fifteen thoufand pounds ; from which take one third for the expence of improvement, the remainder is ten thoufand pounds, the near annual improvement.

. If to the IMPROVEMENT of draining, &c. that of WATERING were added, in places where it is practicable, at a moderate expence, this annual increafe might be very confiderably augmented.

In a country where landed gentlemen are fo minutely, and fo ftrenuoufly, attentive to their own intereft, it is aftonifhing they do not fet about fuch *real* improvements as would, in the inftant, render them refpectable, and bring, in the end, a *durable* increafe to their rentrolls; rather than continue to dwell upon thofe, which have already brought down fo much diftrefs upon their tenants, and obloquy upon themfelves.

However, with refpect to the improvement of meadows, the tenants are equally culpable with their landlords : even a twenty-one year's leafe is not enough to encourage them to make the requifite improvement.

The fact is, the landlord and tenant are jointly interefted ; and the expence in this, as

in

in almoſt all caſes of improvement upon a
leaſed eſtate, ought to be joint. On granting
a leaſe, the landlord ought to advance, or
allow, ſome certain ſum of money towards the
improvement; which he, or his agent, ought
to ſee executed, accorʼling to agreement, previouſly entered into by the tenant.

III. Marshes. This ſpecies of natural
graſsland is, on the eaſtern ſide of the county,
confined to the neighbourhood of Yarmouth;
where an extenſive tract of marſhes lie on the
banks of the Breydon; which, formerly, was
probably, an arm of the ſea, but is now a
mere dilatation of the Yare; which, at Yarmouth, regains the river form. This valuable
tract of land, with its preſent ſtate and application, being fully deſcribed in Minute 118, it
is unneceſſary to dwell upon it in this place.

IV. Fens. Under this head I claſs the
ſwampy margins of the rivers and lakes which
abound in the ſouthern part of this Diſtrict.

Their natural produce is reed, gladdon*,
ſedge, ruſhes and other aquatic and paluſtrean

* Gladdon—Typha latifolia et anguſtifolia,—cats-tail.

plants;

plants ; their upper fides being frequently out
of the water's way, affording a proportion of
grazable land : hence, probably, they are provincially termed " marfhes." This, however,
is not only contrary to the common acceptation of the term ; but the produce and principal ufe of a fen are totally different from thofe
of a grazing marfh.

The profits of a fen arife, in general, from

Reed and gladdon, cut for thatch, for buildings ;

Sedge and rufhes, for litter ; and thatch, for
hay and corn ricks, and fometimes for buildings ;

Coarfe grafs, for fodder, and fometimes for
pafturage ;—and

Peat for fuel*.

The *laft*, if made the moft of, is a very valuable article,—as appears in Min. 54.

* The proprietors of manors are alfo proprietors of the
fifh in fuch parts of thofe frefh-water lakes as lie within
their refpedive manors ; and the right of fifhing is frequently let off to men who make an employment of taking
the pike (fome of them of immenfe fize) and other fifh
with which " the broads" abound.

The ufe and value of REED have been fpoken to, amply, under the head BUILDINGS AND REPAIRS.

GLADDON is of a fimilar ufe, but lefs value; its duration being much fhorter than that of reed.

The other articles require no explanation.

For an inftance of burning *antbills*, fee MIN. 6.

For an inftance of a *grazing ground* being more nutritious to heifers than to fteers, fee MIN. 39.

For the Norfolk method of *opening drains*, fee MIN. 44.

For the method of "geckling" *antbills*, fee MIN. 50.

For general obfervations on Norfolk *mea-dows*, fee MIN. 51.

For general obfervations on *fens*, fee MIN. 54.

For a ftriking inftance of the prefent bad management of *meadows*, fee MIN. 65.

For the method of cutting *reed*, fee MIN. 89.

For a ftriking improvement of *meadow* land, fee MIN. 96.

For a defcription of the *Yarmouth marfhes*, &c. fee MIN. 118.

Befides thefe Minutes on provincial practice, I find fome relating to a fpecies of grafsland, different from any of thofe above enumerated; namely, a young perennial lay; the herbage principally ray grafs and white clover; the foil a tolerably rich loam; the fituation cooler than that of Norfolk arable land in general; but warmer than what is called meadow; forming a fuite of dairy grounds; which, lying round the houfe I refided in, fell immediately under my own eye; and the management of them was frequently conducted under my own directions. See MIN. 108.

For inftance of profit by *mowing the broken-grafs* of paftured land, fee MIN. 7.

For an evidence of *fheep* being inimical to *cows*, fee MIN. 8.

For the effect of the *fhovellings of a fheepfold* upon grafsland, fee MIN. 10.

For an experiment on the *time of manuring* grafsland, fee MIN. 127.

36. CATTLE.

36.

C A T T L E.

IN TREATING of this species of live-stock, it will be proper to consider, separately,

1. The species, or breed.
2. Cows, and the management of the dairy.
3. Rearing cattle.
4. Bullocks, or fatting cattle.

I. THE SPECIES. The present breed of cattle, in this District, is not less peculiar to the country, than its breed of horses was formerly (fee HORSES), and is strongly marked with the same leading characters.

The native cattle of Norfolk are a small, hardy, thriving race; fatting as freely, and finishing as highly, at three years old, as cattle in general do at four or five.

They are small-boned,—short-legged,—round-barrelled,—well-loined,—thin-thighed—clean-chapped; the head, in general, fine, and the horns clean, middle-sized, and bent

Y 2　　　　　　up-

upward : the favorite colour, a blood-red, with a white or a mottled face.

The breed of Norfolk is the Herefordshire breed in miniature ; except that the chine and the quarter of the Norfolk breed are more frequently deficient.

This, however, is not a general imperfection. I have seen Norfolk spayed heifers sent to Smithfield, as well *laid up*, and as *full in their points*, as Galloway or Highland cattle usually are : and, if the London butchers be judges of beef, there is no better *fished* beasts sent to Smithfield market.

These two qualifications ; namely, the superior quality of their flesh, and their fatting freely at an early age, do away every objection to their size and form. Nevertheless, it might be adviseable to endeavour to improve the latter ; provided those two far superior qualifications were not by that means injured. But it might be wrong to attempt to increase the former, which seems to be perfectly well adapted to the Norfolk soil.

The medium weight of a well-fatted three-year-old is forty stone (of fourteen pounds each).

Bulls

Bulls of the Suffolk polled breed have, at different times, been brought into this District: and there are several instances of the Norfolk breed being crossed with these bulls. —The consequence is, an increase of size, and an improvement of form: but it is much to be feared, that the native hardiness of the Norfolk breed, and their quality of fatting quickly, at an early age, are injured by this innovation; which was first introduced by gentlemen, who, it is probable, were unacquainted with the peculiar excellency of the true Norfolk stock; and the mongrel breed, which has arisen from the cross, yet remains in the hands of a few individuals.

A few years ago, a Highland Scotch bull was brought into this neighbourhood, by a man who stands high in the profession of grazing; and who has crossed his own stock of the true Norfolk breed, with this bull.— The produce of this cross proves, that if the genuine breed can be improved, by any admixture of blood whatever, it is by that of the Highland breed. The chine is, by this cross, obviously improved; and the hardiness, as well as the flesh, and proneness to fat *at a*

certain

certain age, cannot receive injury from this admixture. The only thing to be feared from it is, that the ſtock will not fat ſo *early*, as will that of the genuine breed; and, if the opinion of the oldeſt, graveſt, and I had almoſt ſaid the beſt, farmer in the Diſtrict has any weight in this caſe, this evil effect is much to be apprehended: he is clear in that a " Scot" does not fat kindly even at *three* years old; much leſs at *two*; at which age many hundred head of cattle are annually fatted in this country.

The fact appears evidently to be, that the Norfolk Huſbandmen are in poſſeſſion of a breed of cattle admirably adapted to their ſoil, climature, and ſyſtem of management: and let them croſs with caution; leſt by mixing they adulterate; and, in the end, loſe, irretrievably, their preſent breed of cattle; as their forefathers, heretofore, loſt a valuable breed of horſes; the loſs of which can, now, be only lamented.

If, through the laudable ſpirit of improvement, attempts be made with *foreign* breeds, they ought to be made with caution. But, from what I have ſeen and know of the Norfolk

folk stock, and what I have since seen of the improvement of the breed of cattle in other counties, it appears to me, evidently, that nothing more is wanted to improve the form of the present breed of cattle in Norfolk than a due attention to the breed itself.

While *such* cows, and *such* bulls, as I have sometimes seen, are suffered to propagate their deformities, no wonder some valuable points should be lowered. But if, in the reverse of this unpardonable neglect, men of judgment and enterprize would make a proper selection; and would pay the same attention to the Norfolk breed as is paid to the long-horned breed, in the midland counties, and to the short-horned, in the north of Yorkshire;—every point might beyond a doubt be filled up, and the present valuable qualities be at the same time retained.

But the great cause of neglect in the breeding of cattle in Norfolk, is, that men of judgment and spirit rather choose to purchase of the Scotch drovers, or of their poor and industrious but less judicious neighbours, than to go themselves through the tedious round of rearing. However, if we consider the present universal scarcity of cattle (1786), and that the Scotch-

men,

men, through recent improvements in their plan of husbandry, are now enabled to fat a part of that stock, which formerly they drove wholly to the southward; it seems highly probable that the Norfolk graziers will, henceforward, find their advantage in encreasing, and improving, their own breed; and they may rest assured, that he who first sets about its improvement will have it in his power to keep the lead; and reap, of course, the highest advantage.

II. Cows.—The prime intention of keeping cows in this country is the rearing of young stock;—the produce of the dairy, unless in the neighbourhood of large towns, being a secondary object,

But the number of cows kept, even by the rearing farmers, is few: eight or ten may be considered as a middling dairy of cows. upon a middle-sized farm;—I mean on the east side of the county.

In West-Norfolk, especially on the marshland side towards Cambridgeshire, large dairies of cows are kept, for the purpose of making butter; which is sent weekly to London under the denomination of Cambridge butter.

This

This is a fortunate circumstance to the Eaſt Norfolk breeders, who draw an increaſe of rearing calves from that quarter of the county: whoſe dairymen, in their turn, are benefited, in being by this means enabled to get riddance of their calves, at an early age; jobbers making it a buſineſs to transfer them from one ſide of the county to the other.

By this means, and by buying up the calves of cottagers, farmers, and gentlemen of the neighbourhood, who do not rear their own, an Eaſt Norfolk breeder is able to rear a greater number of calves than the number of his cows amount to.

Ten or twelve calves may, perhaps, be conſidered as the medial number reared at preſent, on a farm of one hundred and fifty pounds to two hundred pounds a year.

In the neighbourhood of Norwich and Yarmouth, cowkeeping is frequently applied to the FATTING OF CALVES for the ped markets (ſee MARKETS).

Alſo, in the neighbourhood of theſe and other towns, BUTTER becomes an object of ſale.

CHEESE

CHEESE is likewise an article of the ped market; where it is generally sold in a crude recent state; especially in the spring and early part of the summer; when it is bought up at a few weeks, perhaps at a few days old, by the working-people; of whom at that season of the year it is the principal food.

With respect to the management of the Norfolk dairywomen, and their skill in butter and cheese making, little can be said which will redound to their credit. However, in extenuation, it may be said, and with truth, that rank meadows, and new lays, in summer, and turneps in winter and spring, are ill calculated for producing the delicacies of the dairy: and it may be added, that where perfection cannot be hoped for, emulation loses its effect.— Besides, custom has been very kind in reconciling their countrymen to those things which a stranger revolts at; so that they have, now, no motive for endeavouring to correct the rankness of their butter, or the rancidity of their cheese.

Nevertheless, in one thing they are extremely culpable: this is in suffering their cheeses to be devoured, year after year, by a

species

species of maggot peculiar, perhaps, to this county, with every appearance of tameness and resignation; as if they were conscious of its being a judgment upon their evil management.

But even in this case, custom is friendly to them: for such is the depravity of taste, when led away imperceptibly by habit, that even the maggots themselves are to some grateful.

This, however, is only a palliation of their crime; for, not unfrequently, the entire dairy, except the ordinary skim cheese, is more or less affected; so that, before Michaelmas, the cheeses would be literally so many bags of maggots, were they not sold off, and consumed, at an age, at which, in any other country, they would not be ranked among human food. I have myself seen a dairy of cheese— that is, the stock then left on hand—in total ruins before that time. An East Norfolk cheese, sound and whole at Christmas, is a rarity; by Ladyday, there is not, generally speaking, a pound of Norfolk cheese, nor even a handful of maggots, to be purchased in the District.

I am

I am the less reserved in my censures of the Norfolk dairywomen in this respect, as I know, from my own experience in the county, that the evil which is here spoken of, and which is a cause of great and unnecessary hardship to the labouring poor, in the winter months, originates, principally, in a want of attention and management. But having in that case, as in others relating to my own experience, minuted the circumstances, as they occurred, or as soon as a regular Minute could be formed of them, I shall not enlarge upon the subject, here, but refer to MINUTE 108,

III. REARING CATTLE.—This subject calls for a threefold division.

 1. Calves,
 2. Yearlings,
 3. Two-year-olds.

'1. CALVES. The rearing of cattle is become, in my opinion, a subject of the first importance to this country: a universal and growing scarcity of neat stock is experienced, more or less, throughout the kingdom. I have therefore paid more than common attention to the rearing of calves (the first and most difficult

cult part of the bufinefs) in this Diftrict: not only as being a primary object in the Eaft Norfolk fyftem, but becaufe the practice here is, in many refpects, peculiar to the country.

The *number* has already been mentioned in general terms: it varies, however, with the quantity of meadow or other natural grafsland belonging to a given farm; and fometimes, but not always, with the time at which the cows happen to come-in.

The time of rearing.—Some farmers "bring up" all the year round;—rearing every calf he has dropt. Others rear in winter, only; fatting his fummer calves for the ped markets; or, at a diftance from them, for the butcher. Norfolk farmers, in general, begin early in winter to rear their calves: fome fo early as Michaelmas; in general, if their cows come-in, before Chriftmas: not only as being fully aware of the advantage of rearing early; but in order that they may rear as many of their own calves as poffible; "drove calves" being always hazardous, and fometimes fcarce.

No diftinction is made as to fex: males and females are equally objects of rearing, and are both, occafionally, fubjected to caftration; it

being

being a prevailing cuſtom to ſpay all heifers
intended to be fatted at three-year-old; but
ſuch as are intended to be finiſhed at two-year-
old are, I believe, pretty generally left "open:"
as are, of courſe, ſuch as are intended for the
dairy.

There are two reaſons for this practice:—
they are prevented from taking the bull too
early, and thereby fruſtrating the main intention; and by this precaution they lie more
quietly—are kept from roving—at the time of
fatting. This may be one reaſon why ſpayed
heifers are thought to fat more kindly at three-
year-old, and to be better fleſhed, than open
heifers.

The method of treatment remains now to be
explained.—This depends in ſome meaſure on
the time of rearing: the winter calves require
more milk than the later-dropt ones do.

The general treatment of a calf dropt at
Chriſtmas may be ſaid to be this: ſucks, twice
a day, the firſt fortnight: has the pail, twice
a day, for the next month or ſix weeks: and
once a day, for a month or ſix weeks longer:
with hay in a rack, and *turneps* in a manger;
and ſometimes, with oats and bran among the
turneps:

turneps: which laft, after a calf has taken freely to them, ferves as both meat and drink.

In this confifts the chief peculiarity of the Norfolk method of rearing calves : which may be faid to be with milk and turneps: the lalt a fpecies of food, which, in every other part of the kingdom, is, I believe, entirely neglected, or unthought of.

As foon as the weather gets warm enough; the calves are turned out, in the day, among the fatting bullocks; or into a patch of turneps, or upon a piece of wheat, or a forward grafs-piece, and houfed again at night: until, the days growing long, and the nights warm, and the clover and darnel have rifen to a full bite, they are turned out altogether; and continue to have the firft bite of every thing, which is good and palatable to them, throughout the fummer.

This, as beforementioned, may be called the general treatment of calves dropt at Chrift-mas; but as the managements of no two far-mers are exactly the fame, I made it my bufi-nefs to attend to the practice of individuals; and as the refult of my obfervations appears in Minutes 53, and 70, I fhall refer the reader to thofe

thofe Minutes for further particulars on thé
fubje ct.

2. YEARLINGS. The lattermath and ſtubbles being finiſhed, the yearlings—provincially "buds,"—are put to turneps: either as
followers to the bullocks, or have fome freſh
turneps thrown to them: in either cafe, they
ſleep in thé par-yard, and generally have a ſeparate par allotted them; though fometimes
they are parred with the two-year-olds.

In the yard, the beſt of the "ſtover" is allowed them, and, perhaps, a little ordinary
hay: it being a maxim pretty generally
adopted among good farmers, to keep their
young ſtock as well as they can the firſt
winter.

In ſpring, and fummer, they follow the
bullocks, and run in the meadows; or, if
thefe be wanting, are fometimes fent out to
fummer graſs in the marſhes or grazing-
grounds. For the agiſtment price, fee the
LIST OF RATES.

3. TWO-YEAR-OLDS. Run in the ſtubbles
and broken graſs till Chriſtmas, or until turneps can be fpared them; when they generally
follow the bullocks. In winter, they are
always

always " parred" at night; fometimes with
the cows; fometimes with the buds; fometimes alone. Good farmers generally keep
them feparate :—if parred with the buds, they
rob them; if with the cows, they are liable
to be " horned," and are never at reft : except
while the cows are eating up the beft of the
fodder.

Some farmers, when turneps run fhort, " put
out" their two-year-olds in winter : and others,
when they are plentiful, " graze," that is, fat
their two-year-olds.

In general, however, they are " kept over-
year," on meadows or lays, or are fent to the
marfhes or grazing grounds, as fituations and
circumftances point out; and, at Michaelmas, are put to turneps as fatting cattle.

The agiftment price for two-year-olds, from
Mayday to Michaelmas, varies with the keep.
See LIST OF RATES. For further particulars
fee the MINUTES referred to below.

IV. BULLOCKS *.—This is the grand object
to which every part of the Norfolk hufbandry
more

* " Bullocks."—This is a general term, in Norfolk, for
all kinds of cattle at turneps, or other food, with an intention

more or lefs tends, and which diftinguifhes it, and has long diftinguifhed it, from the huf-bandry of all other countries.

The practice of fatting bullocks on turneps is, however, now beginning to creep into every part of the kingdom : but it may be faid to be ftill in a ftate of infancy every where, except in Norfolk; and an accurate account of the practice of this parent county cannot fail of being ufeful to every other turnep-land Diftrict.

Impreffed with this idea, I fpared no pains, nor let flip any opportunity, of making myfelf acquainted with the fubject. The refult of my obfervations and enquiries I regiftered as they occurred, and appear in the Minutes. All, therefore, that remains to be done in this place, is to make a general analyfis of the fub-

tention of being fatted ; whether they be oxen, fleers, heifers, or cows. A fimple general term is much wanted in this cafe ; and, although the term bullocks may not be entirely free from objection, I fhall, in this place, adopt it. Dr. Johnfon defines it " a young bull ;" but the moft general acceptation of it, at prefent, is—" an aged ox." Upon the whole its meaning is vague, and it may, without much impropriety, be applied to fatting and fatted cattle.

ject,

ject, and to delineate its outline, fo as to place
it in a regular and clear light ; and thereby
prepare the reader to go through the Minutes
with the greater eafe and advantage.

The four grand divifions of the fubject
are,

1. The fpecies of bullocks fatted.

2. The method of obtaining them.

3. The method of fatting them.

4. The method of difpofing of them.

1; Species.—The only fpecies of cattle fatted in Eaft Norfolk may be faid to be " homebreds" and " Scots." Some " Irifh beace"
have, at different times, but not regularly,
been brought into the country, and have generally done very well. In Weft Norfolk,
great numbers of Lincolnfhire and Yorkfhire
oxen were formerly, and fome few, I believe,
are now, fatted ; but in this Diftrict they have
always been confidered as much inferior to
the Scotch and home-bred ftock.

Home-breds confift of

Steers,

Spayed heifers,

Open heifers,

Barren cows,

" Running calves."

The

The laſt is a ſpecies of fatting cattle peculiar, perhaps, to this country. They are
calves, which are ſuffered to run with their
dams until they be a twelvemonth or more
old : the cow being all the while at " head
keep," of which the calf partakes, as well as
of the milk of its dam : which, herſelf, in the
mean time, generally gets fat enough to be
ſent to Smithfield, with her calf (perhaps, as
heavy as herſelf) by her ſide.

The Scotch cattle fatted in Norfolk
conſiſt of what are here called

> " Galloway Scots ;"
> " Lowland Scots ;"
> " Highlanders ;"
> " Iſle of Skys."

Galloway cattle are large, thick, ſhort-legged,
moſtly hornleſs, and of a black or brindled
colour : the fleſh well grained ; and the form
altogether beautiful:—chine full;—back broad
and level;—quarter long and full at the nache ;
round barrel;—deep girt ;—and the bone,
head, and chap, in general, fine.

Such, I apprehend, is the genuine original
" Galloway Scot ;" and a principal part of the
bullocks brought into Norfolk under that name
are

are of this defcription :—but the droves are generally adulterated with a mongrel fort ;—the produce of a crofs with a long-horned breed.

This fpecies of adultery is faid to be committed and encouraged by the nobility and landed gentlemen of the countries they are bred in ; but the fact appears to be, that they have already one of the fineft breed of cattle in the world upon their eftates : and it behoves them to hand it down to pofterity as pure at leaft as they received it.   In this age of improvement, it might be laudable to endeavour to improve it to the utmoft : not, however, by foreign admixtures; but by giving the moft beautiful females to the moft beautiful males of their own breed. They appear to me to have much to lofe, but nothing to gain, from croffing,—not even with the prefent long-horned breed of the midland counties..

This fpecies of Scotch cattle appears to be originally of the county of Galloway, which forms the fouthern extremity of Scotland ; but they are now, it is faid, propagated in other

Z 3   parts

parts of the Lowlands, especially in the rich-
land counties of Lothian, in the neighbourhood of Edinburgh. I have known them fatted to eighty stone ; and have been informed, •
from authority which I have no reason to
doubt, that they have been known to reach
near one hundred stone (of fourteen pounds
each).

Lowland cattle. The ordinary breed of
black cattle, in the Lowland counties, are a size
below the Galloways,—and appear to be a
mixture between these and the Highland breed.
Sixty stone is a good weight for a Lowland
ox. His form and inclination to fat partake
of the Galloway breed : the former, however,
is seldom so near perfection as is that of a " true
Galloway Scot." Lowland cattle are some of
them horned, some of them polled : their colour black, or brindled, or dun.

Highland cattle. This seems to be a distinct
breed. The size is beneath those of the Lowlands : forty to fifty stone is the ordinary weight
of a Highland bullock. In form, flesh, and
fatting quality, the Highland breed resemble
much that of Galloway ; except that their
backs in general are coarser, their bone proportionably

portionably larger, and in that they have, in general, but not always, horns,—of the middle fize, and moftly bent upward,—like thofe of the Welfh cattle—but finer.

In general appearance there is a ftrong re-femblance (their horns apart) between the Highland breed and the black cattle of North Wales; but with refpect to flefh and fatting quality,—the main objects,—the comparifon is greatly in favor of the Scotch breed; which the gentlemen of North Wales are faid to fetch annually out of Scotland, or to buy them up at the Englifh fairs, to be fatted for their own tables.

The Ifle of Skys appear to be only a *variety* of the Highland breed; contracted by foil, or climature, or both. They are, in point of fize, the loweft in the gradation. But with regard to flefh, fatting, and growth while fatting, they may be faid to ftand foremoft. I have known an Ifle of Sky fteer, bought at two years and a half old for lefs than forty fhillings, reach, in about twenty months, to fortyfive ftone *.

At that age their " growth" in England is aftonifhing; owing, perhaps, not more to

* But this was the head bullock of a lot of half a fcore, and is, perhaps, a fingular inftance.

their

their nature, than to a change of climature, and
a change of food. Much, however, depends
upon their age. If they be intended for immediate fatting, four years old is the propereft
age. An Ifle of Sky or a Highland fteer at
two or three years old will grow, but he will
not fat; at five or fix he will fat, but he will
not grow while fatting, equal to a four-year-
old bullock. At this age, the weight of Ifle
of Skys, when *fat*, varies, from twenty to forty
ftone.

These are the four *species*, or *varieties*, of
cattle which are brought by the Scotch drovers to the Norfolk fairs, and which are bought
up and fatted by the Norfolk farmers, under
the foregoing names. There may be other
breeds, and admixtures of cattle, propagated
in Scotland; but not being fent to this market, they are foreign to the prefent fubject.

2. THE METHOD OF OBTAINING BULLOCKS
for fatting.—This is either by

Rearing, or by
Purchafe.

Some farmers rear all their own fatting ftock;
others purchafe the whole. But the more general practice is to rear part, and buy in part.

Much

Much depends upon fituation ; but more, perhaps, upon judgment : and ftill more, perhaps,
upon an ample and regular fupply of the *means*
of purchafe.—It is allowed that the affluent fortunes, which were·formerly made by fome few
Norfolk farmers, were chiefly acquired through
a fuperior fkill in the purchafe of ftock ; fe-
conded by a full fupply of money ; by which
means they were always able to time their
purchafe to the beft advantage. But in men
of inferior judgment, and who have not money
at their command to purchafe when the price
of ftock is low, it is undoubtedly prudent to
rear the whole, or a principal part, of their own
ftock ; for, in doing this, they travel a beaten
track, and tread on fure ground.

The purchafe of homebreds is chiefly at the
fairs ;—or at the breeders' houfes ; or on the
" caftle hill" at Norwich, where there is a
weekly market ;—fometimes pretty full of
different forts of live ftock.

The purchafe of Scots is, in this Diftrict,
chiefly at the fair of St. Faith's, a village near
Norwich ; to which the Scotch drovers bring
annually great numbers.—See MIN. 27. and
134.

Thefe

These Scotch dealers have a succession of fairs, which keep them some months in the country; during which time a continued stream of cattle is kept flowing from its various sources in Scotland to its general efflux : which is judiciously removed from place to place, that the diffusion may be the more regular and easy.

The sale begins the 9th of September, at *Harleston*, in South Norfolk ; where its stay is about a fortnight. From Harleston it moves on to *Welpit*, in Suffolk ; and returns to *Seching*, near Lynn in Norfolk, the 10th of October. From " Seche" it is removed to *St. Faith's* (its grand station) near Norwich, the 17th of October. Its stay, here, is uncertain : a fortnight, or three weeks, or as long as the demand lasts. There is a fair at *Halesworth*, a few miles within Suffolk, the beginning of November ; but this seldom, I believe, closes altogether St. Faith's fair. The 22d of November it recommences in Norfolk at *Hempton-Green*, in the northern part of West Norfolk : where continuing a week, or longer time, it is finally removed to *Hoxone*, on the borders of Suffolk, the beginning of December;

ber; and there continues open until near
Chriftmas.

Eaft Norfolk, as obferved above, is principally fupplied at St. Faith's. The northern
Hundreds fometimes draw an additional fupply
from Hempton-Green; and the fouthern ones
from Halefworth and Hoxone; which, with
the other fair in Suffolk, lie within the reach
of the Norfolk farmers.

The Highlanders and Ifle-of-Skys are chiefly or wholly oxen; but the Galloway, and
other Lowland Scots have a mixture of fpayed
heifers; a fpecies of fatting-cattle which is
coveted by judicious graziers.

The moft common age is four years old;
but many of the Scotch cattle brought to thefe
fairs are probably much older: fome of them
have been worked: even fome of the Highland oxen are faid to be worked at the col-
lieries. There are alfo many three-year-olds,
and fome two years old, or under. Thefe are
bought to be kept "over-year" in the meadows, marfhes, and grazing-grounds.

For the fame purpofe, two-year-old homebreds are alfo-purchafed, the firft days of thefe
fairs, as well as at others.

But,

But, for immediate fatting, the defired ages are three years old for homebred, and four years old for Scotch.

3. THE METHOD OF FATTING.—This has been already fpoken to in defcribing the application of TURNEPS; to which the reader is referred; as well as to the MINUTES mentioned at the clofe of this article, for individual practice. It will neverthelefs be proper in this place to take a general view of the fubject; thereby endeavouring to place it in a light as perfpicuous as may be. The firft thing to be confidered is,

The *proportion* of bullocks to a given quantity of turneps. This depends on the fize of the bullocks, and the quality of the turneps.— The general calculation is a middle-fized bullock to an acre of good turneps. Taking turneps on a par, a fatting bullock and a follower come, perhaps, nearer the real proportion.

The *time* depends on the growth of the turneps and the poffefiion of the bullocks: the homebreds are ufually put to turneps about Michaelmas: the Scotch as foon as they are purchafed. It is obfervable, here, that notwithftanding a Scotch bullock, efpecially of
the

the fmaller kind, never faw, perhaps, a turnep;
yet, when thrown to abroad, in company with
two or three homebreds, he generally foon
learns to break his turneps. Some particular
bullocks, however, will receive a check before
they take to them.

The *place* for fatting bullocks on turneps
appears, under the article TURNEPS, to be
either

> The field,
> The yard,
> Sheds, or hovels.

The firft requires leaft attendance and attention, and is highly beneficial to light land:
the fecond makes a great quantity of manure,
but a wafte of ftover: the laft requires lefs
litter; but incurs a greater portion of labour.

In a dry, open feafon, bullocks at turneps
do beft abroad: in wet, pinching weather,
beft under cover.

Out of thefe eftablifhed facts arifes an obvioufly eligible plan of management, where
circumftances will admit of it. In autumn, fo
long as the weather continues moderate, let
bullocks remain abroad; but, whenever it fets
in very wet, or very fevere, take them up
under

under cover;—and there let them remain until they be finifhed, or until the warmth of fpring calls them abroad again.

But the moft eligible method of fatting depends on a variety of circumftances:

The foil and fituation;
The conveniencies in the yard;
The feafon; and
The fpecies of ftock to be fatted.

Cattle which have been accuftomed to lie abroad in a fevere climate, will ftand the winter in the field better than thofe which have been ufed to a fheltered yard, in a warmer climate.

No general plan of management can, therefore, be laid down. All that can be done is, to point out the various modes in ufe, and leave every man to confider well his own particular circumftances, and make his election accordingly. See TURNEPS, page 287.

4. THE MARKETS FOR BULLOCKS. The confumption is divided between the metropolis and the county. The proportion I never heard gueffed at. Perhaps three fourths, perhaps no more than two thirds, of the bullocks fatted in Norfolk, are fent to the London market.

Norfolk

Norfolk is a populous county; not more through the Norwich manufactory, which diffuses itself over a principal part of it, than from the circumstance of Norfolk being an arable country.

The *places* of sale are,

Smithfield;
St. Ives*;
The fairs; and
The farmer's yard.

Bullocks for the London market are chiefly sent directly to Smithfield: many, however, go by the way of St. Ives; and some few are bought up in the country by the London dealers.

Those sent to London and St. Ives are put under the care of drovers, and generally sold by the salesmen of the respective markets.— Some farmers follow their bullocks to these markets; and sometimes, but very seldom, stand the market themselves.

The advantage of sending bullocks by the way of St. Ives is, that if that market prove a bad one, they are driven on to Stevenage; and if this does not suit, are driven through to the

* St. Ives, in Huntingdonshire.

London market. But while they are thus driven from place to place, they are not only accumulating expences, but are fhrinking in carcafe. From the north-weft quarter of the county confiderable numbers of bullocks are, I believe, driven to St. Ives, and there is one drover from the northern part of this diftrict.

But the grand market for bullocks fatted in Eaft Norfolk is Smithfield: to which, in the feafon, they are driven weekly, or twice a week; according to the fupply, and the ftages of the feafon.

Smith of Erpingham has long been the common drover of *this* Diftrict. He generally begins, about Candlemas, to go once a fortnight: in the latter part of February, and the month of March, once a week: in April, May, and June, generally twice a week: and in Auguft or September, he ufually makes one or two journies to take off the furplus of the home confumption, and the "harveft beef," fatted in the marfhes, grazing-grounds, and lays, during the courfe of the fummer.

His place of rendezvous is St. Faith's; where, or in his road to it, the farmers meet him with their refpective lots.

For

For the Monday's market, he sets out from St. Faith's on Sunday, and reaches London the Sunday following. The distance one hundred and twelve miles.

At Mile-End he is met by the salesmen; who mark, and take, from that time, the charge of the lots which are respectively consigned to them. Sometimes the choice of a salesman may be left to the drover; but, in general, every farmer has his own salesman.

If the owners of the bullocks do not attend the market themselves, it is the drover's duty to see (were it possible) that justice be done to his employers; and to receive the neat proceeds from the salesmen; who deliver accounts in this form:

——— " Three Tuns, Smithfield.

Seven beasts sold for Mr. ——— the 10th day of June 1781.

1 Waterman -	14 0 0	Selling (at 1s. 6d.)	0 10 6
1 Beeton -	13 0 0	Toll & expences	0 2 1
1 Andrews -	12 10 0	Help - - -	0 1 9
1 Sewel -	12 0 0	Grass - - -	0 0 0
1 Alexander -	12 0 0	Drover, J. Smith,	1 15 0
1 Brown -	12 0 0	Paid yourself -	86 0 8
1 Brown -	13 0 0		
			£88 10 0
7	£88 10 0	(Signed) S—l P—n;	
		Beast and sheep salesman."	

The expences are, and have been for many years, invariably the fame ; namely, feven fhillings and a penny halfpenny a bullock,—great or fmall ; unlefs when very large heavy bullocks are fent off, a day or two before the drove, as they fometimes are to eafe them on their journey ; in which cafe the expence of the drift is fomewhat more.

Thefe accounts, which are payable at the falefmen's bankers, are delivered to the owners of the bullocks, if they attend ; if not, to the drover ; who formerly brought down the whole amount in money; but now, principally, in bills, at a fhort date, upon the Norwich bankers.

The drover's place of payment in this neighbourhood is North-Walfham; the firft market day after the fale. The farmers go to his Inn, where their accounts and cafh are ready for them. See Min. 117.

MINUTES ON BREED.

For an inftance of the excellency of the *Ifle-of-Sky cattle*, fee MIN. 40.

For an opinion comparative between the *Scotch* and the *Norfolk* breeds, fee MIN. 69.

For

For an evidence in favor of the *Suffolk* breed, fee Min. 69.

For an opinion that *three-year-old Norfolk* will fat as kindly as *four-year-old Scotch*; fee Min. 72.

For an inftance highly in favor of the *Irifh* breed, fee Min. 110.

For an inftance of the excellency of the *Norfolk* breed, fee Min. 119.

MINUTES ON GENERAL MANAGEMENT.

For an inftance of a grazing ground being more friendly to heifers than to fteers; fee Min. 39.

For reflections on the rearing of cattle, fee Min. 53.

For obfervations on the practice of diftributing rubbing pofts in paftured and teathed inclofures, fee Min. 66.

For an inftance of the number and fpecies of cattle kept on a middle-fized farm, fee Min. 70.

For general obfervations on the winter management of ftore cattle, fee Min. 74.

Minutes

MINUTES ON COWS AND THE DAIRY.

For inftances of fheep being unfriendly to cows, fee MIN. 8.

For an opinion that turneps are an excellent food for cows in the fpring, fee MIN. 83.

For general obfervations on cheefemaking, fee MIN. 108.

For general obfervations on making butter, fee MIN. 109.

MINUTES ON REARING CATTLE.

For an evidence that young ftock will pay for good keep, fee MIN. 46.

For a method of rearing calves, fee MIN. 53.

For an evil effect of not fpaying heifers clean, fee MIN. 69.

For various methods of rearing calves, fee MIN. 70.

For obfervations on the winter management of young ftock, fee MIN. 74.

MINUTES ON BULLOCKS.

Species.

For the comparative value of different *breeds* of cattle for fatting, fee MINUTES ON BREED, above referred to.

For

For obfervations on fatting the Norfolk breed at one-year-old, as " running calves," fee Min. 69.

For reflections on fatting them at two-years-old, fee Min. 112.

Buying.

For an account of the Scotch bullock-fair of St. Faith's, fee Min. 27. and 134.

For an inftance of buying the Norfolk breed at Holt fair, fee Min. 39.

For general obfervations on buying bullocks, fee Min. 110.

For further information on this fubject, fee Min. 113.

Fatting.

For a fingular circumftance of the grazing grounds of Foulfham being more nutritious to heifers than to fteers, fee Min. 39.

For an incident on the fatting of Ifle-of-Skys with great fuccefs, fee Min. 49.

For an incident on the quantity of turneps eaten, and the procefs of fatting bullocks *in the yard*, fee Min. 56.

For an incident on the proportion of bullocks to turneps *in the field*, fee Min. 57.

A a 3　　　　　For

For obfervations on fhed and out-door bullocks, fee Min. 69.

For various inftances of individual practice,
fee Min. 69.

For a method of curing fufflation, fee
Min. 72.

For the manner in which bullocks break
their turneps, fee Min. 84.

For obfervations on fhed and out-door bullocks, in fevere weather, fee Min. 93.

For an incident of practice particularly attended to, fee Min. 97.

For further obfervations on this incident,
fee Min. 102.

For fome account of the Fleg grazing, fee
Min. 106.

For further obfervations on the abovementioned incident of practice, fee Min. 110.

For a further progrefs in the fame incident,
fee Min. 111.

For an inftance of bullocks doing well at
grafs, though the weather was wet, fee Min.
113.

For fome account of grazing in Blowfield
Hundred, and in the Yarmouth marfhes, fee
Min. 118.

Selling

Selling.

For an inftance of fale . at Smithfield, fee MIN. 102.

For an account of Walfham bullock-fair, fee MIN. 105.

For an account of Worftead bullock-fair, fee MIN. 107.

For another inftance of fale, and the uncertainty of Smithfield market, fee MIN. 111.

For an account of Ingham bullock-fair, fee MIN. 112,

Obfervations on a lot fent off to Smithfield, fee MIN. 113.

For the drover's method of paying the farmers: with obfervations on that lot, fee MIN. 117.

Profit.

For an inftance of great profit by the Ifle-of-Sky cattle, fee MIN. 40.

For calculations of profit, from the quantity of turneps eaten in the yard, fee MIN. 56.

For a calculation on the quantity eaten in the field, fee MIN. 57.

For an inftance of low profit by Scotch cattle, fee MIN. 102.

For fundry inftances of great profit by Scotch and Irifh cattle, fee MIN. 119.

A a 4   For

For an evidence that profit depends chiefly
on management, fee MIN. 110.

For another inftance of moderate profit by
Scotch cattle, fee MIN. 111.

For an inftance of great profit by homebreds, fee MIN. 119.

It may be proper to obferve, that the inftances of *profit*, which are here adduced, are;
taken collectively, much above par. If, in a
common year, a bullock, of forty ftone, pay
half a crown a week for fatting, he is thought
to have done tolerably well. Suppofing him
to take fix months " time ;" and, in that time,
to eat an acre of turneps ; the grofs produce,
on this calculation, will be three pounds five
fhillings ; from which deduct fifteen fhillings
for ftraw and attendance, the remainder is
fifty fhillings for the neat produce of the turneps ;—exclufive of the value of the teathe,
or the dung arifing from the confumption.

But it being evident (at leaft to my mind)
that very much depends upon management, I
am clearly of opinion, that, by a judicious
attention to breeding, or a proper choice
in purchafing ;—by laying-out farms conveniently,

veniently, and adapting the mode of fatting to
the given foil and fituation;—by finifhing the
bullocks highly, and conducting the fale judicioufly, the prefent par price of two.fhillings
and fixpence a week, for a bullock of forty
ftone, might be raifed without extraordinary
exertion, to three fhillings or three fhillings
and fixpence a week:—and, confequently, the
neat par produce of an acre of turneps, on the
above calculation, to three pounds, or three
pounds ten fhillings an acre. To this muft
be added the TEATHE, which, upon the lighter
lands, is one of the main fupports of the Norfolk fyftem of hufbandry.

37. SHEEP.

37.

S H E E P.

NO CIRCUMSTANCE in the Norfolk husbandry surprized me more than that of finding the country in a manner destitute of sheep.

In one of my journies to Gunton, I purposely rode, on horseback, through the center of the county—by Thetford, Watton, Dereham, Reepham, &c. in order that I might catch a general idea of its rural economy.

From the nature of the soil, and from the prevalence of the turnep husbandry, I had conceived it to be the land of sheep: but from the time I crossed the river at Thetford, until I arrived within a few miles of the end of my journey, *I did not see one sheep!*

In the north-west quarter of the county, considerable flocks are kept: but in the eastern and southern divisions the number kept, in the summer months, is trifling; except upon commons, or about the residences of gentlemen; and, except upon some few capital

farms,

farms, upon which over-year flocks are kept. But Eaſt Norfolk farms, in general, are, in the months of July, Auguſt, and September, as free from ſheep as elephants;—except, perhaps, ſome few kept on until harveſt for, what is called, " harveſt beef;" namely, to be killed for the work-people in harveſt.

In and round the park of Gunton, a conſiderable flock was kept; and it is chiefly from obſervations on this flock, that I gained my information reſpecting the Norfolk breed of ſheep.

The BREED of Norfolk horſes was not formerly, nor its breed of cattle at preſent, more ſingular than is its BREED OF SHEEP; which, it is highly probable, has long been preſerved in purity;—I mean without adventitious mixture of blood.

There are two *varieties* of this SPECIES of ſheep: the one larger (weighing from fifteen to twentyfive pounds a quarter), which is the common ſtock of the county:—the other ſmaller (from ten to fifteen pounds a quarter), which are bred chiefly upon the heaths in the neighbourhood of Brandon and Methwold, in the ſouth-weſt quarter of the county. Theſe

go

go by the name of " heath fheep;" but differ in no refpect from the common fort; except in that of their being fmaller, and in that of their wool being finer.

The characteriftics of a Norfolk fheep are thefe:

The carcafe long and flender.

The fleece fhort and fine.

The legs long, and black, or mottled.

The face black, or mottled.

The horns—of the ewes and wedders, mid- dle-fized, and fomewhat ftraight; refembling thofe of the Dorfetfhire ewes, fo well known, now, in different parts of the kingdom, as the mothers of houfe lamb;—but thofe of the rams are very large, long, and fpiral, like the horns of the Dorfetfhire ram.

The loin of a Norfolk fheep, of the beft mould, is wide, and the hind quarters fuffi- ciently large for the general make; but the fore quarters, in general, are very deficient.— The fhoulders low, the back aukwardly high, and the chine fharp, and unfightly.

This is, at leaft, too generally the cafe; I have, however, feen fome of them with tole- rable backs; and I am confidently of opinion,

that

that if the Norfolk breeders of sheep would
pay less attention to their "countenances"
(that is, the colour of their faces) and more to
their carcases, the present breed, viewed in a
general light, might be very highly improved :
not, however, by the introduction of strange
breeds, and unnatural crossings ; but by a judicious choice of the males and females of their
own breed ;—which, taken all in all, even at
present, appears to be singularly well adapted
to the soil and system of management prevalent
in this country.

They may be bred, and will thrive, upon
heath and barren sheepwalks, where nine
tenths of the breeds in the kingdom would
starve : they stand the fold perfectly well : fat
freely at two years old: bear the drift, remarkably well, to Smithfield, or other distant markets ; and the superior flavor of the Norfolk
mutton is universally acknowledged.

, Therefore, the Norfolk husbandmen, in
their sheep, as well as in their cattle, have
much to lose : and the almost only thing they
have to gain is a better chine ; which, with a
judicious attention to their own breed, might
beyond

In ; as well as to every other rich inclofed grafsland country; and confequently may not be
unfit for the paddocks of gentlemen in this or
any other Diftrict; nor, perhaps, altogether
improper for the *Eaft* Norfolk farmers, who
keep only a few fheep, for the purpofes above-
mentioned. But, taken in a general light, as
a breed for the county at large, they appear to
me to be wholly unfit.—*I believe* they will not
live upon the heaths, and open, extenfive, unproductive fheep-walks of Weft Norfolk, fo
well as the prefent breed of heath fheep of that
country : *I know* they will not ftand the fold fo
well, nor travel fo well to the London market,
nor fell for fo much by the pound when they
arrive there, as will the prefent breed of Norfolk fheep in general ; which, aukward in form
as they undoubtedly are at prefent, appear to
me, from a knowledge of different breeds, to
be better adapted to the foil, fituation and
fyftem of management of the county at large,
than any other breed at prefent exifting in the
Ifland.

THE GENERAL ECONOMY or fyftem of management of fheep in this country is mentioned in MIN. 122, on the fheepfhow of Caw-
ſton ;

ston; in which also the particular practice of
this District is so far pointed out as relates to
the lambs and crones bought at that fair; which
with those of Kenninghall and Kipping, also
held in the summer months, form the grand
communication between the two sides of the
county.

If a farmer do not lay in his intended stock
at these fairs, he buys hoggards at the spring
fairs; letting them run in the fallows, lays, and
stubbles until autumn; and finishing them with
turneps the ensuing winter.

For the method of fatting them on TURNEPS,
see that article.

For the admeasurement of a *sheepfold*, see
MIN. 1.

For an evidence of sheep being *inimical to
cows*, see MIN. 8.

For an instance of advantage of *sheepfold* to
barley, see MIN. 11.

For an experiment and observations on the
time of putting the *ram* to the ewes, see
MIN. 17.

For an experiment with *sheepfold* for wheat,
see MIN. 18.

For

For an incident of *sheepfold* checking the turnep-fly, fee MIN. 21.

For an evidence that different *breeds* of sheep affect different species of *food*, fee MIN. 75.

For obfervations on *ewes lambing*, fee MIN. 76.

For an inftance of the effect of good keep on young *lambs*, fee MIN. 78.

For an incident on *croffing* Leicefterfhire ewes with a Norfolk ram, fee MIN. 82.

For an inftance of *prolificknefs* in the Norfolk breed of fheep, fee MIN. 86.

For an inftance of *cutting ridgil* lambs, fee MIN. 99.

For a further evidence of an almoft total privation of fheep in Eaft Norfolk, fee MIN. 106.

For obfervations on *Cawfton fheepfhow*, fee MIN. 123.

38.

R A B B I T S.

THE SOIL of this county, viewed at large, might be termed a rabbit foil ; and it is highly probable that, before its prefent fyftem of hufbandry took place, a confiderable part of it was occupied by this fpecies of liveftock.

At prefent, however, they are, in this Diftrict, wifely confined to the heathlets, and the barren hills upon the coaft. A level country is unfit for rabbit warrens, but convenient for the plow : on the contrary, rabbits delight in the fides of fandy hills ; which, where turnwrift plows are not in ufe, are extremely inconvenient for tillage ; and, when cultivated, are generally unproductive.

The rabbit, on level ground, finds it difficult to makes its burrow ; the excavated mould is all to be dragged *upward* to the furface : hence a piece of ground, altogether level, can feldom be ftocked fuccefsfully with rabbits ;

unlefs

unlefs it be firft laid up, by art, at a great expence, into inequalities.

On the contrary, againft the fide of a fteep
hill, the rabbit has no difficulty to encounter :
the declivity affords him a ready vent for his
mould ; his work is all *down-hill* : and—unlefs
the foil be too ftubborn, or too rocky, for the
rabbits to work freely among,—a broken hilly
country may generally be ftocked with advantage ; provided a tolerable market for the car-
cafes can be had within reach.

There are, perhaps, few fandy or other
loofe-foiled bills, which would not pay better in
rabbit-warren than under any other courfe of
hufbandry.

For an Inftance of an improvement by con-
verting unproductive fandy hills into rabbit-
warrens, fee MIN. 79.

39.

S W I N E.

THE NUMBER of fwine reared and fat-
ted in Norfolk is very confiderable : the dairy
in fummer, the ftubbles in autumn, and the
barns and ftables in winter, furnifh a conftant
fupply of fuftenance ; while the great quantity
of buck raifed in this country furnifhes an
ample fource of fatting.

In Norfolk, however, as in other Diftricts,
farmers differ widely about the proper number
to be kept, upon a given farm, under given
circumftances. It may neverthelefs be faid
that, in general, they are fully aware that a
moderate number well-done-to, are more profitable, in the end, than a greater number
badly kept;—yet there are fome few men,
even in Norfolk, whofe half-ftarved herds are
nuifances to the neighbourhoods they are kept
in ; without affording either pleafure, or extraordinary profit, to their refpective owners.

The

. The fpecies of fwine, which formerly was univerfal throughout the country, is, like the fheep, a flender long-legged animal; but, like thofe, is of quick growth, and prone to fat at an early age: I have feen them, at fix months old, near three quarters grown, and as fat as pigs in general are, at nine or twelve. Their fize is not large : fifteen to twenty ftone (fourteen pounds) is a good weight for a fat wellgrown hog.

But the "old original fort" is now nearly loft; the Chinefe and Berkfhire breeds have of late been introduced; fo that, at prefent, Norfolk exhibits the fame motley mixture of breeds, which may be feen in almoft every other county in the kingdom.

Farmers in general rear their own pigs: keeping, according to the fize of their farms, one or more fows, which in general are fatted young, *and fpayed before they be fatted*: through which means their flefh is thought to be much improved.

They are fatted almoft univerfally on buck; which is fometimes crufhed, and fometimes given to them whole. It is a quick good fat-

ting; somewhat similar to barley; not so good
as peas.

The consumption lies principally with the
county: some few, but I believe no great number, are sent to the London market.

They are in general killed as porkers,—and
either carried to the ped market, or pickled
for family use; not put down in tubs, for keeping, in the south-of-England manner; but only
immerged in brine, for present use; and in this
manner are continued to be temporarily preserved, from time to time, throughout the
year: a species of household management I
have not met with elsewhere.

For a singular instance of fatting hogs loose
in a yard, see MIN. 52.

40. POULTRY.

40.

P O U L T R Y.

NORFOLK is celebrated, and juftly, for its TURKIES. The fpecies is large; their flefh, neverthelefs, fine; and the number reared greater than that produced in any other Dif-trict of equal extent; owing, perhaps, to one circumftance. It is underftood, in general, that, to rear turkies with fuccefs, it is neceffary that a male bird fhould be kept upon the fpot, for the fame purpofe that a gander, a drake, or a male fowl is kept; namely, to impregnate the eggs individually. This deters not only cottagers, who are afraid of the expence of keeping a gluttonous turkeycock the year round, but many farmers, who diflike the noife and troublefomenefs of thefe animals, from breeding turkies. But the good houfewives of this country know that a daily intercourfe is unneceffary; and that, if the female be fent to a neighbouring male previous to the feafon of exclufion, one act of impregnation is fufficient

for one brood. Thus relieved from the
expence and difagreeablenefs of keeping a
male bird, moft little farmers, and many cottagers, rear turkies. This accounts for the
number: and the fpecies, and the food they
are fatted with (which, I believe, is wholly
buck) account for their fuperior fize and quality.

With refpect to GEESE, DUCKS and FOWLS
of this country, nothing is noticeable; except that they are, in general, below the
common fize, and that it is a practice to put
young goflings upon green wheat: a piece of
houfewifery which perhaps is peculiar to the
country.

Poultry of every fpecies are fold, in the markets, ready picked and fkewered fit for the fpit;
and are, in general, fo well fatted, and dreffed
up in fuch neatnefs and delicacy, as fhew the
Norfolk houfewives to be miftreffes in the art
of managing poultry.

41. DECOYS.

41.

D E C O Y S.

THE LAKES, and large pools, which abound in the fouthern Hundreds of Eaft Norfolk, are the nurferies of innumerable flights of "wildfowl," of various fpecies, but principally ducks; which are taken in great numbers in decoys, formed on the margins of thefe waters; and which, in eligible fituations, may well be confidered as objects of rural economy.

Much judgment is requifite in forming and managing a decoy. A gentleman in this · neighbourhood had a perfon out of Lincolnfhire to make one for him. But, after a great expence of cutting pipes, fixing fkreens, nets, &c. it proved unfuccefsful. The pipes were too ftraight, too clofe and confined, and too narrow at the mouth; without any banks for the wildfowl to bafk upon. Upon the whole, it was too much *like* a trap to be taken.

The

The leading principles of a decoy are thefe:
The wild duck is a very fhy bird, and de-
lights in retirement. The firft ftep, therefore,
is to endeavour to make the given water a
peaceful afylum, by fuffering the ducks to reft
on it undifturbed. The fame love of con-
cealment leads them to be partial to waters
whofe margins abound with underwood and
aquatic plants: hence, if the given water is
not already furnifhed with thefe appendages,
they muft be provided; for it is not retirement,
alone, which leads them into thefe recefies,
but a fearch after food, alfo.

Neverthelefs, at certain times of the day,
when wildfowl are off their feed, they are
equally delighted with a fmooth, grafly margin, to adjuft and oil their plumage upon. On
the clofe-paftured margins of large waters frequented by wildfowl, hundreds may be feen
amufing themfelves in this way: and, perhaps, nothing draws them fooner to a water
than a conveniency of this kind:—hence it
becomes effentially neceffary to fuccefs to pro-
vide a grafly, fhelving, fmooth-fhaven bank at
the mouth of the pipe, in order to draw the
fowl, not only to the water at large, but to the
defired part of it.

Having,

Having, by these means, allured them to
the mouth of the pipe, or canal, leading from
the water to a tunnel net, fixed at the head of
it; but hid from the sight among trees and
aquatic plants; the difficulties now remaining
are those of getting them off the bank into
the water, without taking wing; and of
leading them up the pipe to the snare which is
set for them.

To get them off the bank into the water, a
dog (the more he is like a fox the better)
steals from behind a skreen of reeds, which is
placed by the side of the pipe to hide the
decoyman, as well as his dog, until the signal
be given.   On seeing the dog, the ducks rush
into the water; where the *wildfowl* consider
themselves as safe from the enemy which had
assailed them.

But among the wildfowl, a parcel (perhaps, eight or ten) of *decoy-ducks* have mixed,
and were, probably, instrumental in bringing
them, with greater confidence, to the bank.——
As soon as these are in the water, they make
for the pipe; at the head of which they have
been constantly fed; and in which they have
always found an asylum from the dog.   The
wild-

wild-ducks follow; while the dog keeps driving behind; and, by that means, takes off
their attention from the trap they are entering.

As soon as the decoyman, who is all the
while obferving the operation through peep-
holes in the reed fkreen, fees the entire fhoal
under a canopy net which covers and inclofes
the upper part of the pipe, he fhews himfelf;
when the wildfowl inftantly take wing; but
their wings meeting with an impervious net,
inftead of a natural canopy formed of reeds
and bullrufhes, they fall again into the water,
and, being afraid to recede, the man being
clofe behind them, pufh forward into the tail
of the tunnel net which terminates the pipe *.

This being the ufe of the pipe, its form becomes obvious. It ought to refemble the out-
let of a natural brook, or, a natural inlet or
creek of the principal water. The mouth
ought to be fpacious, and free from confine-

* I was told by the proprietor of a decoy, who is
himfelf fond of the diverfion, and whofe veracity I have
no reafon to doubt, that he has, in this way, caught
" nine dozen at a pufh."

ment,

ment, that the wildfowl, on their first rushing into the water, and while they have yet the power of recollection, may be induced to begin to follow the tame ducks; and for the same purpose it ought to be crooked, that its inward narrowness, and nets, may not, in the first instance, be perceived. The lower part of a French horn is confidered as the best form of the pipe of a decoy.

One material circumstance remains yet to be explained. It is the invariable nature of wildfowl to take wing with their heads toward the wind; and it is always imprudent to attempt to take them in a decoy, unless the wind blow down the pipe: for, while their enemy is to leeward of them, they have lefs fcruple to go up the pipe, making fure of an efcape by their wings. But, what is of still more confequence, if the wind fet up the pipe, when they take wing under the canopy net, fome of them would probably efcape (a circumftance always to be dreaded), and thofe which fell again into the water would fall, of courfe, with their heads toward the wind, and would, with greater difficulty, be driven into the tunnel.

This

This circumſtance is ſo well known, by de-
coymen in general, that every decoy is, when
circumſtances will admit of it, furniſhed with
three or four different pipes, pointing to diſ-
tinct quarters of the horizon, that no opportunity may be loſt on account of the wind.

42. BEES.

.

42.

B E E S.

A CONSIDERABLE quantity of honey is collected in Norfolk; but, in general, it is of an inferior quality: owing, as it is generally believed, to the quantity of buck which is annually grown in this country, and which is highly grateful to bees; affording them an ample supply of honey.

It does not, however, appear clear to me, that the inferior quality of the Norfolk honey is owing to its being collected from this plant. It resembles, in colour and smell, the honey of the north of England, collected from the heaths, moors, and fells, which abound in that part of the island: and it appears to me probable, that the brownness and rankness of the Norfolk honey is owing to the same cause; namely, heath;—which not only abounds on the little heathy wastes, which occur in almost every part of the county; but seems to

.   .   be

be a natural production of the foil in general ;
frequently rifing, even in good foil, on ditchbanks, and other uncultivated places ; fo that
the evil, if not wholly, is, in part, occafioned
by the heath , which, it is a notorious fact,
affords much honey, but of a bad quality.

I will not, however, infer from this, that
buck is productive of fine honey, and that it
has no fhare in the debafement of the Norfolk
honey.   The flowers of buck have no doubt a
powerful, lufcicus fmell, which is *difagreeable*
to many people ; but are not thofe of beans
equally powerful, equally lufcious, and to fome
perfons equally difagreeable ? I only wifh
that the evil effect of buck upon the quality
of honey may be *doubted*, until it be *proved*, by
accurate experiments.

For an inftance of a depopulated hive being
taken poffeffion of by a new colony, fee
MIN. 126.

LIST

L I S T

OF

RATES and PROPORTIONS

IN

N O R F O L K.

THE MOTIVE for forming a register of rates and proportions was, principally, my own practice. A man who sits down to practise in a District whose customs he is a stranger to, has many difficulties to encounter. An ignorance of the current prices of materials, labour, and produce, is not one of the least; and he finds it expedient to make himself acquainted with these particulars, as soon as possible.

Vol. I.   C c   My

My motive for endeavouring to perfect the lift, and for publishing it, is threefold. First, it will be a proper, and, in some measure, a necessary appendage to the present volumes. Second, it may be a guide to the inexperienced: A gentleman, or any man, who undertakes the management of an estate, or a farm, without having been regularly initiated in the employment, stands, in his own country, in a situation similar to that which a practitioner finds himself in, when he first enters a fresh District: and the present List may not be found useful to the inexperienced in Norfolk, only; but may serve, in some measure, as a guide to those in other countries: for although the prices of labour and produce vary in every District; yet an authentic register of those of any *one*, may serve to lessen the number of impositions which gentlemen are liable to, on their first entrance into the field of practice. And, lastly, a *collection* of registers of rates of labour, in different and distant Districts, will not only be a still better guide to the beginner; but may be found useful to practitioners in general; in assisting them to regulate their respective lists of prices.

The

.The particulars which I collected in Norfolk fall, aptly, under the following heads:

I. BRICKLAYERS WORK.
    1. Materials.
    2. Labour.
    3. Proportions.

II. CARPENTERS WORK.
    1. Materials.
    2. Labourers.

III. THATCHERS WORK.
    1. Materials.
    2. Labourers.
    3. Proportions.

IV. WOODLANDS AND HEDGES.
    1. Produce.
    2. Labour.

V. HUSBANDRY.
    1. Yearly servants.
    2. Day labourers.
    3. Road team-work.
    4. Soil procefs.
    5. Manure procefs.
    6. Seed procefs.
    7. Vegetating procefs.
    8. Harveft procefs.
    9. Barn management.
    10. Markets.
    11. Grafsland.

I. BRICK-

I. BRICKLAYERS WORK.

1. Materials.

Common red bricks *, 15 to 16s. a thoufand.

Hard-burned, 16 to 17s. a thoufand.

Stone-coloured, 21 to 23s. a thoufand.

Flooring bricks, 9 inches fquare, 8s. a hundred.

————————— 12 inches fquare, 18s. a hundred.

————————— 18 inches fquare, 50s. a hundred.

Common pantiles, 50s. a thoufand.

Glazed pantiles, 90s. a thoufand.

Plane tiles, 16s. a thoufand.

Ridge tiles, 80s. a thoufand.

Pipe-drain bricks, 14 to 18s. a hundred.

" Dreeps"—offset bricks, 20s. a thoufand.

" Lumps"—barn-floor bricks, 30s. a thoufand.

————large ditto, 50s. a thoufand.

Old bricks (half-bricks, half-bats), 12s. a thoufand.

Old foundation-blocks (rough maffes of brick and lime cemented together), 2s. 6d. a load.

* Gage,—nine inches long; four inches and a quarter wide; and two inches and one-eighth thick.

Cafting

Cafting and carting the clay, and making and burning bricks, 7*s.* a thoufand.

—————pantiles, 30*s.* a thoufand.

Taking down brick walls, and cleaning the bricks, 2*s.* 6*d.* a thoufand; reckoning two bats for one brick.

Cleaning loofe bricks, 2*s.* a thoufand.

Price of fea ftones, 1*s.* to 1*s.* 6*d.* a load.

Pulling down old fea ftone walls, and clearing and forting the ftones, 5*s.* a fquare ftatute rod (namely, about 30 fquare yards).

Lime, 9*s.* to 10*s.* 3*d.* a chaldron (of 32 bufhels).

Cafting and carting marl and burning it into lime, 18*d.* and beer, or 20*d.* a chaldron.

One chaldron of coals (36 bufhels) burn 7 chaldron of lime (32 bufhels).

Clay, 1*s.* a load.

Hair, 1*s.* to 14*d.* a bufhel.

Sap laths, 14*d.* a bundle.

Pantile laths, 7*s.* a bundle.

2. LABOUR.

Journeymen's wages, 20*d.* and beer, or 1*s.* 11*d.* a day.

Labourer's wages, 1*s.* and beer, or 1s. 3*d.* a day.

Lay-

Laying bricks, 10*d*. a square yard, (of 14 inch work ; that is, one and a half brick thick).

Foundation, 1*s*. (the same thickness).

Labour and lime, 20*d*. a yard.

Laying pantiles on interlaths and mortar, 4*s*. a square (of 100 square feet).

Plaistering, 2*d*. a square yard.

Ceiling, 4*d*. a square yard.

Rendering, that is, one coat of plaistering) between spars, 1*d*. halfpenny a yard.

Laying brick floors in mortar, 3*d*. a yard.

Laying barn floors with clay, 4*d*. halfpenny to 6*d*. a yard.

Laying hay-chamber floors with ditto, 4*d*. halfpenny to 6*d*. *.

Daubing on studwork, 4*d*. halfpenny a yard.

Stopping and plaistering old daubing, 1*d*. a yard.

3. PROPORTIONS.

A square yard of 9 inch work (that is, a brick in length thick) takes about one hundred and twenty bricks (the gage small).

One chaldron of Norfolk lime will lay about two thousand bricks.

* Tempering the clay and dressing the floor included.

One

One load of fea ftones will pave about ten fquare yards.

One load of clay will lay (in the Norfolk manner) about eight fquare yards of barn-floor.

II. CARPENTERS WORK.

1. MATERIALS.

Oak timber as it ftands, 3*l.* 3*s.* to 4*l.* a load (of forty feet).

Ditto in the ftick, 50*s.* to 60*s.* a load.

Afh as it ftands, 40*s.* to 50*s.* a load of 44 feet; allowing 4 feet for bark.

Ditto, in the ftick, 30*s.* to 40*s.* a load of 44 feet.

Poplar, as it ftands, 30*s.* to 40*s.* a load of 44 feet.

Alder, as it ftands, 20*s.* to 30*s.* a load of 44 feet.

2. LABOUR.

Journeyman carpenter's wages, 18*d.* and beer, or 21*d.* a day.

A foreman carpenter's wages, 2*s.* and beer, or 2*s.* 3*d.* a day.

A joiner's wages, 2*s.* 3*d.* and beer, or 2*s.* 6*d.* a day.

Cc 4

III. THATCHERS WORK.

1. MATERIALS.

Reed, 3*l.* to 3*l.* 3*s.* a hundred fathom (of 6 feet).

Cutting and binding reed, 25*s.* a hundred.

Cutting and binding gladdon, 30*s.* a hundred.

Taking off old reed and binding it, 10*s.* a hundred.

New "tar-rope" (three strands), 3*s.* 6*d.* to 4*s.* a stone (of fourteen pounds).

2. LABOUR.

Day's work of a man and boy, 2*s.* 6*d.*

Laying reed, a halfpenny a foot ; or, 4*s.* 2*d.* a square.

Laying straw, the same.

Setting on " roofing," 3*d.* to 4*d.* a foot in length.

3. PROPORTIONS.

A hundred of reed covers five square :

A load of straw about two square.

A square of reed takes about five pounds of tar-rope.

A load of straw will make about 25 feet of " roofing."

IV.

IV. WOODLANDS AND HEDGES.

1. Produce.

For prices of timber, fee CARPENTERS WORK.

Oak bark, 10*s*. to 12*s*. each load of timber.

Top wood, 8*s*. to 10*s*. each load of timber.

Round wood, (the naked boughs) 12*s*. to 15*s*. a waggon load*.

Bakers' faggots, 15*s*. to 18*s*. a hundred (of one hundred and twenty).

Spray faggots, 12*s*. to 14*s*. a hundred (of one hundred and twenty).

"Bufhel blocks†"—10*s*. a load (of forty blocks).

2. Labour.

"Grub-felling‡" timber from 1*s*. to 18*d*. a load of timber, together with the "ground-firing;" that is, the roots.

---

* A full waggon load of round wood piled up rough (not cut into lengths) meafured on a par, nine feet long, four and a half feet wide, and four and a half feet high.

† Rough firing blocks cleft out of decayed pollards, roots, or other offal wood; each block being *fuppofed* to be the fize of a bufhel.

‡ Partially grubbing.—See PLANTING.

Cutting

Cutting off the round wood, 1s. a load.

Tying wood faggots, 2s. 6d. to 3s. a hundred (of six score).

Tying furze faggots, 2s. to 2s. 6d. a hundred (of six score).

Riving bushel blocks, 4s. a load.

Riving half-bushel blocks, 5s. to 6s. a load (of eighty blocks).

Riving half-bushel from short ends, when little sawing is wanted, 4s. a load.

Riving small billet, 1d. a score.

Riving plaistering laths, 6d. a bundle.

Tolerably good white-thorn layer, at 4s. a thousand.

Oaken layer, three or four years old, to lay into hedges, 1s. a hundred.

Gathering haws, 8d. a bushel.

Gathering acorns, 1s. a bushel.

Gathering ash keys, 6d. a bushel, heaped and pressed down *.

Double-digging two spits and a crumb, 1s. a square rod (of seven yards).

Price of furze seed, 15d a pound.

---

* These prices vary of course with the plenty or scarcity of the different articles in a given year. The above are low prices.

Making

Making a new fix-foot ditch, planting quick, and fetting a hedge, 1s. and beer, or 14d. a rod (of feven yards).

Re-making an old ditch, fcouring, facing, backing, and fetting a hedge, 7d. to 10d. and beer.

Cutting thorns, 1s. a waggon load.

Backing and hedging, 5d. a rod.

Backing without hedging, 3d. a rod.

Grubbing up hedges and borders, 6d. to 1s. a rod and the "fmall firing," that is, the chips and fmaller roots. See p. 112.

V. HUSBANDRY.

1. YEARLY SERVANTS.

Yearly wages of a head man, 8l. to 10l.

Yearly wages of a fecond man, 4l. to 6l.

Yearly wages of a harrow boy, 40s.

Yearly wages of a woman, 3l. to 3l. 3s.

Yearly wages of a girl, 30s. to 40s.

2. DAY LABOURERS.

Day wages of a common man*, in winter, 1s. and beer.

Day wages of a common man, in fummer, 1s. 1d. and beer.

* A teamer man is allowed 1s. a week extra, for "horfe money."

Harveft

Harveſt wages, 35s. to 40s. and board during harveſt, whether it be ſhort or long.

Day wages of a woman, 6d. and beer, and in
harveſt alſo board.

3. ROAD TEAM-WORK.

Five horſes, one man and waggon, 10s. a
day *.

Teamerman's road allowance, 6d. a day's
journey.

4. SOIL PROCESS.

Plowing,—whether it be breaking up a fallow or ſtirring it, 2s. 6d. an acre for man and
horſes.

Seed-plowing (eſpecially for wheat in narrow ridges) ſeldom done by the acre.

5. MANURE PROCESS.

Caſting marl, 3d. to 6d. a load †.

---

* Inſtance of four horſes one man and two waggons in
hay time, for 7s. 6d. a day.

† One individual gives 4d. in leiſure-times, and 6d. in
turnep-hoing, a load for caſting; beſides the uncallowing, which he pays for extra by the day. One man and
big boy fill twelve loads a day; the team (five horſes one
man) carrying that number a ſhort diſtance. Total expence about 18d. a load.

Another gives 3d. to 4d. for caſting (beſides uncallowing). A team carries ſix loads about half a mile.—
One man fills by the day.

Filling

Filling marl, 2d. a load.,

Spreading marl, 9d. to 1s. an acre.

" Outholling" (scouring out the rich mould from the bottoms of ditches), 1d. to 2d. a rod (of seven yards).

" Turning up borders," (that is, digging up the topsoil, and laying it in a ridge with the grass-side downward) 1d. a rod, for a yard wide, if free from roots or other obstructions.

Filling mould,—generally done by the day.

Turning up muck in the yard,—by the lump.

Turning muck heaps, 1d. a load.

Filling muck, 1d. a load.

Spreading muck, 8d. to 10d. an acre.

6. SEED PROCESS.

Wheat, generally sown by the day.

Barley, &c. 2d. an acre.

Turneps, 2d. an acre.

Clover and ray-grass (mixed), 2d. an acre.

7. VEGETATING PROCESS.

Hoing turneps,—first hoing, 3s. 6d. to 4s.
—second hoing, 2s. to 2s. 6d.—the two hoings, 6s. an acre, and beer.

Weeding, 6d. and beer; or 6d. to 5s. an acre.

Stonepicking, 2d. an acre.

8. HAR-

8. HARVEST PROCESS.

Mowing clover and ray grafs, 1s. to 18d. an acre, and beer.

Mowing grafs, 18d. to 21d. an acre, and beer.

Sweeping broken grafs In paftures, &c. about 1s. an acre:

Reaping wheat, 5 to 6 or 7s. an acre.

Mowing barley, &c. 1s. an acre.

Dragraking, 2d. an acre.

Thatching ricks, 8d. a fquare; or more commonly 6d. a yard, in length, for both fides, whether the roof be deep or fhallow:

9. BARN LABOUR.

Thrafhing wheat, about 1s. a coomb, and beer.

Thrafhing barley, oats, and buck, 6d. to 8d. a coomb, and beer.

Thrafhing peas, 9d. a coomb, and beer.

Thrafhing clover feed, 6s. a bufhel.

Sifting cleaned corn, 1d. a coomb.

Skreening and putting up fuch corn, 6d. a laft.

Cutting chaff, 18d. to 20d. a fcore; or 18d. a day and board! (the machine in ufe a bad one.)

10. MARKETS.

10. MARKETS.

The Norfolk bushel, eight and a quarter gallons.

Eighteen stone a coomb, of four bushels, is esteemed a good weight for wheat: twenty stone has been produced; that is, sixtythree to seventy pounds a bushel, of eight and a quarter gallons; or about sixtyone to sixtyeight Winchester.

11. GRASSLAND.

Agistment price for the summer; namely, from Mayday to Michaelmas; in marshes or grazing ground, at head keep;—

 For two-year-olds and small Scotch cattle, 30s. to 35s.

 For yearlings, 18s. to 21s.

Agistment price for the summer, in meadows, or at second grass;—

 For two-year-olds, 18s. to 20s.

 For yearlings, 10s. to 12s.

Agistment price, by the week, in summer;

 For bullocks, at head grass, 2s.

 For sheep, at head grass, 3d.

Agistment

Agiſtment price, by the week, after Michaelmas;

    For fatting cattle, at head, 1s. 6d.

    For two-year-olds, dry cows, &c. at ſe-
      cond graſs, 1s.

    For yearlings, at ſecond graſs, 8d.

    For ſheep, 2d.

Cutting open drains in moory meadows,
three feet wide, 2d. to 4d. a rod (of ſeven
yards); and beer.

Scouring ſuch drains annually, a halfpenny
a rod.

Scouring main drains (five or ſix feet wide)
annually, 1d. a rod.

Scouring main drains the ſecond year, 2d. a
rod.

Scouring main drains the third year, 3d. a
rod.

www.ingramcontent.com/pod-product-compliance
Lightning Source LLC
Chambersburg PA
CBHW032316280326
41932CB00009B/829